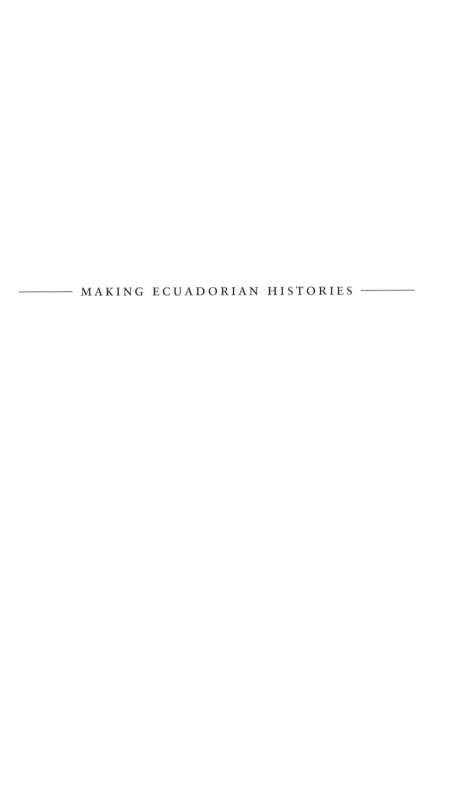

MAKING ECUADORIAN HISTORIES

MAKING ECUADORIAN HISTORIES

Four Centuries of Defining Power

~

O. HUGO BENAVIDES

UNIVERSITY OF TEXAS PRESS

AUSTIN

Printed in the United States of America
First edition, 2004

Requests for permission to reproduce material from this work
should be sent to Permissions, University of Texas Press, P.O. Box 7819,
Austin, TX 78713-7819.

The paper used in this book meets the minimum requirements of
ANSI/NISO Z39.48-1992 (R1997) (Permanence of Paper).

Library of Congress Cataloging-in-Publication Data

Benavides, O. Hugo (Oswald Hugo), 1968–
Making Ecuadorian histories : four centuries of defining power / by
O. Hugo Benavides.—1st ed.
      p.   cm.
Includes bibliographical references and index.
      ISBN 0-292-70229-9 (cloth: alk. paper)
      1. Indians of South America—Ecuador—Antiquities.   2. Indians
of South America—Ecuador—Historiography.   3. Archaeology—
Ecuador—History.   4. National characteristics, Ecuadorian.
5. Political anthropology—Ecuador.   6. Ecuador—Historiography.
7. Ecuador—Antiquities.   8. Ecuador—Politics and government.
I. Title.
F3721 .B46   2004
986.6'01'072—dc22

                                                      2003016603

For Gregory Lamont Allen, "who is all Poetry and Love."

CONTENTS

ACKNOWLEDGMENTS

A work is never completed except by some accident such
as weariness, satisfaction, the need to deliver, or death:
for, in relation to who or what is making it,
it can only be one stage in a series of inner transformations.

— RABIH ALAMEDDINE (1998)

This project has benefited from the support of the following institutions, which funded either the fieldwork or the writing: National Science Foundation (Dissertation Improvement Award), Wenner-Gren Foundation (Small Grant), Social Science Research Council Pre-Doctoral Grant (Mellon Minority Fellowship), Magnet Dissertation Writing Grant (City University of New York, CUNY), Ames Faculty Grant (Fordham University), and Alumni Writing Grant (CUNY).

I wish to extend my gratitude to my doctoral committee for its support of this initial project. I am particularly grateful to my advisor, Prof. Leith Mullings, who provided support and wisdom throughout the process, even after my career as a graduate student ended.

I also want to thank my colleagues at Fordham University. All of them, including the chairs of the sociology and anthropology departments, Dr. Rosemary Cooney and Dr. Orlando Rodríguez, have made the environment one of true camaraderie and fellowship. I want to especially acknowledge Dr. Jeanne Flavin for her undying friendship and concern; there is no doubt that she has made the path worth traveling. A special recognition to Father Gerry Blaszczak for his unrelenting spirit, which has almost reconciled me with my Catholic childhood. Thanks also to Rosa Giglio and Paula Genova for keeping the department going, and to Ed Gallagher for being the graduate student par excellence. I also wish to thank Mary Weismantel for her support and the *Journal of Latin American Anthropology*, in which part of chapter 4 was published as an analysis of Guayaquil's sexual history.

To G. A. (Gregory Allen), who, in Marguerite Yourcenar's (1963) words, is "that someone who bolsters our courage and approves, or sometimes disputes, our ideas; who shares with us, and with equal fervor, the joys of art and of living, the endless work which both require, never easy but never dull; someone who is neither our shadow nor our reflection, nor even our complement, but simply himself; someone who leaves us ideally free, but who nevertheless obliges us to be fully what we are." Gracias.

To Elissa West, whose vision has continued to provide me with a realistic assessment of my existence and validation of my work.

To my fellow travelers, now more than ever—G. Melissa García, Jannette Bramlett, Aseel Sawalha, Bernice Kurchin, Murphy Halliburton, Mike Muse, Judy Kried, and Molly Doane, thanks for your love.

To my friends in the field—Marco Vargas, Leonor Buri, Duvant, Eduardo, the staff at Cochasquí, the librarian at the Universidad Católica in Quito, and everybody else who made my stay as comfortable as was humanly possible—my gratitude.

To all my colleagues and friends who provided their support during different stages of the process, one, as they know, that was fraught with difficulty and hardship—Bassam Abed, Peter Sieger, Diana Agosta, Carmen Medeiros, Tracy Fisher, Ana Aparicio, Charles Price, Belkis Necos, and Arlene Dávila (and those whose names I forget)—thanks for making this writing experience possible.

Special thanks to two outstanding women whose initials both happen to be BB: Dr. Barbara Bowen and Dr. Beverlee Bruce. Without Barbara's support I would never have even allowed myself to dream about becoming an academic; without Beverlee's inspiration I would not be the hopeful scholar I am today. To both, sincere thanks from the bottom of my heart and soul.

To my editor, Theresa May, for believing in this project, for her patience, and, above all, for her humanity.

To Alejandro Sanz, Cesária Évora, Marisa, Sade, Miguel Bosé, Simone, Gal Costa, Joan Manuel Serrat, Diane Schuur, Billie Holliday, Shirley Horn, Marc Anthony, Simply Red, Jamiroquai, José Feliciano, Kronos Quartet, among many others.

And finally to my love: as Bosé says, "Te amaré mientras respire."

1. Back View of Pyramid 9

2. Central View of Pyramid 9

3. Side View of Pyramid 13

4. Frontal View of Pyramid 13

5. Closeup of Pyramid 13

6. Closeup of Pyramid 13 (Construction)

7. *Afro-Ecuadorian Group at Cochasquí*

8. *General Festivities at Cochasquí*

9. *Entrance sign to site*

10. *Smaller sign at site-entry shack*

11. Civil unrest in Quito (February 1997)

12. Continued Protests
(February 1997)

13. *Outside Ecuadorian Congress (February 1997)*

14. *Protests at the Congress (February 1997)*

MAKING ECUADORIAN HISTORIES

INTRODUCTION

The Indians have had no voice for five hundred years.
Little by little, they are feeling like protagonists in history.

—LUIS RICCHIARDI, ROMAN CATHOLIC PRIEST

In the 1990s Ecuador saw a reappraisal of indigenous identity that coalesced into the country's most important social movement since the turn of the century. The Indian movement, under the leadership of the Confederación Nacional de Indígenas del Ecuador (National Confederation of Indigenous Nationalities of Ecuador, CONAIE) and the Pachakutik Nuevo País party, provoked a serious rupture in Ecuador's ideological belief that it had maintained concerning its historical identity and its indigenous heritage. Since the 1990s the Indian movement has been able to paralyze the country for weeks on end, has forced two governments to reconsider their application of the International Monetary Fund's (IMF) structural-adjustment policies, and has successfully aligned itself with the military to overthrow Jamil Mahuad (in 2000).

The Indian movement is the most powerful of a number of social movements (and fragmented social subjects)—women's associations, the gay and lesbian movement, and ecological organizations—that are questioning Ecuador's traditional national identity within the wider cultural and economic concerns of globalization. Each of these groups has justified itself, in varying degrees, by assessing a history that situates the group in a powerful position vis-à-vis the nation and the state. In this respect, history has become a contested commodity and is as important in claiming national narratives as in securing international funds or planning mobilization strategies. History more than ever is being envisioned by these social movements, including the state, as being where it has always been—at the center of national hegemonic contention and articulation.

As a result of this national political battle, the claim of the nation-state and of the new social movements to pre-Hispanic identity as a powerful historical legitimization of national objectives is a debate of considerable importance, suspiciously and tellingly absent from most political and academic forums. Most archaeological sites in Latin America and pre-Hispanic archaeological discourses in general have traditionally been understood as having very little impact in terms of defining a country's national hegemonic discourse. At best, pre-Hispanic sites have been consistently given greater attention only when nation-state ideology and bureaucracy, for example, in Mexico and Peru, have explicitly constructed a national ethos around indigenous cultures to uphold a more modern sense of identity and citizenship (see Patterson 1995a; see also Mallon 1995).

This book takes a more radical approach by sustaining that most, if not all, pre-Hispanic sites and discourses are subtly, and sometimes quite explicitly, articulated in historical productions that are pivotal to the national production of the contemporary Latin American nation-state. These historical discourses, which are routinely subsumed under a myriad of contested interpretations, are so essential that, without them, no nation-state would be able to fulfill its hegemonizing role successfully.

Recent research documents the central place of history in the construction of nationalism and the nation-state (Anderson 1983; Domínguez 1986; Foster 1990; Fox 1990; Friedman 1992; Handler 1988; Herzfeld 1982, 1987; J. Hill 1988, 1992; Hobsbawm 1990; Lowenthal 1985; Malkki 1995). No nation can endure without a history that legitimizes its existence (Renan [1882] 1990). The past, including the pre-Hispanic one, therefore readily becomes a contested landscape in which actors compete for authority, representation, and power (Bond and Gilliam 1994). Archaeology is an important element in this competition because it contributes the material needed to construct these histories (Rowlands 1994). Thus, I maintain that the pre-Hispanic past is a contested terrain in which actors strive to embody national histories that contribute to the operationalization of the nation-state. I argue that historical invention is essential, not only for the nation-state itself, but also for all national communities and social movements that are contesting political authority and power. Furthermore, I maintain that contesting or alternative histories are not detrimental, but, rather, essential for the consolidation of any national movement, including that of the nation-state.

The role of historical memory and the pre-Hispanic past in the modern Latin American nation-state has received little critical analysis, however (see Patterson and Schmidt 1995 and Castañeda 1996 as two exceptions to this trend). This book addresses this complex relationship for Ecuador, that is, the mutual dependence of the pre-Hispanic past and the nation-state in the production of contemporary nationhood. It explores how the pre-Hispanic past informs the present and is transformed into authoritative national histories that are articulated by a series of identity components that compete in a constant hegemonic project in the making (Joseph and Nugent 1994). I ultimately question the notion of historical truth per se and point to the multilayered contexts in which all historical versions are, and must always be, produced.

My research included a yearlong ethnographic study (during 1997) of the archaeological site of Cochasquí (Lumbreras 1990) as well as analysis of other pre-Hispanic historical discourses such as those of the Indian movement and Ecuador's print media. At Cochasquí, I attached myself to the Programa Cochasquí (Cochasquí Research Program) team at the Consejo Provincial de Pichincha (Pichincha's Provincial Council). The Programa Cochasquí is the regional organization in charge of the administration of the archaeological site of Cochasquí. My research strategies included interviewing the personnel involved in the creation and maintenance of the site, interviewing members of the *comuna* (local community), examining the site archives, recording the guided tours, analyzing the site museum, administering questionnaires to the tourists, and participating in daily activities at the site.

The site of Cochasquí is just fifty-six kilometers north of Quito, Ecuador's capital, only an hour-and-a-half's drive north of the city. The site is also very close to a cluster of small landholders who make up the *comuna* of Cochasquí. The *comuna* itself comprises a series of barrios (neighborhoods), with the most important one being centrally located with respect to all the others and at a significant distance from the site itself. However, the site area is not easily accessible, since it is at a notable distance from the main highway (an eight-kilometer steady climb). Although it is a stone-paved access road (*empedrado*), the twenty-minute ride is quite demanding on car and kidneys; by foot it would be a two- to three-hour uphill hike, depending on one's speed and endurance (Mantilla N.d.).

The difficulty of getting to Cochasquí seems to add to the allure of visiting the site, an important element, as we shall see, in its social production. As an article in *El Comercio* (1997b) notes, visiting the pre-Hispanic pyramids at Cochasquí is almost literally "a trip to the past." Since its initial opening to tourists in the late 1970s, under the auspices of the Programa Cochasquí, the site has become one of the most frequented archaeological sites in the country, averaging around twenty thousand tourists a year—nationals, foreigners, and researchers from academic institutions (Programa Cochasquí 1997; see also Corporación Ecuatoriana de Turismo [CETURIS] 1972).

As initially described by the German archaeologist Max Uhle (1939: 5), "The ruins are located to the west of the old path (tradition has it that this was part of the royal Inca road that connected Otavalo to Quito) that comes down the Mojanda from the town of Otavalo and which was followed by Cieza in his trip to Quito. This is the most extensive and most important complex of archaeological ruins and mounds in northern Ecuador."

As a result of Uhle's initial research, as well as later excavations (Oberem 1980) and descriptions by the Programa Cochasquí, three archaeological components have been defined at the site: (1) fifteen pyramids (nine with and six without ramps); (2) over twenty funeral mounds and domestic mounds; and (3) a central "domestic" space of approximately four hectares, defined as the *zona pueblo* (town zone), between the southern mounds and the northern pyramids (Mantilla N.d.). In total, the present legal boundaries of the site exhibit five to six mounds, although over thirty round mounds have been defined at the site (Benavides Solís 1986; Wurster 1989). The pyramids have been labeled from one to fifteen going from east to west and north to south.

The three pyramids considered the most important are nos. 9, 14, and 13, in order of importance. By far the largest is no. 9: ninety meters long north to south, eighty meters wide east to west, and twenty-one meters high at its tallest point. It is also the one that has endured the most looting, suffering a severe cut in the early 1930s that detached the two hundred meter–long ramp from the body of the pyramid. The next-largest pyramid is no. 14, which also possesses the longest ramp (250 meters) and is the one most often selected for traditional and shamanistic rituals and ceremonies. (During my fieldwork, a wedding took place on this pyramid.) It is described by many as having the greatest "energy" of all the pyramids. Pyramid no. 13 is also interesting in that two hardened earthen platforms on its top, discovered during the 1962–1963 German excavations of the site, are open for public display.

The pre-Hispanic site of Cochasquí is a locus of constant dispute and negotiation. Far from being a monolithic historical monument, Cochasquí presents multiple histories that play an active part in the production of the site. As an archaeological and historical drama (local, regional, and national), Cochasquí has a full set of characters, some playing more important roles than others, but all equally involved in its "production" or "invention" (Anderson 1991; Hobsbawm 1990; Hobsbawm and Ranger 1983). The archaeological site of Cochasquí is produced in the same manner that any other historical site is produced (Bender 1998; Handler 1986, 1988; Handler and Gable 1997; Silberman 1982, 1989, 1995). That is, no single person, event, or even institution can ultimately be hailed as being exclusively responsible for the site's construction as such. Rather, a complex cast of characters and events is intricately involved and actively competing and negotiating in the maintenance and representation of the site. As Handler and Gable (1997: 9) describe Colonial Williamsburg, the site of Cochasquí can also be appreciated as a "social arena in which many people of differing backgrounds continuously and routinely interact to produce, exchange, and consume messages." Never-ending interaction and disputes define the ever-changing dynamics of the site.

This dynamic historical production is apparent in the multiple functions claimed for the site simultaneously by tour guides and tourists: (1) because of its size, the site is hailed as a major agricultural and urban center; (2) because of its panoramic view and control of surrounding areas, it is said to have been a military garrison; (3) because of astronomical research, it is seen as an observatory (Yurevich 1986); (4) because of its large size, it is considered a ceremonial center; (5) because of personal "religious" (spiritual) experience, it is a major ritual and esoteric center for UFO sightings. All functions, as we shall see, receive nearly equal attention and official sanction, depending on the context in which the narratives have been produced or are being told.

I do not look to exhaust the historical elements at work at the site or the complex interaction between the different pre-Hispanic narratives in Ecuador at any given time. Rather, my main objective is to provide an understanding of the multiplicity of histories inherent in the production of the archaeological site of Cochasquí and pre-Hispanic narratives that subtly inform Ecuador's national identity. To this end, this book examines how Cochasquí and other pre-Hispanic archaeological narratives are represented and offers different rationales for their maintenance of the nation-state in their furnishing of the raw material for the production of an Ecuadorian heritage and identity.

THEORIES OF HISTORY,
NATIONALISM, AND HEGEMONY

I am concerned with assessing the part played by the pre-Hispanic past in Ecuador's national production. I view historical memory as closely aligned to the hegemonic structure that both supports and reinforces a national identity and the nation-state's contemporary status quo—that is, highly unequal class, racial, and gendered/sexual social structures. Since hegemony is not static or monolithic (Sayer 1994), one must locate the historical productions and cultural representations that serve the dominant structure at particular moments and not at others. Because of this specific historical and political problem, I examine the manner in which national communities are dynamically (and necessarily contradictorily) consolidated and maintained (Wylie 1995) and the essential role that not only a communal imagination (Anderson 1991) but also, more precisely, a historical imagination plays in this regard (see Comaroff and Comaroff 1992).

Culture is an integral part of historical imagination. As a pivotal component of communal memory and historical narratives, culture and cultural forms are inextricably intertwined with the different positions that look to, and must, imbue history with authority if it is to be successful (see Baldwin 1990: 480–481). It is not so much that culture becomes a highly political tool as that it is already present as a highly political enterprise intersected by varying degrees of power, control, and mechanisms of domination (Foucault 1980, 1991). All national communities, social movements, and even the nation-state find themselves struggling over notions of cultural authenticity as a particular cultural form intimately linked to historical production.

It is because of this contested cultural dynamic that authenticity has become so widely accepted, even in the "First World," thereby allowing traditionally oppressed Indian groups finally to express their socioeconomic grievances in universal cultural terms. This "opening" has allowed Latin American social movements (Escobar and Álvarez 1992) to identify successfully with a global human rights agenda, but it is based not only on a platform of cultural authenticity but also on one that is enabled by a postmodern global developmental discourse (García Canclini 1992a, 1992b). As a result, the Indian movement and, more specifically, the CONAIE are but one of the many Latin American social movements that have been able to capitalize on this postmodern global turn of events. This global process also provides an insight into why the Indian movement, in Ecuador as well as in many other postcolonial nation-states, has been able to critically gain visible levels of political control and autonomy, even after five centuries of systematic physical decimation, economic exploitation, and racial oppression (see Hall 1997).

ARCHAEOLOGY'S NATIONALIZING ENTERPRISE

Being a nation implies getting your history wrong (Renan [1882] 1990), and in this respect, Ecuador is no exception. Historical invention, or "making history" (Patterson and Schmidt 1995), implies rewriting, changing, and transformation, that is, the representation of the past being described. This transformation takes place as a result of both the attitudes and the preferences of the people constructing, describing, and participating in the historical narrative (Castañeda 1995, 1996; Sider and Smith 1998; Trouillot 1995) and the level of support offered by an array of social institutions, such as the state, to the historical versions being created (Abrams 1988; Alonso 1988; Gable, Handler, and Lawson 1992; Handler and Gable 1997; Abu El-Haj 2001).

Both processes are equally present and effective at the site of Cochasquí and in the different versions of Ecuador's national histories. As I discuss in the following chapters, the institutional characteristics of Cochasquí, that is, state funding and state support of the site, provide a dominant structure that strategically solidifies a particular version of Cochasquí's past. This history, the program's (i.e., the official) version, is legitimized almost as soon as it is produced. This structure serves as a dialectical support system in which the official version is legitimated by the state while the nation-state and its history are legitimated by the program's version of history at Cochasquí (see Althusser 1977 for similar discussion).

The national appropriation of the archaeological site of Cochasquí is part of a greater narrative by means of which the Ecuadorian nation-state is able to represent a historical continuity that transcends time by being embedded in a communal ethos of homogeneity and essentializing naturalness (Alonso 1988; Foucault 1991). As discussed below, analysis of the national appropriation of the archaeological past at Cochasquí and discussion of the different national histories enable one to understand how Ecuador's history is afforded agency and takes a hegemonic stance (Mallon 1995). Ecuador, like all nation-states, must represent itself within a unique national history. However, as discussed above, no such singular national history exists at any particular moment or in terms of the historical elements being represented. Multiple versions of the past are "nationalized" according to the social, economic, and political agendas that are essential to the state's maintenance of the nation and its constitutive communities. Therefore, there is no single archaeological past—pre-Hispanic or of any kind—in Ecuador; rather, multiple pasts are integrated into diverse national narratives, which are then presented as a unique national history at particular political moments, in particular arenas and settings.

Exploring this process is complicated, however, since the incorporation of the archaeological past into Ecuador's history is not simply an issue of historical objectivity per se (as has been traditionally argued); instead, it is related to a larger web of social relations that condition and are conditioned by the nationalizing process itself. An example of this is the progressive stance taken by many Ecuadorian (Ayala Mora 1983; Benítez Vinueza 1986; Marcos 1986c) and foreign historians (Meggers 1966), who envision the nation's history as beginning with the indigenous occupation of the territory and not with the Spanish colonization of these same indigenous communities. The potential of this interpretation to disrupt the historical legitimization and internalized racial and class oppression of the majority of Ecuadorians by a small white/mestizo governing elite is evident (Ayala Mora 1985b). However, an Indian origin for the nation is not inherently disruptive and, in some ways, maintains the oppressive figure of the nation and the state.

In contrast, the traditional historical establishment (Andrade Reimers 1995; J. M. Vargas 1953, 1964, 1982) has adopted the idea of the indigenous origin of Ecuadorian history, but as an origin devoid of actual (and therefore contemporaneous) Indian historical subjects. In this sense, the establishment has constructed a narrative that lacks an actual and authentic genealogy (Muratorio 1994, 1998) and, instead, presents a narrative that claims continuity between a static and glorious Indian past and the sacred ideals of the contemporary nation-state.

In contrast, many Indian communities, activists, historians, and social researchers presented a different reinterpretation of this same process (Pakari 1994). Their rendering has reached a wider national audience through its dissemination by the Indian movement and the CONAIE (1989, 1997). In this alternative narrative, the Indians reconstruct their own historical continuity among indigenous communities, past and present. In this version, it is the white/mestizo groups that are historically illegitimate and simply represented as the oppressors and usurpers of history.

As I discuss in detail, historical interpretations are singularly constructed and have direct political implications for the contemporary makeup of the nation. The active struggles of the multiple hegemonic readings at Cochasquí and in Ecuador's different national histories display the eminently political nature of any reconstruction of the past. Both at Cochasquí and in the other national histories, the political dimensions and implications represented by different interest groups are essential to determining the structure of the narrative and its ultimate meaning. The political and socioeconomic contexts in which Ecuador's national histories are produced and narrated are essential for understanding how each of these histories is presented to a national audience within particular settings (Agoglia 1985; Ayala Mora 1985a; Quintero López 1997; Silva 1995).

As many have argued (e.g., Bond and Gilliam 1994; Kohl and Fawcett 1995; Kuklick 1991; Patterson and Schmidt 1995), the reconstruction of the past is not a neutral enterprise, but is, quite to the contrary, charged with implicit and explicit notions of cultural authority and authenticity, as well as of national and territorial legitimacy. In the process of reconstruction, the past will always offer certain groups natural rights and power over others and legitimize, or delegitimize, territorial conquest (Silberman 1995: 256). It is this same factor that has contributed to many nations' interest in archeology as a means of constructing a "modern" history to legitimize their national and state objectives. Clearly, archaeology is one of the most effective ways of inventing a modern nation's history (Foster 1990). Within contemporary Western discourse, systematic surveys, radiocarbon dating, and archaeological excavations have become synonymous with scientific truth. This fact in itself transforms any archaeologist into a potential nationalizing agent whose scientific analysis may enable the modern nation-state to construct a history that is accepted as valid at the local and international levels (Elon 1997; Silberman 1995; Silberman and Small 1997).

In a practical sense, the political malleability of all archaeological discourse is a direct result of the impossibility of ever fully knowing exactly what the past was really like (Hodder 1982, 1986; Shanks and Tilley 1987a, 1987b). Interpreting the past, either archaeologically or historically, is always a project of understanding the past as precisely and objectively as possible. However, no matter how objective the reconstructions might be, history is not and should never be confused with the "real thing." History is never the past itself, but is, instead, a present-day narrative and understanding of it (Handler and Gable 1997: 223).

It is precisely this contemporary characteristic of historical production—the relationship of the study of the past with the present—which allows for this dynamic production of multiple histories (Benavides 1994). Therefore, it is these multiple histories that question the very notion of "real historical facts," of historical reality, and of a quest for "real" history (Wylie 1995: 269). This questioning is not necessarily in the suprarelativistic sense of there ever having been a "real" past, but, rather, in the sense that what is offered as the history of that "real" past is not only invariably colored, but, above all, also sanctioned by contemporary elements of our own making, independent of the past we are describing and striving to represent (see, e.g., Handler 1988; Handler and Gable 1997; Kuklick 1991; Wylie 1995). As Alonso (1988: 37) suggests: "Historical description, 'what really happened,' is not the result of self-evidences which we gather and string together but instead, the product of a complex interpretive process which, like any practice, is inflected by broader social projects, by relations of domination which seep into the private sphere of even the most 'civil' of societies." This is very much the case in the discussion of Ecuador's national histories, where "national" signifies different, and even contradictory, elements and meanings of the country's past.

The relationship between history and nationalism has been the object of dutiful research (e.g., Anderson 1983; Bhabha 1990; Hobsbawm and Ranger 1983) which has focused especially on the emergence, development, and legitimating power of national histories (e.g., Alonso 1995; Herzfeld 1987; Joseph and Nugent 1994; Karakasidou 1997; Mallon 1995). This has led many scholars to agree with Hobsbawm (1990) that historians in many ways are what poppy growers are for heroin addicts: the providers of the raw material needed for the active construction of a product (see also Foster 1990). This is not a minor concern when you take into consideration the power of nationalism in shaping the political contours of the contemporary world, in Chiapas and Kosovo, among other places. This political reality has most likely contributed to increased research since the 1980s into the workings of nationalism (see, e.g., Anderson 1983; Gellner 1983; Hobsbawm 1990; A. Smith 1983, 1987, 1995; Wolf 1982).

It is within this vein that the archaeological underpinnings of nationalism and national identity have begun to become the focus of research. For Silberman (1997: 18) this interest in the national politics of archaeology has provided for "a sociology of knowledge that seeks to understand the social and political strategies underlying archaeological research and the subsequent utilization of archaeological data, that is, how archaeology is used by modern institutions and nations to create a socially meaningful understanding of the past." This sociology of knowledge has been made possible by an influx of different intellectual traditions, such as neo-Marxism, critical theory, poststructuralism, literary criticism, and cultural studies. These intellectual currents have encouraged the analysis of archaeology as a modern discourse constituting contemporary contentions and conflicts over cultural heritage and authenticity (Trigger 1995), a debate which is essential in terms of the modern representation of the nation-state (Kohl and Fawcett 1995). This archaeological discourse incorporates more than individual concerns; it includes those of archaeology as a discipline and those of archaeology as part of much larger social processes implicated by nationalism itself (Silberman 1997).

In many ways, the epistemological crisis of the last decade, brought about by the postprocessual movement in archaeology (Hodder 1986; Shanks and Tilley 1987a, 1987b), and highlighted by the World Archaeological Congresses (Layton 1989a, 1989b; Ucko 1987), has also made it easier to focus on archaeology's discursive constraints. However, the subtle relationship between the nation-state, different forms of nationalism, and archaeology, which is the focus of this book, needs further attention. Analysis may be lacking because scholars who carry it out, such as philosophers of science (Saitta 1988; Wylie 1992, 1995) and archaeologists (e.g., Gero 1990; Patterson 1995b; Silberman 1997; Vidal 1993), are shunned by the academic archaeological establishment for having abandoned the discipline's fieldwork base.

The analysis of archaeological research as a discourse has led several scholars (among them, Arnold 1990, 1992; Kohl and Fawcett 1995; Layton 1989a, 1989b) to assess the state's manipulation of archaeological research as a potentially powerful tool for ideological legitimization of its own agenda of domination and oppression. This view, however, has fortunately given way to a more dynamic understanding of archaeology's relationship with nationalism and the recognition that archaeology not only is instituted by fascist or dictatorial states, but also is a characteristic of any modern "democratic" nation-state or national movement contending for political survival (Patterson and Schmidt 1995; Scham 1998; Silberman 1997).

NATIONAL SITES AND HEGEMONIC HISTORICAL NARRATIVES

The study of specific archaeological sites, such as Cochasquí, as part of the nation-state's agenda points to a broader understanding of archaeology's nationalistic implications and constraints (Bender 1998; Kuklick 1991; Peterson 1995). The invention of a national past in Ecuador exemplifies the routine manipulation (or collaboration) of archaeological knowledge as part of the representation of a homogeneous community and an authentic past—a representation that is essential for the political maintenance of the nation. It is this political context that makes the historical reconstruction of Ecuador's archaeological past a highly relevant national enterprise. As one of the largest archaeological sites in the northern Andean highlands, Cochasquí is a locus of subtle mechanisms of representation which are important to the regional and national maintenance of the Ecuadorian nation-state. The analysis of Ecuador's multiple histories enables one to understand the intricacies involved in the politics of the past and in the production of history (Trouillot 1995; Wylie 1995). The analysis of Ecuador's national past also provides evidence against the portrayal of archaeology as a neutral, free enterprise, solely concerned with the past, that is, of archaeology as a purely objective scientific approach, merely influenced by contemporary hermeneutic concerns (Moore and Keene 1983; Spriggs 1984; Wylie 1992). As Blakey (1995) states, the myth of being engaged in "real history" is in itself another form of domination, inherent in all postcolonial populations and nation-states that are struggling to free themselves from a colonial heritage (see also Blakey 1991).

This book suggests that, in many ways, the past is continuously under construction because of the nature of historical research and hermeneutics in general (Alonso 1988; Foucault 1991). The past, both the nation's and our own, is never the same as we originally saw and thought of it (see Hellman 1980; Kincaid 1997). My analysis suggests that variations in an archaeological discourse at a site and within national communities develop within specific historical, social, and territorial contexts.

Bender's (1998) analysis of Stonehenge exemplifies the context specificity of archaeological sites. She delineates Stonehenge's growing role as a status and class marker within the British nation and its ability to represent the nation's past. She explores how this past has become sacralized through the nation's investment in the site's importance and meaning. Only the aura of a nation explains the religious undertone in both the state's official and the alternative (new age) groups' claims of the site's importance. There is a fetishizing of the signifier (the archaeological site), which allows it to be more important than what it signifies (the nation-state's past) (Barthes 1972, 1982, 1992; Taussig 1992b). With the site now off limits to everyone, its representation of the past is no longer only an emblem; it has become more important than the past itself. Stonehenge has been constituted as the past, even though this substitution is produced by the privileging of a set of contemporary contentions (Bender 1998).

It is this partly "religious" aspect of archaeological heritage that has made Silberman (1997) interpret the visiting of national sites as a secular form of the traditional practice of religious pilgrimage. We can also appreciate this practice at Cochasquí. Within the modern-day representation of the nation-state, visiting sites that are presented as essential bearers of the national spirit is a form of national pilgrimage during which one's faith and belief in the national ideal are rekindled. These secular pilgrimages to archaeological sites imply a form of physical effort in which the visitors make an explicit physical action (penance) for an abstract, intangible (spiritual) goal, in this case, national archaeological/historical knowledge; allow visitors to participate in something more cohesive than their own existence—an imagined community, if you will (Anderson 1991); and after the visit, afford the ideological weapons with which to fight the traitors who question the nation's historical reasons for being and its existence (Silberman 1995). These elements, as we will see, are inherent in the tourist's visit at Cochasquí and are part of how the site's history is appropriated through one's physical effort to cohere to the contemporary representation of the nation-state.

Silberman (1995, 1997) also points to the fact that a commercial push for large national sites may make archaeological sites into a historical commodity thrown ruthlessly into the global market. It is not a coincidence that at sites like Cochasquí, small cabins for weekend tourists have been built (Leonor Buri, personal communication). This is also the case at sites such as Pompeii in Italy and Colonial Williamsburg in the United States, which seem to be the archaeological version of what Dávila (1997) calls "sponsored identities" in her study of commercial backing of Puerto Rican national cultural festivals.

Unlike Bender's (1998) analysis of a European site, Kuklick's (1991) analysis of an African site, Zimbabwe, documents the importance of both the site and its multiple interpretations for the country which chose to take its name from the site. Using the site of Zimbabwe, Kuklick examines the large signification value placed on archaeological sites in constructing a national ethos against colonial symbolisms, in this case, the name Rhodesia. As Kuklick elaborates, the use of the site to justify colonial rule is evident in the denial for decades of any evidence that might point to the construction of the site by one of the known indigenous national groups of southern Africa, the Bantu. The denial of this interpretation, even as a possibility, was so strong that when Rhodesian archaeologists elaborated an indigenous theory for the emergence of the site, they were fired from their posts and their theory was attacked as evidence of political infiltration of the archaeological enterprise:

> The constant theme of the pamphlets, now, reflects totally unproved assumptions substantiating Pan-African claims that for centuries Rhodesia was the centre of a sophisticated Negroid "civilization." The political implications are clear; if the claims are justified, there should be no legitimate opposition to a Black take-over of the country. It is no accident that the banned nationalist groups refer to Rhodesia as "Zimbabwe." . . . Fortunately, the National Monuments Commissions and the museums (and their associated archaeologists, whether professional or amateur) fall under the Ministry of Internal Affairs, and if that Ministry can ensure that the new Guide to Zimbabwe *is a wholly factual presentation* of the country's ancient history . . . it will at least remove yet another pretext for hostile political propaganda. (Unsigned October 1971 article from the Rhodesian paper *Property and Finance,* in *Antiquity* [1977]: 1; my emphasis)

What the writer of this article, and the Rhodesian government, did not understand is that archaeology, as part of history, is always a political venture (Blakey 1995; McGuire 1992; McGuire and Paynter 1991; Patterson and Schmidt 1995; I. Vargas 1995, 1990; Wylie 1995; Zimmerman 1989). That is, it was not the presentation of a new interpretation of old evidence which supported Bantu occupation of the site; instead, archaeological interpretations that had helped the white government stay in power had been a politically involved venture all along (Kuklick 1991). This is similar to the situation in Ecuador, where a minority of whites and mestizos benefit from the continuous retelling of the archaeological past in a myriad of forms, all of which, in one manner or another, serve to maintain the nation-state's agenda.

I argue for recognition that we have no evidence for believing in an ultimate archaeological truth or that the truth will finally win in some teleological sense; rather, the historical truth, like any truth (see Foucault 1991), is a product of conflict, negotiation, and contradiction and, as such, is implicated in constant change. This is true even though each time an archaeological interpretation reaches a hegemonic stance (see Mallon 1995), it presents itself as the truth and hides the hermeneutics of its own production and representation (Foucault 1991; Taussig 1992a). Only in this manner can archaeological truths be presented as historically self-evident and natural and legitimate the national ideals being actively produced and contested.

Analysis of archaeological discourse demands the withdrawal of hegemonic objective truths and awareness of the devices which have allowed these truths to flourish and claim their authoritative positions. In this regard, what is needed is not only an assessment of the truth, but also the production of knowledge that enables archaeological and historical truth to be presented as such. This was also the conclusion of the School of American Research's seminar on alternative histories and archaeologies (Patterson and Schmidt 1995). Ultimately, seminar participants preferred to use the concept of "making history" because it more accurately portrayed the reflexive stance inherent in any political positioning needed to fruitfully assess the master narratives, their analytical categories, and their knowledge claims from a variety of standpoints. One needs a reflexive strategy if one is interested in unmasking the conditions under which historical knowledge is produced and serves to legitimize political domination. This strategy is reflexive because it must incorporate the shifting political underpinnings inherent in the reconstruction of the past (Patterson and Schmidt 1995: 12–13).

History is never linear, nor does it inherently express causality by itself; instead, it is our own renderings of it, as defined by the hermeneutics of historical production, that structure historical accounts (Foucault 1991). In this sense, individuals and institutions, without exception, constantly incorporate archaeological interpretations into master narratives that reinterpret and meaningfully connect the nation's present with its past. The master narratives then overlook the breaks and discontinuities that make smooth transitions impossible and that therefore would delegitimize the whole national historical enterprise.

The need for historical continuity is particularly evident in colonial settings, where the new leaders are keen to present themselves as the natural heirs of the dominated group and territory (Kuklick 1991: 165). Colonialism always implies an artificial and violent break from the immediate past and a necessary legitimization of the new order as natural and ever-constant. In this enterprise, archaeological interpretations are used to obliterate the break and present a new, unproblematic extension of the archaeological past into the political present.

Cochasquí is no exception. It elaborates a complex discourse of colonial conquest, first, by the Incas over a thousand years ago; second, by the Spaniards fewer than five centuries ago; and most recently, by the white/mestizo elite, whose position of political, economic, and social privilege is continuously reinforced. In this manner, national histories homogenize cultural diversity by "permanently removing generations of [local] history from the landscape and creat[ing] a national historic rootlessness under official state sponsorship" (Patterson and Schmidt 1995: 20).

Even though legitimated national renderings of the archaeological past, such as Velasco's history of the ancient Kingdom of Quito (see chapter 1), might be much easier and perhaps more gratifying to deconstruct, alternative versions, such as the CONAIE's historical claims of Indian authenticity, are also produced within similar constraints. All historical versions, in their own fashion and for their own gain, strive to overlook the discontinuities in their archeological rendering of the past. National archaeological narratives, official or not, are always about presenting a smooth history where there are only accidents; a continuous subject where there is only discontinuity; a homogeneous nationality where there is a heterogeneity of communities; and historical truth where there is only subjugated knowledge.

THE PAST, THE POLITICAL PRODUCTION OF CULTURAL AUTHENTICITY, AND DEVELOPMENT

Anthropological studies of the role played by historical memory and archaeological knowledge initially addressed the question of representational politics from the standpoint of cultural exhibitions and museums (Clifford 1988, 1992; Gable, Handler, and Lawson 1992; Handler and Gable 1997; Haraway 1989; Price and Price 1995; Stocking 1985; Young 1995), including that of large international cultural fairs (Mitchell 1988; Muratorio 1994). These studies examine the issue of power, authority, and authenticity in the national display of cultural artifacts and the construction of homogeneous cultures (Rosaldo 1989). However, other work addresses archaeological research more explicitly (Beach 1998; Bender 1998; Castañeda 1996; Harke 1998; Morse 1994; Abu El-Haj 2001; Oyuela-Caycedo 1994; Patterson 1989; Peterson 1995; Silberman 1982, 1989; Wilk 1985). Bender's (1998) work at Stonehenge, Silberman's (1982, 1989) and Nadia's (1995) work in the Middle East, and Castañeda's (1996) work in the Yucatan peninsula highlight the close relationship of archaeology and nationalism in states that openly recognize the value of the former in legitimizing its religious, territorial, and political claims. Although it does not deal with archaeological knowledge per se, Rappaport's (1994) work in Colombia's Andean highlands demands particular notice because of her analysis of the communities' use of indigenous historical memory in the production of their identity. Her work allows one to begin to assess how historical memories, especially pre-Hispanic ones, are not only emblems of local resistance but also hegemonizing enterprises that make homogeneous notions of the local and the national, of resistance and domination, problematic, since these notions are intersected by complex discourses of history, culture, and power (see Dirks, Eley, and Ortner 1994).

In the following chapters, I take into account these works as I analyze how official, alternative, and local perceptions of the archeological evidence at Cochasquí and other pre-Hispanic narratives are used to construct particular pasts and histories that support the interests of the individuals and communities involved. In this regard, I am interested in the more common situation in which the state is not necessarily directly involved in archaeological research, yet benefits from the historical discourses without exposing its national interests, which are so problematic that they are erased, hidden, or denied. However, these pre-Hispanic discourses are not created in a cultural void; rather, they are caught within a wider global dynamic of a developmental paradigm. Within this developmental framework, it is impossible to think of, or to represent, the contemporary world and therefore its history, outside of this uneven cultural model. Postcolonial (Third World) nation-states are expressed as either communities lacking development or, in more positive terms, as in the process of developing, which places them in an inherently inferior position wherein they lack the elements that the developed (read "First") world already possesses and controls. It is not difficult to see the "coloniality of power" (see Quijano 1993) of this pervasive contemporary developmental framework (Heyer, Roberts, and Williams 1981). What is harder, though, is to understand how this neocolonial paradigm exerts its control, and how notions of power, domination, and resistance are intimately inserted into the communities' daily life (Escobar 1995; Ferguson 1994).

One manner in which this neocolonial power is articulated is within the mythical discourse of a pristine cultural authenticity. In this regard, the past serves as an invaluable tool. National communities, social movements, a whole array of fractured historical subjects, and the nation-state itself are actively immersed in representing and contesting notions of cultural authenticity that will validate their political existence. The nation-state has a primary stake in this contest, since losing would mean, and has meant, the disappearance of its hegemonic national production. However, before the nation-state is able to articulate its national discourse of cultural authenticity, the different communities must produce their own cultural traditions, which are, highlighted or not, reinforced, actively remembered, or forgotten by the state at specific junctures. The nation-state never actually expresses a static, homogeneous identity, since that would signify its death. Rather, it represents a monolithic identity while maintaining active deployment of validating alternative, even contradictory, traditions that will be unevenly and ambiguously expressed when needed. A critical revision of any nation-state's history is a testament to this ambivalent historical process (Bhabha 1990; Renan [1882] 1990).

If the nation-state is actively invested in regulating the representation of cultural authenticity, however, the different national communities are equally involved in a necessary dynamic reconfiguration that will enable their political goals. In Ecuador, this has meant the powerful reworking of an indigenous discourse that has, logically enough, both shaken and legitimized the contemporary nation-state. Groups like the CONAIE, Pachakutik Nuevo País, the women's movement, and gay, lesbian, and transgendered organizations have expressed themselves in terms of authentic cultural traditions. Through the reigning developmental discourse, they have obtained international assistance, aid, and political validation. In a sense, they have had no choice but to express themselves in culturally authentic terms, and yet, in another sense, they have been empowered to become "natives" by a developmental paradigm that needs natives in order to develop, and a nation-state that also needs natives to secure international funds. In this postmodern framework, homogeneous postcolonial nation-states are out of the picture, not because they have never existed, but because this reality would translate into an economic debacle and their political demise.

Because of these particular postmodern global processes, I have not limited myself to the site of Cochasquí, but have extended my analysis to other pre-Hispanic discourses, especially those actively deployed by the Indian movement in Ecuador. The alternative histories represented at Cochasquí and other histories actively deployed by the CONAIE present an interesting intersection of individual, local, regional, national, and global relationships that are neither neat nor merely binary. Rather, neocolonial forms of control and political power are exerted in a myriad of fashions, including in forms that are (or would seem) contrary to their own colonizing objectives (see Foucault 1990). This complex articulation of power and domination highlights the role of hegemony and history in the consolidation of national identities, and ultimately in the legitimization of the political power of the contemporary nation-state in Latin America. My analysis is directed toward understanding the hegemonic role of the past in the historical legitimization and modern functioning of the Ecuadorian nation-state so as to provide insights into similar processes throughout the continent.

NATIONALISM AND HEGEMONY

The problematic articulation of hegemony, varying forms of nationalism, and national histories is central to my understanding of the role of the pre-Hispanic past in Ecuador's national production. My central argument in terms of the contested and dynamic nature of hegemonic domination is most indebted to Foucault's (1988, 1990, 1994, 1995) insights into the workings of discourse and control apparatuses in the appearance of modern European social institutions. In this regard, Wylie (1995), among others (e.g., McClintock, Mufti, and Shohat 1997), has pointed to the need of alternative national discourses for the "officialization" and legitimization of any nation-state's political identity. Histories, including alternative or neutral ones, might be stumbling blocks, but they are essential for the nation-state's hegemonic articulation.

Nationalism has been the object of research since it was recognized and analyzed in the nineteenth century (Renan[1882] 1990). The approaches used to research it have tended to be largely influenced by the political trends of the period (Bhabha 1990). In the 1980s there was a renewed interest in nationalism in the social sciences (Gellner 1983; Hobsbawm 1990; Hobsbawm and Ranger 1983; A. Smith 1983, 1987), including Anderson's (1983) influential *Imagined Communities*. In 1991 Anderson addressed many of the concerns raised by other scholars (e.g., Fox 1990; Lomnitz-Adler 1992; Malkki 1995). Although a political scientist, Anderson imbued his study of nation with an anthropological understanding. For him, the nation, like all other social phenomena, does not have an intrinsic empirical reality. It is "imagined," much as our kinship ties or gender roles are "imagined." It is the fact that this imagined reality would seem natural and fixed that is at issue and worthy of intellectual exploration. Assessing the form imagining takes then becomes the primary question, not whether the nation is "real" or a mere political façade.

With this original approach, Anderson was able to shift the discussion of nationalism to a more analytical level, which still begged for an interpretive model to explain the construction of the nation. Anderson proposed a model in which members of the elite, mainly through the print media and educational institutions, were the most influential and viable agents in the nation-building process. According to Anderson, it was the ruling elite's political project that allowed the nation to come into existence. Using Italy and other postcolonial and European nations as examples, he concluded that the idea of the nation was, and must be, present before there was a politically constituted nation-state (Anderson 1983).

In regard to Anderson's (1983) use of Spanish America as a vital element and quasi-precursor of European nationalism, Lomnitz-Adler (1992) has raised some interesting concerns. For Lomnitz, Anderson's definition of nationalism on the American continent suffers from at least three vital shortcomings: (1) his use of the term is not historically accurate in relation to the colonial period of the Americas; (2) he emphasizes horizontal webs of association in disregard of central, vertical ones, that is, hierarchical webs that are essential in the communities' organization; and (3) in many instances, he defines national sacrifice less as a result of national ideals than as exploitative hierarchical social relations and explicit physical coercion. Despite Lomnitz's insightful analysis, Anderson's work is still profoundly paradigmatic for assessing national productions of any kind.

Anderson's work is interesting in its connection with Gramsci's (1971) notion of hegemony. Anderson understands that national histories are not only necessarily self-deceiving, but also the backbone of every nation-state. Hegemonic national histories are constructed in such a way as to make them seem right and natural. Sustained by the state, these national histories take on mythic qualities that secure their atemporality and therefore allow for their adaptation to the nation's changing conditions. In this sense, history becomes a mechanism for suppressing time; this mechanism supports certain groups' authority over others and strives to neutralize other possible versions of the past (Herzfeld 1987; also see Fabian 1983).

Foucault's 1990 work outlines how these far-from-monolithic authoritative histories manage to incorporate many counter-hegemonic descriptions and internal contradictions. His work on European and Western social discourses of sexuality (1990), medicine (1994), science (1972), madness (1988), and prisons (1995) constructs a much more dynamic understanding of hegemony and its construction. His analyses move us away from a simple understanding of authoritative discourses and inform them with a much more nuanced array of players and active contestation. Although his analysis is Eurocentric (see Stoler 1996), it demonstrates that an authoritative discourse is never merely the creation of the ruling elite.

Asad (1985) argues that for a hegemonic discourse to be successful, the ruling elite and the rest of the population must be convinced of its reality. This concept implies that none of the groups involved, including the elite, could conceive of this discourse as a simple plan for domination.

Both Foucault and Asad seem to question and complicate Anderson's (1983) model of an elite that relies on a hegemonic information apparatus for inventing imaginary cohesion and sense of belonging. At the same time, the political reality of present-day national struggles, for example, in Chiapas, Mexico, and the difficulty isolated individuals or large-scale social movements like the CONAIE have in simply dismantling national discourses seems to further validate Foucault's and Asad's arguments.

This has led to theoretical reworking of the very concept of hegemony (Alonso 1988; Bommes and Wright 1982; Corrigan and Sayer 1985; Domínguez 1986; Popular Memory Group 1982; Scott 1985; Silverblatt 1988; Stephen 1989; Wright 1985), including by a significant group of historians concerned with Mexico's past (e.g., Joseph and Nugent 1994). For this group of scholars, the power of hegemony can no longer be understood exclusively as ideological control; more specifically, they look at it as it is expressed in its capacity to constitute itself as a regulatory system supported by contrasting state-formation processes. In this sense, hegemony is not a finished ideological product, but a constant struggle for domination, a dynamic nation-state project in the making. It works because it is not a single thing, but a set of multiple realities with different meanings that can adapt to the times and the people that are constructing and are immersed in it. In this manner, it incorporates everything around it, including the analytical work done to understand it (Bommes and Wright 1982; Foucault 1980; Roseberry 1994; Sayer 1994).

The application of this analytical model to Mexico's past (e.g., by Joseph and Nugent 1994) brings up both the nature of the relationship between nationalism and hegemony within a Latin American context and the question of postcolonialism. Most important, the application of Anderson's model (1983) to the Latin American reality is fraught with difficulties and tensions, which exposes some of the model's weaknesses (see Lomnitz-Adler 1992; Rowe and Schelling 1991: 24–27). So far, Carol Smith (1990) and Mallon (1995) have provided the most general critique of the application of Anderson's model to Latin America. Both seriously question the elite's unique interest in creating a national spirit, especially in places such as Guatemala and Peru, where the group has clearly been more interested in maintaining and, to a large degree, creating greater ethnic differences among the populations. For Mallon, the depiction of the impoverished in Peru as "traitors" is due more to issues of representation and power than to the elite's actual interest in a national ideal. In this sense, nonelite groups contribute to nation building in more dynamic and subtle ways than Anderson would have it. As the Ecuadorian case indicates, a fragmented nation-state is an economic and political asset in the international-development arena.

In a similar vein, Carol Smith (1990) argues that in Third World settings like Guatemala, the elite struggle for the construction of a coercive state that reinforces greater ethnic division. This divisive strategy is particularly evident when the elite benefits more from capitalist development than from a popularly supported state, in other words, in a state buttressed by the legitimacy of the nation. Smith's argument seems to warrant a rethinking of the relationship between state formation and nation building as being not necessarily straightforward. Rather, there would seem to be a greater need for understanding the history and processes involved in each of the state's and the nation's constructions as interrelated and not a single entity.

This postcolonial retuning of Anderson's debate has provided for a rich and interesting intellectual production (Chatterjee 1986, 1993; Harrison 1991; McClintock 1995; McClintock, Mufti, and Shohat 1997; Minh-ha 1997; Patterson and Schmidt 1995; Spivak 1988, 1992; Young 1995). Postcolonial theorists have reworked century-long discussions of race, ethnicity, and sexuality and infused them with a more sophisticated understanding of their roles in hegemonic constructions within postcolonial national contexts. In this sense, their work reiterates much of the national-liberation literature of Cabral (1974a, 1974b), Fanon (1965, 1966, 1967), Freire (1992), C. L. R. James (1933, 1938), Memmi (1991), and Ribeiro (1972, 1988), among others. Although postcolonial studies have been brought to the forefront in the 1980s and the 1990s, mainly by Indian scholars (Chatterjee 1993; Guha and Spivak 1985) and writers (Rushdie 1981, 1989, 1994; see also *New Yorker* 1997), and are intricately related to India's recent independence from colonial rule, they now also form part of a much larger cultural-studies agenda (Appiah 1997; Bhabha 1990; Gilroy 1987; Hall 1981, 1986). Even though Latin America gained political independence over a century and a half ago, many factors still reflect its close relationship with its colonial structure and mark its neocolonial economic and cultural dependency. In this regard, the application of postcolonial theory to Latin America is fruitful and timely, since the continent's reality presents many fascinating postcolonial aspects to explore (see Barbero 1987, 1993; Coronil 1997; Franco 1991; García-Canclini 1992a,1992b, 1993; Rowe and Schelling 1991).

The analyses of pre-Hispanic discourses developed at Cochasquí in the Indian movement and the national print media provide insights into the mechanisms of national production and hegemonic articulation. The pre-Hispanic discourses that inform Ecuador's political identity are traversed by processes of identity formation that struggle at different levels to present coherent cultural pictures. How are these different identity formations, which feed and affect Ecuador's national ethos, formed? How is some level of balance or even the appearance of stability created while identities are changing constantly? To address these questions, we must explore the identity-formation process that popularly expresses the postmodern condition of the "fractured subject" (Hall 1997). It is this process of identity formation, particularly contemporary categories of social class, gender and sexuality, and race, that forms the last point of the theoretical focus of this book.

THE NATION-STATE'S FRACTURED SUBJECTS

The anthropological analysis in this work looks to broaden understanding of how historical perceptions of gender, race, sexuality, and class are integral to the nation-building and state-hegemony project. My contribution to this debate falls along historical lines, especially with regard to the political revision of national subjects as evidenced in Indian, women's, and gay and lesbian movements and organization. Rather than seeing archaeology and history as inconsequential in the debate over the creation of nationally engendered, sexualized, and racialized subjects, I stress the central role of the past and pre-Hispanic memory in the contemporary production of national citizenship. The Ecuadorian case study emphasizes the historical burden of these fractured social categories (i.e., in terms of class, race, gender, etc.) and the pivotal role of genealogical relationships in both their creation and their maintenance. Even though continent-wide analyses are complicated by the breadth of the logistical and research demands, these fractured social categories owe most to continent-wide ideological discourses(e.g., about *mestizaje*) and strategic idiosyncratic realities.

Although I concentrate on Ecuador's fractured subject, I hope my findings will be applicable to other Latin American states and projects. I look to contribute to the "critical" literature on the emergence of hegemonic articulations of race (De la Cadena 2000; Poole 1997) and gender and sexual constructions (Lancaster 1996; R. Parker 1991) throughout the continent. Surprisingly enough, maybe in a kind of academic revenge for their initially Marxist inclinations, critical class analyses are less prevalent than ever, and class itself is no longer treated as an exclusive and privileged identity marker. As in many other poststructural analyses (e.g., Foucault 1991), class is now subsumed as an inherent category in the exploration of other levels of social inequality. This approach has shifted the line of inquiry from one that merely assesses the existence of class to one that is more interested in defining ways in which social classes are actively deployed.

Nation-states rely on implicit truths (or lies) about the class, ethnic, racial, gender, and sexual components of national identity (Mosse 1985; A. Parker et al. 1992). Most, if not all, Western nation-states claim a white, male, heterosexual image as the civilized ideal; alternative sexual forms and gender identities are not disruptive ("a strategic marginality"; see Anzaldúa 1987; Mallon 1996), but are kept in check by all nation-states (Andrade 1995, 1997; Benavides 1998). In this respect, Ecuador is no different. Many recent research contributions point to a need to explore the processes by which these sexual categories are deployed, regulated, and, ultimately, expressed, as a way of analyzing a vulnerable locale of the nation's discourse (Abelove, Barale, and Halperin 1993; Cobham 1992; Gutmann 1996; Lancaster and di Leonardo 1997; Mallon 1996; McClintock, Mufti, and Shohat 1997; Rubin 1984).

It is not surprising, therefore, that "sexuality appears to be a volatile symbol in debates about the character of national identity" (Beriss 1996: 191). However, it is also becoming apparent that placing all the responsibility on the state for controlling and reproducing sex and gender identities is too simplistic, just as laying the complete burden of class regulation on the state proved to be less predictive than Latin American revolutionaries believed. Recent analysis (e.g., Murray and Handler 1996) also seems to show that the state imposes certain policies and guidelines which people must contend with, but what the people select or imagine lies largely outside the realm of coercive state power (Domínguez 1996: 304).

In this respect, research should not only focus on the normative capacity of the nation-state, but should also incorporate a problematization of regulatory agents in each society, or among the individuals who make up the different national communities (Schein 1996: 199). Particularly revealing in this regard is how traditionally exploited groups, such as Indians, women, and transgendered individuals, are at the height of the social movements' political debate in Latin America (see Escobar and Álvarez 1992).

These new, textured approaches are strongly informed by Foucault's analysis of sexual discourse (1990) as a much more complex and dynamic struggle for power and political domination than previous studies indicate. However, future research also needs to incorporate the colonial and subaltern critiques, which are thoroughly lacking in Foucault's analysis (see Spivak 1988; Stoler 1996), that take into account the relationship between the categories of sex and race and that understand that every sexualized being is also a racialized one. In other words, the postcolonial body, as a national body, is both sexualized and racialized and serves to create mores or geographies that help map the nation-state's and its citizens' fractured existence (Stoler 1996).

Race and class, in this sense, are pivotal identity markers. Unlike studies of gender and sexuality, analyses of race and class have a longer intellectual tradition in the continent (Knight 1990; Quintero and Silva 1991; Savoia 1988; Wade 1993, 1994). In this regard, my interest lies not in adding to this research agenda, but in focusing on how all of these identities are intimately woven, deployed, and, in some sense, "acted out" (Butler 1997a, 1997b). This is a particularly difficult, yet necessary, objective because of the constant elaboration of a postmodern fractured subject that is successfully represented, and even represents itself, along singular identity lines. Part of this representational burden is linked to the postmodern developmental concerns highlighted above. However, most important, the lived-in experience of Latin American communities is far from that of the typically represented fractured subject; rather, lives are dynamically embodied to fit public concerns that are intricately related to a wide range of personal experiences and social categories.

The objective, and perhaps the impossibility, of describing social experience as lived in has been aptly debated in recent social science and humanities debate (Rosaldo 1989; see also Arce and Long 2000; Williams 1977; and chapter 7 here). However, these constraints must be examined in terms of scholarly analytical projects when it comes to understanding the postcolonial Latin American subject. My analysis of historical discourses addresses many of these concerns and provides insights into the ways in which social categories are unevenly represented and related to a national ethos. This is particularly relevant because all historical narrative must use fractured subjects to express their stories and ideas. Without race, class, gender, and sexual markers, there would be no Ecuadorian history left to narrate. Therefore, discussion of pre-Hispanic narratives in Ecuador in different national settings illustrates the uneven utilization, production, and exclusion of certain identity markers in specific political settings, including in those made official by the national communities that make up the nation-state.

Class is particularly problematic because of its traditionally privileged setting in the dominant Marxist and revolutionary analyses of Latin America. Rather than highlighting class as a separate marker, I will emphasize how class, as a formative process, is necessarily linked to race, gender, and sexuality in the production of social and economic inequality. Thus, class is not absent from, but thoroughly structures, the field on which other social categories are inscribed, reinforcing uneven access to national resources and imagery and making this inequality appear natural. It is through this interactive analysis that I maintain that the discussion of historical memory at Cochasquí, the Indian movement, and other historical narratives is particularly useful in questioning official history and assessing political domination. How are official histories at Cochasquí linked to inherently unequal social dynamics? How is the Indian movement's understanding of the past imbued with not only racial constraints but also powerful gender and sex imagery? How, ultimately, is the Ecuadorian national enabled to "auto-produce" himself or herself as both a homogeneous and a fractured subject at one and the same time?

OVERVIEW OF THE CHAPTERS

This book is composed of seven chapters. Chapter 1 introduces the national process of historical formation in Ecuador, in particular, how class and race discourse informs the national understanding of the past and the production of a national identity. Particularly important in this regard is the double-sided discourse of *blanqueamiento* (whitening) and *mestizaje* that expounds an ideology of whiteness while purporting to celebrate a mythical, ancient Indian past. Although present throughout Latin America, *mestizaje* exhibits unique characteristics in the Ecuadorian context, which are explored in chapter 1. I also briefly discuss Ecuadorian archaeological discourse as epitomized by two central figures, Juan de Velasco y Valverde and Eugenio de Santa Cruz y Espejo. Their work exemplifies the class, gender, and race dynamic central to the nation-state's historical discourse. Finally, I introduce Cochasquí and the major theoretical processes of state formation and nation building that allow the site to be politically reproduced as nationally significant.

Chapter 2 explores the national dimensions of pre-Hispanic historical discourses at Cochasquí. In this chapter I discuss how the archaeological evidence and narratives are interpreted within a wider web of national ideology that regulates but still does not completely define the site's historicity. Both the program that runs the site (Programa Cochasquí) and the *comuna* of Cochasquí are described. These descriptions allow further exploration of Cochasquí's place in national imagery and two of the most nationalizing discourses present at the site: one which highlights and successfully situates Cochasquí as an Ecuadorian site; and a second which also successfully establishes the role of the site as culturally "authentic" and a nationalizing state enterprise.

Chapter 3 explores how official notions of history, heritage, territory, gender, ethnicity, and race are interwoven and actively appropriated. The chapter begins by examining the dynamic scripts of the past at the site and the role played by the Ecuadorian state and the Programa Cochasquí in making a particular historical narrative official. This historical process is closely examined within the dual operation by which a particular version is produced within a context that legitimizes the state's nationalizing enterprise. I also analyze the historical representation of the later occupations of the site by the Incas and Spaniards and how these two groups are ambiguously interwoven in the narratives to further support a pristine national identity. I pay particular attention to the way in which expressions of territory, gender, and ethnicity and race utterances become part of Ecuador's cultural heritage. Interesting in this regard are the modes of appropriation, which, as I discuss, are essential to the site's success as a national symbol. All of these narratives exemplify how the nation-state, far from curtailing different historical production, uses the many narratives to increase its control and political domination.

Chapter 4 addresses the interstices of these social categories in Ecuador's hegemonic production. The chapter takes as its starting point a novel published in 1976 by Ecuadorian Jorge Enrique Adoum, *Entre Marx y una mujer desnuda* (Between Marx and a naked woman). The novel underlines both the leftist revolutionary and the heterosexual parameters of Ecuadorian citizenship toward the end of the twentieth century. I question this traditional stance as it was originally understood from both Foucault's poststructural viewpoint and by the successful transgendered approaches to the founding of a heteronormative Latin American culture. I review the narratives told at Cochasquí and the historical representation of the *enchaquirados* (a pre-Hispanic male religious harem) to illustrate the ongoing contested relationship between social identities, historical representation, and people's daily lives as well as the changing conditions of the nation's social identities.

Chapter 5 addresses the powerful Indian movement in Ecuador and its understanding of the nation's past. The Indian movement, particularly under the leadership of the CONAIE and Pachakutik Nuevo País, has accomplished what no other social movement has been able to do in almost a century of trying: it has contested the state's dominion. The Indian movement has used traditional civil disobedience and general strikes and has developed a new social identity that expresses ancient grievances in a postmodern form. It is this discourse, which has allowed many Indian groups in Ecuador to attract international resources and recognition, that is closely examined in terms of its own national production and its impact on the representation and maintenance of the modern Ecuadorian nation-state, and, most dramatic, on its own hegemonic implications.

Chapter 6 further explores the nature of officializing discourses from different historical interpretations, this time within the context of the national print media. To this end, I analyze the traditional role of the national print media and their relationship to historical production and the state's agenda. I discuss newspapers' pursuit of objective reporting on Ecuador's pre-Hispanic past. I then focus on the coverage of the struggle over the final resting place for Saint Biritute, a pre-Hispanic monolith deity. Newspaper coverage of this issue illustrates the dialectical nature of the print media's historical coverage—coverage that furthers the nation-state's agenda, albeit ambiguously and indirectly.

Chapter 7 attempts to, first, highlight the major findings of the previous chapters, particularly the manner in which archaeological discourses about the pre-Hispanic past are intricately woven into the national discourse and are glossed over either as natural or normal while their vital political contribution is strategically represented as inconsequential. Second, I address the role of political representation and social movements in the relationship between counter-hegemonic production and hegemonic constraints. More specifically, I engage the larger theoretical question of what liberating contribution, if any, counter-hegemonic concerns play in the rupture of national hegemonic discourses. The comparison of the Indian movement, the site of Cochasquí itself, and the controversy over Saint Biritute provides rich material. Finally, I address the issue of nationalism. Although an enormous part of my research (and this book) concentrates on history and hegemony, I think both are central to the production of nationalism not only in Ecuador but throughout Latin America. I end by discussing what I believe to be the most promising insights from my research in terms of thinking nationalism through in a new postmodern Latin America and Caribbean.

ONE

ECUADOR'S POLITICAL HEGEMONY
National and Racial Histories

⁓

[The nation] had seduced everyone and everything,
even History herself.

—MARGUERITE YOURCENAR (1963)

HISTORIES AND ARCHAEOLOGY:
THEORETICAL AND NATIONAL CONSIDERATIONS

The Construction of a National History

In 1937 Alberto Muñoz Vernaza's *Orígenes de la nacionalidad ecuato-*
riana (Origins of Ecuadorian nationality) was published. In this work,
Muñoz explored the historical underpinnings and emergence of the social formation called Ecuador, barely over one hundred years old. What
is most striking about Muñoz's work is, first, that it is one of the earli-
est works to deal with the historical foundations of Ecuador and, second, that its tone in defending an Ecuadorian nation is unapologetic.
Even the foreword by a foreign scholar demonstrates a patriotic fervor
that voices many of the implicit discourses surrounding the appearance
and maintenance of the nation-state and, most important, the role of
history in the national enterprise (1984: 60; my translation):

> The professor of the Normal School of Cartebourg, in his "Treatise on
> Methodology," has synthesized the importance of these studies in careful
> and true words: "History well understood," he says, "is par excellence the
> school of patriotism. She is the one that allows us to know and admire the

Nation [*la Patria*] in the past; that makes us love and serve it in the present and the one that guarantees its future. In effect, it defends the integrity of the national character, whose disappearing or weakened qualities in future generations would strongly threaten the country's independence, suppressing its reason to exist as a separate political entity."

What is apparent in this quotation and throughout Muñoz's book is the dynamics of historical production as an essential element in nation building and its occupation of a vital place in the national discourse. An at times explicit, at other times implicit, nationalist vein has run through Ecuadorian historiography. The national characteristics of historical production have been there from the days of the struggle for independence from Spain (Velasco [1790] 1841), through the early Republican period (Cevallos 1870; González Suárez 1878, 1890, 1892), to the present day (Ayala Mora 1983, 1985a; Efrén Reyes 1967).

Muñoz's explicit linking of history and a national ethos is not new; rather, it points to the centrality of this relationship even before the appearance of the modern nation-state in 1830. This centrality is even present in critical contemporary histories such as the histories of Ecuador published by Salvat (Holm and Crespo 1980) and the Marxist-inspired *Nueva historia del Ecuador* (The new history of Ecuador [Ayala Mora 1983]). These two edited histories are by far the most ambitious attempts to assess Ecuador's past and, as historical works, both are, by definition, equally invested in the reproduction of the nation. In both works, Ecuador's authenticity is never questioned; instead, its empirical essence as a coherent social whole is projected back millennia. This backward imagining allows historians to talk about a pre-Hispanic past as an integral analytical unit and shows that questioning the Ecuadorian nation would disrupt historical analyses. In other words, no historical text can afford not to be seduced by the nation, since its own survival or that of its analysis depends on this seduction.

This linkage between historical production and national invention is easier to comprehend when one takes into account Anderson's (1983; see also Introduction here) notion of imagining the nation. Understanding the nation as an imagined or invented entity in no way denies its existence, but exposes its complex and multiple realities. Following Anderson's lead, then, makes it necessary to understand how nations are imagined or invented rather than to fruitlessly plot their deconstruction. If the nation does not have an empirical existence as much as an imagined one, then the importance of legitimizing it in historical works is of utmost importance and urgent for the nation's survival.

At the same time, if the state can be viewed as a political project in and of itself rather than as a static entity that carries out political projects, the nation itself has a vested interest in proclaiming its existence as loudly and as often as possible, since it is in this claim of authenticity that the nation is most readily present (Abrams 1988; Anderson 1983; Sayer 1994). The nation's claim to a coherent wholeness is vital to its survival. It is the nation's unquestioned imagined existence that supports works that look to assess its historical evolution.

Historians treat the nation as a given, since, otherwise, they would run the risk of not having anything to study. In Ecuador, as in many other postcolonial nation-states, one of the distinct styles of imagining the nation includes the characteristics of historical production. This "national history" is national above all in its objective of reaching the widest possible audience—the different national communities—and of attributing to itself a general representation of the social formation which is claimed to be the nation. But what is this national history, and how is it really formed?

There is no doubt that this national history has changed over the centuries to adapt to changing conditions. That it has changed is not surprising; what is surprising is that its transformation has gone unnoticed. That is, a national history has been able to metamorphose constantly while appearing to be static, unchanged, natural, and, therefore, relentlessly hegemonic. Over the last two centuries, the Ecuadorian nation-state has benefited from perceived historical unity even though its history has not been unified in any way other than in its hegemonic objective. The multiple contradictions within Ecuador's national history have never been pondered or been an object of study, and their invisibility has facilitated the smoothing over of any plausible or dramatic conflict between national histories. The denial of historical pluralism is not unrelated to the fact that questioning the national history or any of its parts would also mean questioning the basis of the Ecuadorian nation-state itself. Therefore, to question the nation's history would be as daunting as it would be life-threatening for the nation and its citizens.

I do not, and cannot, equate the official history found in state-sanctioned textbooks with a single national history. It is simply one more element in the nation's multiple histories and, in that sense, like any of the other histories, is vital in the far more dynamic hegemonic project which Ecuador's imagined national history comprises. Ecuador's official history as expressed in its textbooks and state-backed discourse (e.g., Velasco's notion of an Ancient Kingdom of Quito—Antiguo Reino de Quito) is far too static to single-handedly constitute the hegemonic discourse, but it contributes enormously, as do the other historical discourses (the alternative, the neutral, and the multivoiced) to the production of an imagined national and hegemonic history that seeks to legitimize (and so far has done so successfully) the Ecuadorian nation-state. In this process, a hegemonic national history secures not only the operationalization of the Ecuadorian state and the maintenance of the Ecuadorian nation, but also the oppression and exploitation of the majority of the population. The nation's history, like the nation itself, is also an imagined reality that is in constant flux, a fragmented reality, even though it appears to be fixed. Most important, it appears monolithic and whole when it is neither, and it presents itself as a single national history when it really represents a multiplicity of histories.

This false representation is evident in the several national histories that I have reviewed. Not only do they present contrasting versions, but they are internally inconsistent, as well. The history of the Ancient Kingdom of Quito presented in all history textbooks and initially put forward by a Jesuit priest, Juan de Velasco, in 1790, for example, is plagued with contradictions and weaknesses, the most powerful being the absence of any independent archaeological or empirical evidence to support the kingdom's existence. In fact, he wrote it while living in exile with the rest of his religious community in Faenza, Italy. Since textbook content is strictly controlled by the Ministry of Education, textbooks represent the nation-state's official version of Ecuador's pre-Hispanic past.

The official story of the Ancient Kingdom of Quito has a whole set of characters and players—imperial rulers, generals, feisty women, and heirs. The men are valiant, warlike, and proud; the women have similar proud characteristics, but are also docile and beautiful. In the state's official account of the Kingdom of Quito, the central narrative is, in many ways, a simple war story, that is, a tale of a smaller polity resisting an invading imperial enemy. It is also a story of reconquest, love, and vengeance, as the defeated Kingdom of Quito eventually conquers the conquerors, the Incas.

In the textbooks, the Incas are first hailed as enemies of the Quito nation (read Ecuador), but, interestingly enough, they are themselves conquered by geography (that of the cities of Tomebamba and Quito) and by the beauty of the local women (e.g., Princess Pacha). The Incas are seduced, leading to the Inca heir, Atahualpa, born on Ecuadorian soil. Atahualpa not only rightfully reigns over the Quito polity, but also usurps the Peruvian throne of the Tahuantinsuyu, once the enemy and plunderer of the Quito state. Through Atahualpa and his mother, Pacha, the Inca conquerors are conquered.

Since the 1700s this narrative has been a source of national pride and identity, even though the existence of this kingdom has never been confirmed by archaeological evidence or independent ethnohistorical accounts (Benítez Vinueza 1986). However, the historical inconsistencies in Velasco's account have never prevented Ecuador's Ministry of Education from supporting the idea of an ancient "Quitu" nation and encouraging the teaching of the kingdom's history in schools. The fictitious Kingdom of Quito is still part of the state's official seventh- and tenth-grade history curriculum and is hailed as "the foundation of the Ecuadorian nation" (Programa Anual 1996, 1996/1997).

The alternative history proposed by the Indian movement and the CONAIE seeks to present a counter-hegemonic discourse and uses many of the official version's devices to support its narrative. The proponents of the alternative history struggle to make their version of history the central one in a revised national discourse.

All of these national histories show that the state is not a consent-manufacturing machine nor is popular culture the repository of an authentic and egalitarian traditional ethos (Rowe and Schelling 1991). Rather, both are caught in a field of force that is both shaping and linking their production (Roseberry 1994: 366). It is within this field of force that national newspapers construct their own historical narrative. The controversy over the rightful home of Saint Biritute, the Manteño-Huancavilca monolithic deity, for example, clearly brings up issues of local and national legitimacy and ownership between forces that are caught in a wider discursive framework than the actors are aware of. All of these historical versions demonstrate that there is no single national history beyond a constant and successful (self)-representation as such and a single-minded quest to silence the narrative's own historical multiplicity and fragmented reality.

In this nationalizing venture, one must not underestimate the power of the repressive political mechanisms available to the state. Force, as pointed out by both Weber and Marx (see Sayer 1994; Scott 1985), is the most efficient way to guarantee the state's political claim to and use of power. However, force is even more productive as it breeds terror and fear, as Taussig (1992a, 1992b) claims. Terror allows continuous production of a national history under the vigilant (masculine) guise of the state and the seductive (feminine) care of the nation.

The constant reappropriation of themes and the reworking of similarly fractured social subjects allows for a smoother transition to political domination and the appearance of permanence. Ecuador's national history has been forged from many recurring themes apparent in the different national versions of the country's history, such as that of the Ancient Kingdom of Quito, the constant threat of southern (Peruvian) conquest, a victorious victim that has been wronged, and an Indian struggle for social justice and equality. All of these themes have provided for an almost endless production of versions of history that have been successfully imagined and reproduced as a sole national history.

As many have pointed out (e.g., Abrams 1988; Corrigan and Sayer 1985; Joseph and Nugent 1994), the state lives in and through its subjects, not merely at an ideological level, but also in the materiality of discourses of state formation, that is, in the buying and reading of official textbooks, in the struggle for political power by, for example, marching, in running for office, and in the printing of one's opinion about the final resting place of a pre-Hispanic artifact/deity. In each of these ventures, there is an implicit adherence to the figure of the state, even though many of them may actually be striving to upset the uneven power relationships. But it is this ambiguity or multiplicity of elements within a single national venture that secures not only the imagination that permits the state's existence, but also its dynamic transformation in response to the changing needs of the nation.

In each of these national versions of Ecuador's history, we are privy to how the past can be reconstituted to project different meanings. But the essence of the problem is that these meanings are understood as either/or instances—as official, alternative, and so on—when, as a result of their internal and external contradictions, they actually constitute instances of both/and. Therefore, the hegemony of the state is the most fragile, since it is based on fundamental contradictions, on people living what, most of the time, they know to be a lie, a normalized performance, or at least a much more contradictory situation than they will readily admit to. Military force, terror, and the sheer ambiguity of all oppressive and subversive social acts force people to participate in this contradictory performance (Sayer 1994).

Clearly, Ecuador is not on the verge of losing its historical legitimacy, as Muñoz Vernaza feared, yet this fear provides one of the many resources for imagining or producing the Ecuadorian nation (1984: 61): "Because Ecuador is a nation of great traditions that must be conserved at any cost, since, through them, it [*la nación*] affirms its nationality, whose social and legal embodiment cannot be exposed to the whims of any immigrant who wishes to change it or injure it, of which there are a series of historical examples."

Muñoz's isolated work builds on that of two other scholars, one white (Spanish), the other mestizo (with strong indigenous heritage), who, although they lived in colonial times, provide great insight into what the future Ecuadorian nation would envision as its historical raison d'être. Of course, both scholars, Father Juan de Velasco and Eugenio de Santa Cruz y Espejo (1791, 1786), had no knowledge of what their colonial communities would evolve into or that they would take on the name of Ecuador in the early 1800s. What is most relevant about their work is not simply their contribution to the ideological imperative of the nation as much as their contribution that later generations of Ecuadorians saw in their work. As always in the production of nationalism, it is not Espejo's and Velasco's contribution that counts as much as the reiterated national representation through generations of their work and their lives in the revolutionary transformation of the colonial territories into an independent nation-state.

Before I return to these two figures, I would like to address two more recent attempts similar to my own. Both Guerrero (1991) and Muratorio (1994) have systematically studied not the traditional "objective" historical rendering of the past, but a much more nuanced understanding of how these histories are tied to contemporary representations of the past and, most important, present-day identity production. I have used Muratorio's work throughout this book, particularly in the introduction and this chapter, since I believe her work highlights how to begin to understand how contemporary notions of revitalizing the past contribute to social conditions that further exploit the traditional Indian populations and the Ecuadorian population at large.

Muratorio's (1998) insights prove vital in assessing the CONAIE's potential for counter-hegemonic disruption as well as hegemonic reordering. She is one of the few scholars to have looked at the Indian movement's challenge in a nonromanticized way.

Unlike the majority of scholars concerned with Ecuador, Guerrero attempts to provide a history of history. This allows him to free himself from objective limitations that obscure rather than highlight the parchment upon which history is written over and over again.

Ecuador's National Archaeological Precursors

The institutionalization of archaeology as a discipline in Ecuador has been addressed only rarely (Echeverría 1995; Salazar 1993/1994, 1995a). Ecuadorian archaeology did not emerge in close relationship with natural history, as was the case in the United States and Argentina (Patterson 1995b), or anthropology, as was the case in Mexico and Peru (Patterson 1995a). Rather, Ecuador's archaeological discourse was embedded in the production of an academic history that justified a *criollo* (mestizo) heritage as opposed to Indian or Spanish. Archaeological investigations in Ecuador may be, in many ways, particularly burdened by the questioned origins of the national territory within the colonial structure preceding the formation of the modern republic. Thus, Ecuadorian archaeology more closely resembles the historical expression of colonial nations like Puerto Rico or recently founded republics like Panama. In this historical venture, a continental typology of archaeological forms might emerge, similar to Trigger's (1984) designation of colonial, national, and imperial archaeologies. However, recent typological attempts seem to warrant more thorough comparative studies as well as theoretical analyses that incorporate different political systems, modes of production, and nations and nation-states. A more detailed comparative approach should avoid the reformulation of simplistic functional categorization of national archaeologies like, for example, those by Oyuela-Caycedo (1994).

The assumed forefathers of Ecuadorian archaeology (and it is no accident that they are fathers and not mothers) are those historians and scholars who were born in present-day Ecuador. These scholars are indisputably seen as part of the Ecuadorian nation and as Ecuadorians. The five seminal figures in Ecuadorian archaeology are Father Juan de Velasco y Petroche (1727–1792) and Francisco Eugenio de Santa Cruz y Espejo (1747–1795) during the colonial period, and Archbishop Federico González Suárez (1844–1917), Jacinto Jijón y Caamaño (1881–1950), and Emilio Estrada (1916–1961) in the republican era.

González Suárez's three-volume *Historia general de la República del Ecuador* (General history of the Republic of Ecuador) (1890), unlike Pedro Fermín Cevallos's (1870), tried to describe the pre-Hispanic period in terms of remains found throughout the Ecuadorian territory of the decimated Indian cultures found throughout the territory. González Suárez's two major archaeological works, *Los aborígenes de Imbabura y Carchi: Investigaciones arqueológicas sobre los antiguos pobladores de la República del Ecuador* (1878) and *Atlas arqueológico ecuatoriano* (1892), make up the first seriously scientific inquiries into Ecuador's archaeological past.

González Suárez was interested in systematizing historical knowledge to allow the institutionalization of the nation-state in what he considered to be perilous times, for example, during Eloy Alfaro's liberal revolution. Through his historical enterprise, González Suárez led the way for professional archeologists who would carry out a national agenda. With this purpose in mind, he surrounded himself with a group of young students, not surprisingly, from the upper class in Quito, to create the first historical society in the country. It would be one of these students, Jacinto Jijón y Caamaño, who would carry on González Suárez's project of making archeology a viable intellectual pursuit (J. M. Vargas 1991).

If González Suárez was the first Ecuadorian to carry out intensive scientific investigations during the republican period, Jacinto Jijón y Caamaño (1912, 1914, 1918a, 1918B, 1919a, 1919b, 1920a, 1920b, 1922, 1927, 1929, 1930, 1933, 1941/1946, 1952) is by far the most important and influential Ecuadorian archaeologist during the republican period (1900–1934), and possibly ever. Jacinto Jijón y Caamaño was born in 1881 into one of the wealthiest textile-producing families in the country. He played a pivotal role in national politics, becoming a leader of the Conservative Party and mayor of Quito. He also had enormous economic and social resources to expend in his archaeological research. He carried out his work with great passion, as was particularly apparent in his final work (1952), *Antropología prehispánica del Ecuador* (Pre-Hispanic anthropology of Ecuador), on which he labored almost until he died. He dedicated a major part of his life to excavating, collecting, researching, and writing about the pre-Hispanic cultures of America. The most important part of his archaeological work—excavations in the country's highlands and coast and in Maranga, Peru—was carried out between 1909 and 1925. Jijón lived in Europe between 1912 and 1916, visiting museums, conducting research in archives, and making academic contacts. He funded the Ecuadorian research in Ecuador of internationally renowned German archaeologist Max Uhle (1922a, 1922b, 1922c, 1923, 1926, 1927, 1928, 1929, 1930a, 1930b, 1931, 1933, 1936, 1937, 1939) for fourteen years (1919–1933), and he developed an impressive library and artifact collection, which is now open to the public as the Museo Jijón in the Pontificia Universidad Católica, and the Fondo Jijón at the Banco Central Library, both in Quito (Collier 1982; Echeverría 1995; J. M. Vargas 1991).

Jacinto Jijón y Caamaño is hailed as the central driving force behind Ecuadorian archaeology (Salazar 1997). Through his groundbreaking archaeological excavations and by the sheer breadth of his intellectual production, Jijón systematized archaeological knowledge in Ecuador into a viable discipline that made it worthy of scholarly pursuit and an essential element in the nationhood debate (Jijón y Caamaño 1992).

Estrada's work embodies many of the elements that made the geographical divide of coast and highlands an important feature of the nation's history (Maiguashca 1994). In this regard, it is instructive to compare Estrada and Jijón, since they shared an interest in the archaeological heritage of the nation, but were informed by completely different regional traditions (Collier 1982): "Jijón was an aristocrat with great inherited wealth, an ethnohistorian, a bibliophile, and a *Quiteño;* Estrada was a successful businessman, a dirt archaeologist, and a *Guayaquileño* who was more interested in world trade and international yachting than in the Archive of the Indies. These differences of temperament and the origin of these two men account largely for the focus on the highland during the Developmental Period and on the coast during the Florescent."

Father Juan de Velasco and Eugenio de Santa Cruz y Espejo

My focus on the first two pivotal figures in archaeological/historical research in Ecuador is not due to their unique intellectual attributes, but, rather, to how they express the greater social forces in which they were embedded and the social forces and representations that worked on them. Juan de Velasco and Eugenio Espejo were not the only persons to be hailed as precursors of an Ecuadorian identity during the colonial period, since this list would include figures like J. Mejía Lequerica, J. J. de Olmedo, and Manuela Cañizares, but they are the ones with the greatest appeal, as evidenced by their continued appearance in newspapers, magazines, and textbooks (*Vistazo* 1997a).

Velasco's account of the Ancient Kingdom of Quito is one of the most influential narratives in consolidating the Real Audiencia de Quito's political authority. The Audiencia was a territorial stronghold that needed to be justified internally and externally in the Spanish crown's eyes because the fame of the rival Inca dynasty symbolically legitimized the Virreynato de Lima's existence (Garcilaso de la Vega 1998; Jijón y Caamaño 1919a, 1919b).

Eugenio de Santa Cruz y Espejo never actually wrote a historical treatise or anything specifically about the pre-Hispanic past. He wrote sociological and medical essays focusing on the inhumane conditions that prevailed during the colonial period. However, in many ways, his Indian ancestry made him a living testament to the pre-Hispanic past that slowly began to pervade the colonial government's and later the nation-state's historical discourse. It is Espejo's Indian heritage and social achievement that make him essential to understanding a national history that is solidly based on a "mestizo" past—a mestizo past which has been significantly and continuously constructed on the re-presentation of Espejo's historical legacy.

These two figures were part of a large group of organic intellectuals, in the Gramscian sense (Gramsci 1971), who voiced a sentiment emanating from the polity in general that, in many ways, described an emerging class fraction that had not yet been able to consolidate itself in the swampy social structure that colonial relations had constructed (see Patterson 1991: 243). Both Juan de Velasco and Eugenio Espejo were born in the Real Audiencia de Quito under the Spanish crown, and thus saw themselves as completely *americanos*. They formed part of an emerging local (*criollista*) elite, which was not content with what it considered foreign domination. As a result, they put forward a historical claim justifying the *criollo*'s initial struggle for self-rule and autonomy. However, even though both Velasco and Espejo were members of a *criollo* elite, they were by no means of equal standing, and their many class, professional, and racial differences affected how they theorized and wrote about their homeland and how they are represented in the national imagery.

Juan de Velasco was born in Riobamba in 1727 into a wealthy household (that is, white, culturally speaking) directly linked to very prestigious European family lines. He entered the Jesuit order in 1747, and was a parish priest in Ibarra by 1761. By 1763 he had obtained a doctorate from the San Gregorio Magno University in Quito, and in 1767 he became a physics instructor in Popayán's high school (Popayán was at that time part of the Real Audiencia de Quito). Velasco and the other Jesuits were expelled from the Audiencia's territory as a result of colonial politics and ended up in Italy. Velasco lived there until his death in 1792. He wrote *Historia del reino de Quito en la América meridional* in Faenza, Italy, in 1789.

Velasco's history of the Ancient Kingdom of Quito has been completely debunked by modern archaeological research and is thought by academics to be devoid of any critical value (Moreno Yánez 1992; Salazar 1988, 1993/1994, 1995b). However, Velasco's account of the fictitious Kingdom of Quito is vivid to most Ecuadorians and is still presented as historical fact in school textbooks (García González 1997; Navas Jiménez 1994). The Ministry of Education's official support of Velasco's history makes it a pillar of their nation's legitimacy for many Ecuadorians.

The durability of Velasco's Kingdom of Quito, even in the face of overwhelming empirical evidence that it is a fiction, is not that surprising if one takes into account the enormous ideological value of his work. Velasco wrote his history of Quito with the objective of reclaiming the human worth of the American people, which had been brought into question by almost three centuries of conquest, colonization, and theoretical elaborations of race. In Moreno's words (1992: 23), as a member of an emerging *criollo* class, Velasco "attempts to apologetically formulate an emerging national ideology and offer his compatriots their 'own' history to justify their roots and hopes for autonomy." It is this ideological value that gives the *Historia del reino de Quito* its enormous mythic power in the founding of the nation, far beyond any empirical validity of its claims or any limited discussion of its accuracy.

Eugenio Espejo's writings, especially his initial newspaper, *Primicias de la cultura de Quito* (Cultural highlights of Quito), are hailed as the foundation of the mestizo essence of the Ecuadorian nation. Espejo was born in Cajamarca in 1747 (which is where the last Inca, Atahualpa, died), of an Indian father and a mulatta (i.e., of African and Spanish heritage) mother (Moreno Yánez 1992). However, the colonial system of caste and racial subordination, which should have doomed his intellectual pursuits, did not impede his obtaining a formal education. He earned degrees in both medicine and law from the university in Quito. His racial distance from the intellectual *criollos* of his period was ever-present in his writing, though, and, as he put it, "in his expertise in the figurative art of hiding" (in Moreno Yánez 1992: 24).

The racial tension Espejo felt is evidenced in his having an Indian nickname, Chusig (Adoum 2000), and is unmistakable throughout his essays. He constantly defends the Indian from the unjust Spanish structure. At the same time, his writings filled the *criollo* elite's need to undermine the oppressive Spanish colonial system, which members of the elite argued was morally unacceptable and, most important, thwarted the dream of self-rule. Espejo's sociological descriptions of corrupt religious orders, inhumane sanitary conditions, and personally experienced racial oppression are filled with an implicit national spirit that seems offended and enraged by Spain's denial of the emerging polities' historical raison d'être and their call for an independent Audiencia.

It is its implicit political and ideological content, not its empirical value, that makes Espejo's narrative central to the contemporary rendition of Ecuador's official national history, as can be observed in the multiple official media that incorporate Espejo into the national historical canon (Efrén Reyes 1967). Espejo's contribution is hailed as important because he made it, in spite of his Indian ancestry, not because of the torturous conditions he faced and describes in his writing. Instead of Espejo's being a confirmation of oppressive racial conditions, he becomes validation of how it is possible to overcome the stigmatization and, if there is an explicitly oppressive condition, of the nation's voice not so much identified with the social context of oppression as with condemnation of that oppression.

By identifying closely with Espejo, the nation sidesteps disquieting ethnic/racial/class inequalities (such as at Cochasquí and within the Indian movement) and instead identifies with the plea for more equal and democratic social relationships. Espejo and Ecuador are one, and unjust racial conditions are to be understood as unpatriotic elements, not as what they are: the nation's founding relationships. The use of Espejo's account as history or of Espejo's figure as historical serves to inflate a national sense of Ecuadorian selfhood and identity and hide oppressive racial relationships.

Although both Velasco and Espejo lived two full centuries before present-day Ecuador came into existence, their work has been appropriated in such a way that it is central to the maintenance of the nation. Their work is interpreted in the official discourse as proving Ecuador's existence from the beginning of time. While Velasco offers us a vision of a pristine "Ecuadorianness," Espejo allows the nation to identify with ethnic and racial subjects and not the state's oppressive class and racial relationships. Both Velasco's account of the Kingdom of Quito and Espejo's early journalistic writings provide an insight into the historically racialized roles and styles of invention utilized in the national production of the Ecuadorian polity (Anderson 1983).

THE FRACTURED SUBJECT'S
REPRODUCTION OF ECUADORIAN IDENTITY

Establishing the Fractured Subject

The unequal socioeconomic and racial conditions, as well as the hierarchical gender structure that currently characterizes the Ecuadorian nation-state, also form part of the subtle mechanisms of identity involved in historical production. Ecuador has suffered under persistent systems of domination, including indigenous ranking systems and the Spanish conquest (Cueva 1987, 1988; Vaquero Dávila 1941). These systems have contributed mechanisms of oppression which have evolved and become accepted as the normal mode of existence for the contemporary Ecuadorian population.

This process is clearly visible at Cochasquí, where, after the Inca conquest and violent decimation of the population, the Spaniards resettled the local populations into two nearby towns. The towns of Malchinguí and Tocachi were founded by the Spaniards in the early part of the seventeenth century to expand their control over an already stratified Indian population that was living in an urban center that reflected its own cosmology and cultural traditions (Larraín Barros 1977; Salcedo 1985). This forced resettlement explains why Cochasquí has no ties with any present-day indigenous community, the founding of one of the largest colonial haciendas (named Cochasquí) in the area, and, interestingly enough, the survival of the pyramids and mounds in the area, which were spared from further Spanish urbanization.

Contemporary Ecuador could be described as a highly stratified society with social power and economic control in the hands of a small elite, most of whom, not surprisingly, are socially defined and perceived as white or white/mestizo. The country suffers from high levels of infant mortality and pauperization, low wages, low levels of education, and poor health conditions, and a majority of the population lives in shanty-towns around the major urban centers and in abandoned rural communities. It is these highly uneven socioeconomic conditions which caused former president Osvaldo Hurtado to state (1981: 293): "It can well be said, then, that economic growth in Ecuador has worked to enable the rich (who have grown in number) to become richer and the poor to become poorer. The great fortunes of yesteryear in no way resemble the consolidated wealth of today's entrenched economic interest groups, which have emerged with a degree of power never before imagined. Seldom have so few, in such a short time, gained so much."

The concern with race, or biological differences, made its initial appearance in the area with the Spanish conquest. As several scholars (Amin 1997; Balibar and Wallerstein 1991; Gregory and Sanjek 1994; Mills 1983) have pointed out, the contemporary discourse of race may be traced back to the moment of the colonial encounter between a European population represented as white and African, American, and Asian populations being defined as black, nonwhite, or of color. In the northern Andes, this colonial preoccupation with race provided an immediate structure of racial privilege that, along with Christianity, served to legitimize the domination of the indigenous populations at the hands of the "white" Spaniard population (V. González 1986; Puga and Jurado 1992). The contemporary racial makeup of the Ecuadorian nation corresponds to this initial establishment of the primary racial categories as white (Spanish), white/mestizo, Indian, black (Afro-Ecuadorian), cholo, montubio, Turco/Libanés (Turk/Lebanese), and Chino (Chinese).

All of these groups, however, are included in a larger racial ideology of mestizaje and blanqueamiento which establishes a racial ideology of whiteness as the highest ideal and symbol of civilization and presents white images as representing the moral, civilizing norm (Muratorio 1994; Stutzman 1981). This hierarchy is reflected in such venues as employment (Roura and Núñez 1991), commercial images (*Vistazo* 1997b), public office, and beauty pageants (Núñez 1998). Whiteness in Ecuador is perceived as an innocent, naïve, transparent, and markedly uncolored identity (Baldwin 1984). Whiteness is not distinguished exclusively as a race per se, but also as a social class or status marker (Babb 1998; Dyer 1997; M. Hill 1997; Lipsitz 1995; Roediger 1991, 1994; Saxton 1990). The oppression of nonwhite populations is so harsh in terms of distribution of wealth, income, assets, education, and general opportunity that escaping racial definition (by being white) is a desired outcome for most Ecuadorians (Ibarra 1992; Núñez 1998).

No doubt because of their lower-class status, Indians and blacks suffer the most from Ecuador's racial hierarchy. These two groups are most significantly barred from influential economic and political spheres. Their exclusion derives from how they are physically perceived and from the meanings attributed to their cultural traditions, that is, their dress, music, language, hairstyles, language, and so on. However, both groups have contested these unjust racial structures throughout the nation-state's existence (de la Torre Espinosa 1996; Girardi 1994; Icaza 1936, 1981, 1983, 1993; Jaramillo Alvarado 1988; Lucena Salmoral 1994; Savoia 1988). Interesting because it defies the pattern is the election of two Afro-Ecuadorian women as representatives to the Miss Universe Pageant in the 1990s (Muteba Rahier 1998).

Within this class- and race-based system of inequality, homosexuals, women in general, and Indian and black women in particular (beauty pageants notwithstanding) have traditionally been the most disadvantaged (Muratorio 1994, 1998). This is the case even though the Ecuadorian nation (*la nación*) used to be portrayed as a caring mother, as I observed at Cochasquí. Scholarship has begun to appear on the impact of gender inequality and sexism in general on Ecuadorian society (Muratorio 1998; Weismantel 1992), but gender issues have yet to be given the analytical attention they deserve.

Far from simply being monolithic or imposed from above, gendered and racialized discourses are active loci of contention, negotiation, and contradiction (Birken 1988; Kinsman 1987; Mort 1987). Thus, gender and race issues are not foreign to Cochasquí and its multilayered interpretations of the past. Gender and racial jokes and stories, as well as complex and subtler negotiations, occur daily at the site. As essential elements of human life, gender and race could not be and, indeed, are not very far from people's minds and are constantly thought and talked about at the site. As a national archaeological site, Cochasquí is also a place where gender and race practices and norms are revealed by their public exhibition and by their contrast with the opinions espoused by the many tourists who visit the site.

The representation of the female warrior Quilago as the last political leader of Cochasquí expresses the ambivalence about gender categories at the site. At one level, Quilago is a symbol of female subversion and rebellion; however, this meaning is co-opted by the larger narrative, which makes her a national icon and which requires her to represent the contemporary sexist ideals of the nation-state. This is also evident in the main racial discourse expounded at Cochasquí (for a more detailed discussion, see chapters 2 and 3).

The site itself represents redemption of the indigenous past, which provides it with a historical agency that has been denied the Indian communities since the Spanish conquest. At the same time, this redemption is incorporated into a narrative that emphasizes a national Ecuadorian ethos in which the Indian past is subsumed and, in a very real sense, stripped of any real agency. The Indian past has been incorporated into a national narrative in which any discussion of contemporary racial exploitation and discrimination is eclipsed by this newly acquired historical truth. The recognition of an Indian heritage neutralizes complaints about Ecuador's racial inequality (which echoes Espejo's racializing legacy), since now everybody is recognized as equal, no matter what their racial or ethnic origin. However, even within these larger nationalizing gender and racial discourses at Cochasquí, continuous ambivalence makes static definition of the discourses impossible and implements the nation-state's dynamic hegemonic processes.

Ecuador's different national histories are also involved in and produced within the nation-state's ambivalent gender and racial discourse. For example, Velasco's Ancient Kingdom of Quito is very much a patriarchal story that utilizes feminine nurturers to provide roots for the national spirit. At the same time, Velasco's narrative of exclusively indigenous protagonists has for over two centuries served to legitimize white and mestizo control over the rest of the population.

Just as in Cochasquí, in Ecuador as a whole, national histories utilize counter-hegemonic race and gender elements to further their own historical agendas and sustain, willingly or not, the oppressive ideals and status quo of the nation-state.

Engendering Mestizaje and Constructing an Indian Present

During the 1970s the then–military dictator of Ecuador, Gen. Guillermo Rodríguez Lara, stated in a speech emphasizing Ecuador's Indian ancestry that there were "no more problems in reference to the Indians. . . . *we all become* white when we accept the objectives of the national culture" (in Whitten 1984: 167; my emphasis). Ecuadorian historian Gabriel Cevallos García (1960) expressed a similar sentiment almost a decade earlier when he argued that Ecuador was made up of Ecuadorians, not of whites, Indians, blacks, or any other racial or ethnic group.

These statements express both contradictions in and anxieties about what it actually means to be Ecuadorian. The Ecuadorian identity is far from being clearly defined or understood, and yet it is constantly espoused in diplomatic forums and during international soccer games, territorial disputes, and national elections (Gallardo et al. 1995; *Hoy* 1997; *El Universo* 1997). Therefore, it is apparently easy, despite some hesitation, to use Ecuadorian national identity to analyze what being Ecuadorian really means, especially in regard to the country's ancestral Indian past.

José Echeverría Almeida's (1995) master's thesis is one of the few exceptions. It analyzes the relationship between an Ecuadorian identity and the nation's archaeological past by examining the manner in which archaeologists' (both national and foreign) theoretical frameworks have affected the interpretation and representation of archaeological reconstructions in several museum exhibitions throughout the country. However, most of the research on Ecuadorian identity has been concerned with the pervasiveness of national hegemonic ideologies (Espinosa Apolo 1995; Guerrero 1991, 1994; Muratorio 1994; Stutzman 1981; Whitten 1965, 1981) and, to a lesser extent, modern constructions of national identity (Acosta et al. 1997; Crain 1990). Although neither of these two areas of concern explicitly deals with archaeological knowledge or the ancestral past per se, they do provide an opening into the study of the complex racial and ethnic issues on which Ecuadorianness has historically been built.

Stutzman (1981), for example, focuses on the ideology of *mestizaje* and *blanqueamiento*. He demonstrates how members of the Ecuadorian national culture, as in many other Latin American countries (see, e.g., Friedlander 1975; Knight 1990), aspire to whiteness as the highest symbol of civilization even as they expound an ideology of miscegenation. This contradiction is further complicated by the continuing oppression of the indigenous population even as national rhetoric refers to the glories of the country's ancestral tradition. Stutzman connects this "glorious past" to an official national history that has taken on mythic proportions.

Muratorio (1994) also notes the problem of a mestizo identity that claims both European and Indian heritage on equal terms. From this contradiction a national culture has developed in which the Indian "other" is portrayed as an aristocratic male Inca while contemporary Indian populations are portrayed as feminine and submissive (see Gould 1996 for discussion of a similar process in Nicaragua). This invention of a mythical Indian "other" not only has strong ethnic and gender implications, but also is devoid of genealogy, of actual historical connections between the present and the past. The official national history attempts to erase this contradiction by including the Indian "other" not as a real contemporary subject but as an archaeological invention.

This process limits the historical dimensions of the Indian to museums, archaeological sites, and past contributions that do not bring into question the current treatment of the indigenous populations by the national culture. In the best cases, museums such as the ones at Real Alto and Salango attempt to revitalize the past and empower the local inhabitants of the archaeological sites (Álvarez 1991; Marcos 1986b, 1986c).

But this task has not been completely successful, as is evident in several of the country's in situ museums, for example, at Rumicucho, Cochasquí, and Salango. The in situ museum at Agua Blanca on the coast might be the best example of how joint work carried out by anthropologists and the community led to the empowerment of the local inhabitants in acknowledging their indigenous heritage and political rights (McEwan 1990; McEwan and Hudson N.d.). However, even at Agua Blanca, there have been no dramatic changes in the regional or national authorities' understanding of the continuity of ethnic identity, and even less in assessing the Indians' contribution to national culture.

As is evident, not all groups are equally represented in this miscegenation process. Indians are seen as closer to the nation's natural history and as having contributed more to the *mestizaje* of the country (see Haraway 1989; Wade 1993, 1994, for other examples in the Americas). The black population in Ecuador, meanwhile, is doubly disadvantaged by a *blanqueamiento* ideology that defines them as inferior and a *mestizaje* ideology that denies their existence, since we are all now mixed (Stutzman 1981; Whitten 1965, 1974). Ultimately, *mestizaje* in Ecuador is about passing as white and becoming less Indian (Espinosa Apolo 1995: 48–54 passim).

The *mestizaje* process in Ecuador has many parallels in other Latin American countries. The idea of a mestizo race superior to its black, Indian, and even white European constitutive components was initially put forward in the late 1800s in Mexico (C. Smith 1996). Vasconcelos (1997) and other ideologues proposed a "cosmic race" to legitimize the aspirations of the local elite in the face of European and North American intrusions and to distance that elite from the country's nonwhite citizens. This mestizo ideal swept through the southern part of the continent, and by the beginning of the twentieth century was an essential part of Latin America, including the Ecuadorian state (Quintero López 1997; Quintero and Silva 1991). In this sense, as Hale elaborates (1996: 2), "*mestizaje* has been a remarkably effective ideological tool in the hands of elite in many parts of Latin America, a unifying myth put to the service of state and nation building. A pervasive effect of this process, in turn, is for alternative or contested meanings to be down played or even erased. *Mestizaje* as an elite generated myth of national identity, it could be said, tends to obscure the conditions of its own creation, to cover its own tracks."

The *mestizaje* process also serves as a pillar in the construction of a national identity and as a viable ideological tool for the maintenance of the status quo and oppression of the majority of the Ecuadorian population (Muratorio 1994; Stutzman 1981). More than a literal reality, the *mestizaje* ideology is an ideal, a wish, and a rhetorical recourse for covering up any differences (racial, ethnic, economic, religious, sexual, etc.) in the country. Difference is seen as dangerous; therefore, its mere presence brings into question and threatens any construction of a national identity. In Ecuador a mestizo ideology has traditionally been employed by the elite to maintain power over the indigenous populations and other national groups. It is as if, through the invention of a national Ecuadorian identity, the elite is attempting to homogenize and hide the "other." Up to now, the country has been based on the exclusion of difference, on the negation or denial of an "other," especially of the Indian as a possible ethnic basis of the nation (Silva 1995: 34).

Mallon (1996) and several other scholars (Anzaldúa 1987; Cypess 1991; Moraga 1986, 1994), however, the majority of whom are women, emphasize the liberating or counter-hegemonic elements of this traditionally exploitative state ideology. They appreciate the contradictory nature of a mestizo ideology that both creates inequality (C. Smith 1996: 149) and liberates from absolute identities (Anzaldúa 1987). It is *mestizaje*'s essentially contradictory nature that becomes a bone of contention and allows for a thorough critique of many of the traditionally accepted social categories from the vantage point of "strategic marginality" (Mallon 1996: 173).

The story of La Malinche (Cortez's Indian lover and partner), who is seen as a traitor from the authentic Indian national perspective or as a liberator from the vantage point of a mestizo nation (see Cypess 1991), and even Rigoberta Menchú's (1985, 1998) uncharacteristic narrative point to the centrality of female sexual discourse in the maintenance of the national status quo. Sexuality, specifically female sexuality, becomes a major locus of contention and domination and the site of boundaries that are essential for maintaining the character of both the nation and the state (Mallon 1996). All of this points to the powerful potential of a strategic marginality to disrupt the traditional categories embodied by the nation-state. This strategic marginality may provide an interesting approach for research into the role of hegemonic devices and myth in the maintenance of the Ecuadorian status quo (see chapter 7).

Silva (1995) suggests that two central myths—the territorial and the vanquished-race myths—have allowed the dominant groups to maintain their control. The territorial myth relates to dominion over the Ecuadorian state's geographic space: the Spaniards (read contemporary whites and mestizos) were able to conquer the Indian groups, who are presented in this myth as never able to fully dominate the territory. The last wars over territory fought with Peru, especially in 1941 and 1981, make it impossible to support this myth any longer; nonetheless, the national rhetoric expounded in the latest border incident with Peru (in 1995) demonstrates significant investment in this myth (Espinosa 1995; Gallardo 1995).

The vanquished-race myth presents Indians as being defeated, first, by geography; second, by the Incas (which is nothing other than the Cuzco version of the contemporary Peruvian invasions; see *El Comercio* 1995); and, third, by the Spaniards. This myth also cracks under the weight of its own ambiguity. For example, the enormous amount of Andean research (e.g., Murra 1989; Salomon 1986) demonstrates that the native polities possessed a complex and singular control of their environment and geography. At the same time, the Inca conquest is no longer unanimously viewed as a foreign invasion; rather, many of the descendants of the groups the Incas conquered now consider themselves direct descendants of the Incas (Pakari 1994). Salomon (1990) has also studied the Cañaris, who, although once the fiercest northern Andean foes of the Incas, now consider themselves the latter's legitimate and rightful descendants. Finally, there is the Indian movement itself, which in the last decade has claimed Inca heritage and, through it, has been able to occupy many of the political spaces that historically have been denied them (CONAIE 1988a, 1988b, 1989, 1997, 1998).

As Crain (1989, 1990) notes, since the 1960s Indians have repeatedly been tempted to allow themselves to be incorporated into a new definition of Ecuador's national culture that would value the group's historical legacy. These attempts were more clearly formulated during the Center-Left governments of Jaime Roldós Aguilera (1979–1981), Osvaldo Hurtado Larrea (1981–1984), and Rodrigo Borja Cevallos (1988–1992). During each of these three administrations, several symbolic demonstrations demanded the incorporation of Indians into a modern economy that would supposedly liberate them from the traditional oppression suffered during both the colonial and the republican periods. Such an economic strategy could be defined as a new form of governmental *indigenismo* (Silva 1995). This trend was continued by Abdalá Bucaram Ortiz during his brief administration (1996–1997), with the creation of the Ministerio de Asuntos Indígenas (Ministry of Indian Affairs) headed by Amazonian Indian leader Rafael Pandam, as a reward for Indian support of Bucaram's candidacy. In reality, Bucaram was probably trying to divide the Indian movement by supporting the Amazonian groups' claim against the CONAIE and other nationally recognized Indian leaders (Macas 1992).

Since national appropriation of local traditions by definition severs them from their historical meaning, however, the new discourse is fraught with contradictions. Thus, national rewritings of native history have been met by a strong indigenous nationalism, such as that of the CONAIE, which seeks to transcend the country's current political borders. During the 1990s CONAIE put forward a radical critique of the Ecuadorian nation-state by struggling for the creation of a multinational state and the right of self-determination for all Ecuadorian nationalities, including Afro-Ecuadorians and other oppressed groups (Kowii 1992; Macas 1992; Quimbo 1992). The CONAIE, through its political arm, Pachakutik Nuevo País, has fought to become one of the leading political forces in the country. The party held a significant number of seats in Congress and in the interim Asamblea Nacional (National Assembly) of 1998, which looked to reform the Ecuadorian Constitution. More important, the election of Lucio Gutiérrez as president in 2002 catapulted the movement to executive power. In fact, one of its leading ideologues, Nina Pakari, has become the country's first female secretary of state.

The CONAIE's larger project of serving as a voice for more disgruntled social movements, however, has not proved completely successful, even though the power of the Indian movement is far from weak. Since 2000 the Indian movement has successfully led popular national uprisings, including one that helped the military overthrow the government of Jamil Mahuad Witt, occupied government offices in Quito, forced the government to disregard IMF structural-adjustment policies, and paralyzed the nation with general strikes and marches (see chapter 5). As the CONAIE continues to bring into question the claim to a homogeneous national identity, a significant group of Ecuadorian scholars (e.g., Acosta et al. 1997) actively disputes the existence of a national identity due to the state's inability to control the national territory and the lack of a national language and culture (Quintero López 1997). For these scholars, Ecuador is still very much "una nación en ciernes" (an emerging nation) (Quintero and Silva 1991).

MAKING HISTORY AT COCHASQUÍ

As we shall see in chapters 2 and 3, the archaeological site of Cochasquí is imbued with implicit and explicit notions of Ecuadorianness and an authoritative history of Ecuador's pre-Hispanic past—essential parts of what Quintero and Silva (1991) refer to as "an emerging nation." As such, Cochasquí embodies contradictions and subtle mechanisms of representation that make analyzing it useful for understanding the complex political hermeneutics of historical production and nation building.

The process of historical production is plagued with questions of representation, authority, authenticity, truth, and political commitment (Bond and Gilliam 1994; Foucault 1991; Handler 1988; Handler and Gable 1997; Jackson 1989). In light of recent research into archaeological knowledge (Kohl and Fawcett 1995; Patterson 1995b; Patterson and Schmidt 1995), researchers acknowledge that pressing social and other discursive constraints are inherent in the production of historical narratives (see, e.g., Sider and Smith 1998; Trouillot 1995). The reappraisal of history and historical truth is a fruitful starting point for understanding the internal logic of power and its forms of domination, since "history is the fruit of power" (Trouillot 1995: xix). Historical production is an eminently politically charged social activity that can offer us an insight into the discourses of power, including that of the state (Popular Memory Group 1982: 213): "Political domination involves historical definition. History—in particular popular memory—is a stake in the constant struggle for hegemony. The relation between history and politics, like the relation between past and present, is therefore an internal one: it is about the politics of history and the historical dimension of politics."

Cochasquí is no stranger to these controversial social processes. As one of the most important and visited archaeological sites in the country, it is seen by many, including the staff responsible for its care and those who visit and study it, as a site of national importance (Mantilla N.d). In the words of many of the Ecuadorian tourists who visit the site, Cochasquí is "marvelous" and it forces Ecuadorians to want to ".defend our treasures" (interview, March 8, 1997); the site ratified "our value as a millenary culture and makes us love our land" (interview, April 15, 1997); it "gave us a greater conscience for protecting what's ours, our roots, our ancestors and culture" (interview, April 25, 1997). The guides also emphasize the national importance of Cochasquí (Pullas de la Cruz 1997: 26): "I would implore, as a peasant who has strong feelings about the site, that primary and high schools, colleges throughout the country, and, why not say it, even at a world level should get to know this site, so important is Cochasquí, that they get to know the roots to which we belong as Ecuadorians." The guide's patriotic rhetoric belies the nation-state's stake in the elaboration of an official Cochasquí, which alternately suppresses and highlights different historical elements.

The site's official story, which is disseminated to schoolchildren, the media, and tourists, is similar to historical narratives from other Latin American communities that are created within the framework of state subjugation and subjective inventions (Alonso 1995). Such hegemonic narratives have three distinct elements: a primordial period with a cohesive and congruent social order; a second disruptive period, or "fall," which marks the transformation of nondominators into the dominated; and, finally, a period of conflict in which, as a result of this transformation, new social relations emerge and are fixed in contemporary life (Alonso 1995).

Cochasquí's official guides and pamphlets produce a narrative that is intertwined with the nation-state's interest in supporting a story of a primordial, pristine past free of domination or subjugation. As Alonso suggests (1995: 232), "The primordial society is located in the time of community origins, the frontier past. Although situated in historical time, however, this past is epic and remote, simultaneously remembered and beyond memory. The outlines of the primordial society are nebulous, eluding sharp delineation precisely because they are the contours of an idealized past, a past from which the effects of power and traces of pain have been effaced so as to conjure up a memory of time in which oppression was not preordained."

In Cochasquí this primordial past is expressed in the site's presentation as being inhabited by the unsullied society of Quitus-Caras, which, remarkably, did not exhibit any signs of political domination. The original inhabitants are depicted in an almost socialist light, echoing Baudin's (1961) benevolent portrayal of the Incas as an overprotective and caring state (Pullas de la Cruz 1997: 27): "Good, let's remember our culture, which was a communal people [*pueblo*], united, they didn't work individually, nobody was richer, nobody was poorer, instead they all worked together, so that everybody had something to eat, so that everybody had something to wear."

The second period, the "fall" of this primordial society (see Foucault 1993: 143), is illustrated in the narrative of the invasion and conquest of the site, first by the Incas, then by the Spaniards. As a result of these foreign invasions, the indigenous inhabitants of the site lost their autonomy and sovereignty and had to pay homage to each of the new ruling monarchs. However, it is clear that the inhabitants and the "queen" (Quilago) of Cochasquí did not give up their freedom lightly, fighting to the death (Pullas de la Cruz 1998: 12–13):

> And therefore she is betrayed by her close aides and they "gossip" the information to Huayna Capac [the conquering Inca leader] so that she falls in the trap of the Incas and then come the white people, the savages that are the Spaniards, with which these people are destroyed, and this area gets abandoned. We know, as some accounts tell us, they talk about many surnames that left because Huayna Capac was furious with the Quitus [original inhabitants of the site according to the narrative], wants to pass them all through the knife, burn them all, so the people of this area go to other places. . . . Finally, a whole bunch of surnames leave here and this area is totally abandoned and the Spaniards take it as the Hacienda of Cochasquí, all this area gets organized as the Hacienda of Cochasquí.

Both the Inca and the Spanish conquests display unique elements that relate them to notions of Ecuadorianness. Once the Spanish conquer both Cochasquí and the Incas, they are able to claim dominion over the land, which they do by redefining the territory as an hacienda, signifying a shift of social and economic relations (Quintero and Silva 1991). These new conditions are associated with dramatic shifts in the racial and ethnic structure of the conquered territory. This explains the contemporary description of Cochasquí's heritage and meaning (Pullas de la Cruz 1997: 26):

> The word *Haira pamushca* means that we represent the three honorable bloodlines of the Quitu-Cara to which we belong as Ecuadorians, Incas, coastal, and Spanish; and returning to the word Quitu-Cara, why should we be ashamed? We must feel proud, with our heads held high, with our

minds clean, and not be embarrassed in any part of the country, in any part of the world to say that we belong to the Quitus; and not be ashamed of this because it was a group of people wise in every way, we give value to other cultures: Mayas, the Aztec culture, and ours, nothing, not even in the history books is it mentioned, or they say very little that can be considered interesting in terms of knowledge about our people.

This synthesis of Cochasquí's official history as presented by the tour guides highlights the hermeneutics involved in any form of historical production. Historical production is inextricably tied to issues of political and territorial legitimatization (Kuklick 1991; Silberman 1995). These underpinnings are enough to make us wary of any narrative, official or not, being presented as an objective rendering of the past (I. Vargas 1995; Wylie 1995). This is especially true since history's authority relies on its being presented as the real thing, as objective truth, even though, by definition, historical narratives are merely that: narrative approximations of the past that is being described (Handler and Gable 1997; Wylie 1995).

This, however, is just the first level of complexity in the process of historical production. As Nietzsche (1989) notes, there are no facts as such; one must always begin by introducing a meaning in order for there to be a fact. This distinction is essential for understanding that historical renderings are not simply a question of individual or social honesty, truthfulness or accuracy; rather, all of these elements are bound up in the production of the historical discourse. That is, history's imperative to re-create the past, to describe or interpret past reality, is, above all, an exercise in creating and sustaining a sense of reality. It is this exercise that "is the major ideological task of the discourse of history, and it involves a mode of representation which denies the act of representing" (Taussig 1989: 11).

Alonso has also tackled this problem in her work on a Mexican community's past (1988: 37): "The paradox is that historical discourses hide their hermeneutics so as to construct their 'credibility' and 'authoritativeness' vis-à-vis their audiences. History is rhetorical in that it aims to convince and in order to do so, it is drawn into misrepresenting its project. Like realistic art, historical narrative pretends to be a copy of an actuality which is 'naturalized,' presented as 'raw data,' as 'hard fact.'" For Alonso, as for many other scholars concerned with historiography (e.g., Foucault 1993; Guha and Spivak 1985; Spivak 1988), this naturalizing technique is essential in understanding history's powerful role in legitimizing or constructing political subjects such as the state, the nation, or the citizenry. History's hermeneutics, based on the discipline's hidden misrepresentation, takes "unusual pain to erase the elements in [the historians'] work which reveal their grounding in a particular time and place" (Foucault 1993: 156). It is this misrepresentation which allows us to impose an order and sense that were not present or could never have been achieved when the original events were being interpreted.

History is able to order and explain because it introduces a secular teleology that looks to meaningfully orient the actions at hand, even though there was never an initial story line other than the events themselves (see Thorpe [1853] 1968). According to Foucault (1993: 152–153), traditional history is able to offer meaning because it relies on characteristics associated with a metanarrative that looks to reconcile the past with the present, is outside of time as it searches for ultimate truths, relies on apocalyptic objectivity, and seeks a continuous and organic development of events.

At another level, history is inextricably linked with power beyond the notions of explicitly coercive domination. Rather, history's credibility relies on its potential authority as truth. Since the ability and power (or will) to know are inseparable, the resulting truth of knowledge is also the truth of power (Alonso 1988: 39). In other words, the social production behind "what really happened" is hidden to offer the authority needed by the historical narrative. Thus, "the effects of truth are also effects of power" (Alonso 1988: 50; also see Foucault 1991). The will to know is characterized by powerful violence and injustice, because it destroys the illusions we have constructed to protect ourselves in the pursuit of happiness: "it sides against those who are happy in their ignorance" (Foucault 1993: 162). Contrary to our perception of knowledge as a quest for truth, the will to know "ceaselessly multiplies the risks, creates dangers in every area; it breaks down illusory defenses; it dissolves the unity of the subject; it releases those elements of itself that are devoted to its subversion and destruction" (Foucault 1993: 163).

The power which both produces and is produced by historical accounts is nowhere more evident than in the national histories elaborated within the social boundaries of large-scale communities, such as the nation-state. As Anderson (1983) and many others (e.g., Fox 1990; Hobsbawm 1990; Hobsbawm and Ranger 1983; B. Williams 1990) have discussed, the nation as an imagined community is privy to a history that makes sense and legitimizes its claims. This community is woven through an imagined kin genealogy in which history both defines and holds a privileged position. The power of this historical genealogy is nowhere more palpable than in the millions of lives lost, many of them willingly, in the defense of the nation, of the purity of one's blood, or of the dignity of one's identity (B. Williams 1990, 1991). The ultimate sacrifice of one's life, demanded and expected by every nation, once again brings home the pivotal role of history as a medium "through which nations are imagined and sovereignty is constructed" (Alonso 1988: 41).

Contrary to what one would expect, however, no historical narrative, in particular, no official one, is able fully to eradicate counter-hegemonic accounts. Rather, nonofficial and dominant narratives live side by side, as is the case of the multiple historical discourses at Cochasquí. The official history merely appropriates essential characteristics within certain constraints and truths. Official and alternative narratives exist in relation to each other, need each other, in a dynamic relationship that changes as the social terrain that produces them is being negotiated and redefined (Alonso 1988: 49; see also Joseph and Nugent 1994).

It is precisely because of this process that counter-hegemonic narratives can never maintain their status as such (Foucault 1993: 151): "The successes of history belong to those who are capable of seizing these rules, to replace those who had used them, to disguise themselves so as to pervert them, invert their meaning, and redirect them against those who had initially imposed them; controlling this complex mechanism, they will make it function so as to overcome the rulers through their own rules." Therefore, once afforded a greater level of normative acceptance, they become hegemonic, no matter how progressive or alternative their claims (see Wylie 1995). It is also for this reason that hegemony presents itself not as an elusive category of deconstruction but as one of dynamic transformation. As many authors (among them, Joseph and Nugent 1994; Roseberry 1994; Sayer 1994; Scott 1985; Silverblatt 1988) strive to illustrate, hegemony is a constant state project in the making, "an ongoing process in which official and popular discourses struggle to advance and to defend social interests and values" (Alonso 1988: 48).

REINSERTING THE STATE

In the nation's imagined existence across time, it is the state that seems to be actively interested in appropriating and officializing histories for the nation (Alonso 1988). Phillip Abrams' 1988 article "Notes on the Difficulty of Studying the State (1977)" (published posthumously) stands out as one of the most impressive modern contributions to understanding the mechanisms of the state apparatus. He revisits Engels and Marx to qualify our contemporary analysis of the state's role and function in society. He claims that we should pay heed to the fact that "the state presents itself to us as the first ideological power over man" (Engels in Abrams 1988: 64); further, "the most important single characteristic of the state is that it constitutes the 'illusory common interest of society'" (Marx and Engels in Abrams 1988: 64).

In this vein, Abrams (1988: 58) proposes that "the state is not the mask that stands behind political practice. It is itself the mask which prevents our seeing political practice as it is. . . . The state starts its life as an implicit construct; it is then reified—as res publica, the public re-ification, no less—and acquires an overt symbolic identity progressively divorced from practice as an illusory account of practice." The state's mask, or supposed absence, is really the state itself, or, rather, its mask does not imply that there is a face hiding under it or that it is not really there (see Wilde's discussion of identity in Browning 1991). This is also Radcliffe-Brown's (1950) (traditionally ignored) argument in the preface to *African Political Systems*. He claims that the state in this sense does not exist in the phenomenal world; it is a fiction of the philosophers.

Neither Abrams (1988) nor Radcliffe-Brown (1950), however, denies the enormous and real power held by the state. Quite the contrary; both authors point to the source of this power as lying not in the state itself, but in our own fictive construction of it, in our own fetishizing of the state as a boundless entity. The state's "ideology displaces power from its real to its apparent center" (Abrams 1988: 78) precisely through this play of images, or this constant looking for further and deeper proof when the state (both as a system and an idea) is right in front of our eyes. The understanding of an enormous state fetish in the making, far from denying the presence of state-imposed oppression and coercion, "directs us to precisely the existence and reality of the political power of this fic-tion, its powerful insubstantiality" (Taussig 1992a: 113).

It is the repressive institutions at the state's service—armies, prisons, national security apparatus—coupled "with the idea of the state and the invocation of that idea that silences protest, excuses force and convinces almost all of us that the fate of the victims is just and necessary" (Abrams 1988: 77). The state always appears as the rightful claimant of domination; very rarely, if at all, does it appear as the practitioner of the terrorism and violent oppression in which it routinely engages and on which it is based. The state allies itself with reason and offers "purposes in a purposeless condition"; it offers "a mind in a mindless world" and therefore becomes yet another "opium of the citizen" (Abrams 1988: 82).

Taussig (1992a: 115) alleges that the intricate relationship between reason and violence, or the violence of reason, is a form of state-sponsored cultural practice. He argues that our own fear of the anomie and chaos that surround us makes us grapple for a reason, any reason, that will deter them. And in that instance we are, if not grateful, at least willing to overlook violence, because we fear even more the void in a world without reason (Baldwin 1984: 20). Our fear, often sheer terror (Taussig 1992b) of the randomness that makes up life, forces us to want to violently deny "a historical sense [that] confirms our existence among countless lost events, without a landmark or a point of reference" (Foucault 1993: 155). This is especially true when we find that "at the historical beginning of things is not the inviolable identity of their origin; it is the dissension of other things. It is disparity" (Foucault 1993: 142). In a way, the fear of violence makes us accept violence regulated by the state apparatus as a matter of life, and death (also see Sider and Smith 1998).

The state, then, not unlike historical production, is also invested in a project of concealment (Abrams 1988: 77): "it conceals the real history and relations of subjection behind an a-historical mask of legitimating illusions; contrives to deny the existence of contentions and conflicts which would if recognized be incompatible with the claimed autonomy." That is why the task of the social scientist is to attend to that demystification, to actually determine the forms in which the state does not exist rather than those in which it does (Abrams 1988: 77).

That is also why the ultimate secret of the state, its hidden agenda, if you will, is that there is no secret, no hidden agenda at all (Abrams 1988: 79). If we listen to history, we find "that there is something altogether different behind things: not a timeless and essential secret, but the secret that they have no essence or that their essence was fabricated in a piecemeal fashion from alien forms" (Foucault 1993: 142). This nonexistent, hidden reality takes us back to the core of what state hegemony is all about, what Sayer (1994: 374–375) refers to as both the strongest and the most vulnerable element of the state:

> Individuals live in the lie that is "the state," and it lives through their performances. Their beliefs are neither here nor there. What is demanded of them is only—but precisely—performances. Like actors (to invoke another metaphor sociologists are prone to employ, without always considering what it conveys) they merely have to behave as if they were the characters they are impersonating. Rituals, we argue in *The Great Arch,* are a crucial dimension of that power that represents itself as "the state" and us as members of a "body politic." Believers or not, participants are by their very action affirming the power of what is sanctified. Hobbes had good

reason for baptizing the state Mortal God. In ritual observances, "His" omnipotence is daily celebrated, even if his existence is, for many members of the congregation personally, a matter of doubt.

It is this fragility of the truth, of artifice, of people daily engaging in practices that support a state entity which they have not necessarily seen, which makes hegemony the intellectual equivalent of the emperor's new clothes (Sayer 1994: 377). It is in this process that individuals and institutions are constituted as historical subjects and are thereby obligated to support the deception which is the state and its hegemonic construction (Taussig 1992a: 132).

This inquiry is closely related to Foucault's interest in analyzing "the question of power by grasping it where it is exercised and manifested, without trying to find fundamental or general formulations; without considering, for example, the presence of a state which would be the holder of power, which would exercise its sovereignty upon a civil society which itself would not be the depository of analogous processes of power" (1991: 164). The state holds power as a result of its reification and keeps it through the good graces of its own citizens and institutions.

The process of "subjection" (Foucault 1991) by which the state is able to constitute historical subjects is inherent in the official portrayal of Cochasquí as an Indian and pre-Hispanic site with an essential Ecuadorian heritage. At the site of Cochasquí, the state is nonexistent except in the Programa Cochasquí's official practices and belief (or cultural performance of a lie) that there is a state figure it can rely on, beyond (and partly expressed through) the financial support made available to them through the state apparatus (i.e., state as system; see Abrams 1988: 58). In this sense, one of the main characters in the historical drama of Cochasquí has always been the Ecuadorian state. And it should not surprise us if the state "brilla por su ausencia" (shines by its absence). The state is nowhere to be seen at the site, and yet in many ways it is the main beneficiary of the discourse expounded there. The entity of the state is constantly reconstructed in the daily, if not hourly, elaborations by tour guides in which Cochasquí is hailed as a treasure chest of Ecuadorianness. Cochasquí openly legitimizes the Ecuadorian nation-state's reason for being by means of the oral and written guides at the site. These allow visitors to pay allegiance to this higher ruling authority, not unlike a secular God imbued with sacred power (Abrams 1988; Taussig 1992b). As I will argue in the next two chapters, it is the Programa Cochasquí's employees, as part of the Consejo Provincial de Pichincha (Provincial

Council of Pichincha), who range from a popularly elected *consejero* to a hand-appointed director to local guides, who are the most visible representatives of the state. These employees can function as representatives of the state because of their subtle creation of that state via the depiction of Cochasquí as a pre-Hispanic archaeological site of great national importance.

∽

THE ECUADORIANIZATION OF
AN ARCHAEOLOGICAL SITE
National Identity at Cochasquí

∽

*To everyone who looks back on his past life it presents itself
rather through the beautifying glass of fancy, than in the faithful
mirror of memory; and this is more particularly the case the
further this retrospection penetrates into the past. Among
nations, the same feelings prevail. They also draw a picture of
their infancy in glittering colors. The fewer the traditions they
have, the more they embellish them; the less trustworthy the
traditions are, the more they sparkel in the brilliancy which
fancy has lent them, the more the vain-glory of the people will
continue to cherish, to ennoble and diffuse them from generation
to generation, through succeeding ages. Man's ambition is
two-fold: he will not only live in the minds of posterity; he will
have also lived in ages long gone by. He looks not only forward
but backwards also; and no people on earth is indifferent to
the fancied honor of being able to trace its origin to the gods,
and of being ruled by an ancient race.*

—BENJAMIN THORPE ([1853] 1968)

COCHASQUÍ: THE PROGRAM AND THE *COMUNA*

The Program

The Cochasquí Program is: an organic structure that is concerned with scientific research; the conservation, restoration, the economic development
of the region; the diffusion, promotion, and carrying out of different agen-

das, scientific and ecological tourism; with the perspective of defining, motivating, and defending our national identity. (Mantilla N.d.)

The maintenance of the site of Cochasquí is strictly controlled and supervised by the Programa Cochasquí, which is under the jurisdiction of the Consejo Provincial de Pichincha. Since 1986 the program has officially been an administrative unit of the Consejo Provincial; before then the program was an independent department in the Consejo Provincial. The program's funding is automatically included in the Consejo Provincial's annual budget, although extra funds for special events are presented separately to the council and approved by the prefecto provincial (provincial prefect). Requests for extra funding are usually received favorably. During my stay in 1997, for example, the program was awarded over one hundred million sucres (twenty-five thousand dollars) to fund two cultural events: an international meeting of shamans, and a week-long memorial to commemorate the thirtieth anniversary of Che Guevara's death.

The Programa Cochasquí's staff is typically composed of nineteen members: a director, five tour guides (two of them local *comuneros*), a site resident, an archaeologist, a sociologist, a secretary, two drivers, four day workers (*jornaleros*), and three local guards. About half of the staff—the director, the secretary, three of the guides, the archaeologist, the sociologist, the site resident, and the drivers—is based in Quito. Most make the trip back and forth to the site daily, an hour each way. The rest of the staff—guards, workers, and two guides—are *comuneros* and live adjacent to the site. The director visits the site an average of two or three times a week, but rarely stays for more than a couple of hours. All positions are appointed by the *consejero* (the head of the Consejo Provincial), who is also responsible for representing the program on the Consejo Provincial. It is ultimately the *consejero* who holds the greatest amount of bureaucratic power in the program.

Since 1979 the Consejo Provincial has been actively involved in the control and maintenance of Cochasquí as a large-scale archaeological site. As a staff member told me, Lenín Ortiz, *consejero* of the Consejo Provincial de Pichincha during my stay there, was the person responsible for the idea of developing the site of Cochasquí. Lenín Ortiz decided to rescue the site and convert it into a life-sized museum.

The program's work started in the late 1970s, when Ortiz and some of his students from the Universidad Central carried out the initial cleaning of the site and the planning and organization of the project. Early on, he also enjoyed the help of other university professors, such as Alfredo and Piedad Costales (the former later became director of the site), ethnohistorian and architect, respectively.

By 1981 the 83.9 hectares that currently make up the site had been completely expropriated from their last private owner, the Hacienda Pirela, and the site of Cochasquí opened its doors to the public. The Consejo Provincial initially obtained fourteen hectares of land, which consisted of a large east-west trench that included just five of the major pyramids. Within a couple of months, the remaining 69.9 hectares owned by the hacienda were taken. The current site contains the fifteen pyramids and the smaller mounds that surround them. Nonetheless, there is evidence of archaeological remains well beyond the currently delimited area (Programa Cochasquí 1991).

The expropriation process appears to have had a negative impact on the relationship between the program and hacienda management. The strained relationship was obvious during my fieldwork in the staff's fear of trespassing on hacienda land or of giving the hacienda owners any reason to legally challenge the expropriation process. These fears are not unfounded, since legal issues have not been completely resolved.

The program initially put forward four main objectives for the maintenance of the site: (1) historical/anthropological heritage; (2) conservation and restoration; (3) socioeconomic (community) development; and (4) public awareness (Programa Cochasquí 1981). These initial objectives have been maintained, with only a minor restructuring while Alfredo Costales served as director in the early 1990s (Programa Cochasquí 1991). The program's most interesting historical reconstruction objective is its wish to include the *comuna* in the site's preservation. From the outset, the Programa Cochasquí proposed a dynamic concept of culture as the essential element in any model of autonomous development of the region (Programa Cochasquí 1981).

The program was initially interdisciplinary, because it looked at the development of Cochasquí not only as an archaeological site, but also as an autochthonous community with many other needs—agricultural, socioeconomic, and medical (Programa Cochasquí 1981; Paredes and Estrella 1989). It also proposed a structure wherein the *comuna* would be responsible for and capable of managing the site directly. This initial cultural objective is still declared by the tour guides: "That is why the program is preoccupied not only with restoring or rescuing the pyramids, but also with everything that is culture, with all the culture" (Vicente, tour guide, February 2, 1997).

During the restructuring of the early 1990s, there was an explicit understanding of three major periods of activity at the site: the first was the initial period of cleaning and preparing the site for public display; the second was marked by the presence of foreign and national experts who served as consultants and studied different aspects of the site (e.g., Lumbreras 1990; Yurevich 1986); and the third was the program's recognition of the difficulty of implementing many of its initial objectives, mainly because of employee turnover (Programa Cochasquí 1991). The program had over seven directors from 1981 to 1998, although only four of them had a major impact on the site, because they held the position of director for more than a year: Lic. Lenín Ortiz (1981–1985); Lic. Alfredo Costales, an architect (1986–1993); a sociologist, Ramiro Mantilla (1994–1996); and Dr. Hugo Vaca, a historian (1996–1998).

Lenín Ortiz is a traditional, self-trained archaeologist who has also been actively involved in politics since the 1970s. He has been elected *consejero* for the Province of Pichincha twice. Although he was the initial proponent of rescuing the site, many of those who have collaborated with him over the years have mixed feelings about his legacy. Several former and current staff members I interviewed implied that, although the site of Cochasquí had benefited immensely from Lenín Ortiz's labor, he had also used it to further his own reputation and economic status. They alleged that he had done this by allowing the site to be used by the public for special events and celebrations, such as the international meeting of shamans, which received more attention and funding than the regular maintenance of the site.

According to a former staff member who worked at the site at the very beginning, Lenín Ortiz was ousted from control in 1985 by an ethnohistorian, Alfredo Costales, who became the director until 1994. It was during Costales's tenure that two museums were opened: the site museum (which was constructed in 1991), and the war museum, which was dismantled in 1995. Ortiz regained his influence over the site when he was reelected as *consejero* in 1994. He was instrumental in appointing sociologist Ramiro Mantilla as director in 1995 and providing for a rhetorical shift in the initial interdisciplinary objectives of the program.

One staff member explained to me that the director at the time of our interview, Dr. Hugo Vaca, was originally a tour guide and later became the site resident before being promoted to director. Ortiz, as *consejero*, demanded Ramiro Mantilla's resignation and that of everyone who supported him. Vaca was then appointed director of the site. Vaca, who served as director until 1998, had Ortiz's full confidence and was one of his personal advisors while the latter was head of the Instituto Nacional de Patrimonio Cultural (National Institute of Cultural Patrimony, INPC).

Vaca had worked for over a decade as head of the Public Relations Department at the INPC, the entity in charge of regulating all cultural work in the country.

Program staff had completely turned over since my first contact with the program in 1995. Only the local staff, the archaeologist, and the site resident remained from the previous administration. The instability of the staff is pointed out by Salcedo (1985) as a central characteristic of the program. For Salcedo, staff turnover is provoked by a whole array of reasons and situations (1985: 103):

> The instability of the staff, who are constantly removed; the confusion of personal conflicts with the general and transpersonal objectives of the Program; the problems of communication between different social and cultural backgrounds; the intangible phenomena resulting from power conflicts; the labor tensions from the working conditions of the Provincial Council and of the program itself; the different ideological tendencies of its members; and the different degrees of interest in the program itself have made it a heterogeneous composition of varied interests and personal motivations, which is why a uniform collective action cannot be implemented.

More important, this instability is a response to structural constraints defined by the country's different ideological currents (Salcedo 1985). The program's position within the Consejo Provincial, a state institution, makes it prey to economic hardships as reflected in low wages, contract problems, transportation deficiencies (cars are always breaking down), and social instability as a result of the constant power plays involving *consejeros* and electoral politics.

Not surprisingly, as I was recently informed by one of the staff members, the personnel have been changed again since my participation in the project in 1997. The director, the sociologist, and the site resident from my time have been removed, and the former president of the *comuna* has been hired as a site guard. At the end of 1998, Ortiz's nephew was appointed director, and a close friend of the new director was hired as site resident. Turnover will most probably only increase with every new government and the attendant political turmoil that new regimes produce in the Consejo Provincial.

The Comuna

I did not go to school, we know nothing here to live, it was all work, it was all service on the hacienda, like we are now, just like what was left after the Incas. (Concepción de la Cruz, *comunera* of Cochasquí, in Moscoso and Costa 1989)

The *comuna* of Cochasquí is located just south of the secondary road that leads to the site from the main highway. The center of the *comuna* is located on a hilltop two kilometers south of the entrance to the site. The *comuna* itself is made up of dispersed farmholdings that are clustered in three barrios—San Francisco, El Cholán, and El Salado—with an estimated six hundred inhabitants and a total of sixty-five families when Salcedo (1985) carried out his study of the area.

Although the population is considered to have an indigenous origin, there is very little Indian identity represented in the community (Costales and Costales 1990–1991). This lack of an Indian identity was also apparent in my conversation with a couple of the *comuneros,* who admitted to having lost their ancient traditions, not speaking Quechua (the native Indian language), and dressing in Western clothes. Rather, as in many other peasant communities in coastal and highland Ecuador, their identity was more directly linked to a rural-mestizo ethnicity and to the towns of Malchinguí and Tocachi, from which 90 percent of the original population came (Salcedo 1985).

Like other Ecuadorian peasant communities (Barsky 1984), Cochasquí suffers enormously from the departure of most of the younger population to the neighboring town of Cayambe or Quito. The year-round population of the *comuna* comprises only 52.5 percent of the estimated population. The lack of work and educational facilities (there is only one primary school) are the two main reasons given for the exodus to the urban centers.

The consequences of this high migration level are evident in the *comuna* members' lives. For example, one of the guides still lives in the *comuna* with his wife while his two sons and daughter are working and studying in Quito. The other guide's eldest son moved to Cayambe by himself to start high school (seventh grade), even though he is only thirteen years old.

The fairly recent influx of flower factories (which are the local version of *maquiladoras*) into the area has brought new job possibilities. However, these companies prefer female to male workers and demand that the worker spend the whole week away from home, since inadequate and unreliable transportation makes a daily commute impossible. In addition, stories about the health risks of the pesticides used in these factories were related to me.

The *comuna* is governed by a locally elected ruling body known as the Junta Directiva, which is composed of a president, a vice president, a secretary, and a *síndico* (treasurer). The Junta Directiva is elected by popular vote of the *comuneros* and has to be officially recognized by the *teniente político* (political authority) of the city of Tabacundo. The officials (all of whom have been men) serve for one year and are usually reelected for another year; some are elected again after several years (Salcedo 1985; also see Allen 1988 for the governing structure of the Andean town of Sonqo).

The elected officials recognize this post as a thankless job ("un trabajo ingrato"), since they have to worry about the needs of the *comuna* and are not recognized for their efforts. Even worse, they are often questioned and accused of wrongdoing (Salcedo 1985). Occupying these elected posts, especially the presidency, means an economic loss but a gain of social capital (Bourdieu 1993). The president often has to use his own money for transportation and other expenses and is never reimbursed. However, this economic loss is translated into social clout and prestige (Salcedo 1985). This would explain how the previous *comuna* president was able to get himself hired in 1996 by the Consejo Provincial as one of the new guards for the site. I was told that a stable job at the site is highly coveted and anyone who secures one is the target of great envy.

The history of the *comuna* is very closely associated with that of the Hacienda of Cochasquí. Before it was forced to sell the land by the 1962 agrarian reform, the hacienda was very large. The *comuneros* told me that the hacienda's holdings were vast, originally starting at the Pisque River (a little farther east from the Panamerican Highway), going all the way to the Fuya Fuya (the top of the Mojanda volcano). In all, it extended for thousands of square kilometers and covered a full thousand meters of fertile land (Moscoso and Costa 1989).

The hacienda grew several crops, wheat, corn, oats, and potatoes being the most important. It also boasted many cows, bulls, sheep, and pigs, as well as mules and horses (Moscoso and Costa 1989). In the 1990s the Calisto family sold a large part of the hacienda to the Pirela Company, which specializes in pyrethrums (an insecticide). Unfortunately, the insecticide had a negative effect on the mound and pyramids because of its harsh impact on the soil (Programa Cochasquí N.d).

The hacienda historically was supported by different forms of labor relations, the two most important being *huasinpungueros* and *arrendatarios*. The *huasinpungueros* (see Icaza 1993) were workers who were given a small plot of land to live on and work with their family in payment for the whole family's service to the hacienda (Moscoso and Costa 1989). Not surprisingly, this form of labor extraction, inherited from colonial times, was a subtle form of slavery, since the *huasipungueros* could never improve their socioeconomic situation (see Benítez and Costa 1983).

As one member of the Cochasquí *comuna*, Virgilio Pullas de la Cruz (1997: 53), notes, *huasipungueros* were "workers who live[d] and work[ed] on a piece of land around their homes, which generally [provided] them with the necessary basic resources for their survival, without there being enough for their reproduction."

Arrendatarios also lived on the hacienda, but paid for the land. This freed the rest of the family from serving the hacienda household. In the words of another *comuna* member (a guard, March 26, 1997), "So, you see, some people had land from way before, like my father-in-law, several years back when this hacienda belonged to the Calistos. They had people on as *huasipungueros* and *arrendatarios*. So that the *arrieros* had to take the produce and grain to Quito, while the *huasipungueros* had to work for the hacienda for free one day a month. They had to go to the hacienda and pay with one day of their labor."

As some, but not all, of the accounts disclose, the *comuneros*' relationship with the hacienda was, unfortunately, one of exploitation and servitude (see Rodríguez 1980 for a more positive interpretation of life at the hacienda; also see Stoler 1996 for a theoretical discussion similar to the one here). Hortencia Sotamín describes the past much as the guard does: "In my father's time, there were schools, but only for white people; for us *naturales* [natives] there was nothing" (in Moscoso and Costa 1989). Pullas de la Cruz (1997: 53) describes how "the owner of the hacienda made people work on Saturdays and Sundays for his benefit. Both fathers and older boys went to do this work, while the daughters worked as house servants for the hacienda. If they refused to work, the owner of the hacienda would imprison them and tie them up. Because of this, the Cochasquí natives left."

Most of the imported workers were from the neighboring towns of Malchinguí and Tocachi, especially during the big harvest periods. However, during the 1960s there was a major selling of plots of land to the *huasipungueros* as a result of the national agrarian reform that looked to dismantle the latifundios (large landholdings). As one of the *comuneros* explained to me (March 26, 1997), "Instead of giving them compensation in the form of money, they were given land. I am not too sure whether six or eight hectares." Since the owner decided which lands would be sold (Moscoso and Costa 1989: 31), the worst and most arid parcels were the ones distributed (Salcedo 1985: 88): "The worst lands were given to us"; "He would tell us that so we could be together and form a town he would give us the land in the *salado* [the most arid parcels; the word means 'salty']."

It was at this point that the *comuna* of Cochasquí as such began to function. The community grew, and elected local *comuna* officials got approval for their legal jurisdiction from the regional authorities in Tabacundo.

In terms of the *comuna*'s relationship with the Programa Cochasquí, conditions have diverged from the original objectives (Paredes and Estrella 1989: 11): "that the peasants who lived in the surrounding area had the social right to participate, not only as workers, but as administrators, since, ultimately, they are the direct descendants of what constitutes Cochasquí." Based on my observations and conversations with both staff members and *comuneros,* it appears that the relationship between the *comuna* and the program has always been contentious. Most of the *comuneros* I spoke with agreed that there was a much closer working relationship at the beginning of the program's existence and that it has deteriorated. As a local *comunero* explained (March 26, 1997):

> That is, before, when the program just began here in the community, there were good relations. That is, there was understanding. Both the community offered its service, such as *mingas* [communal labor]. Any work that needed to be done, the community would go out and do it, but all with one objective the people would offer their work. Then they would help when it was the secretary's, treasurer's, or the president's turn from here [the *comuna*]. The people would offer their service so that the program would help the secretary, treasurer, and/or president, giving them transportation so that they could carry out the paperwork to benefit the community. That is, there was an even exchange. . . . But now it's not like that. I am not too sure, but since Costales was in charge, and he said that the program was on one side and the community was on the other. Since then the people decided to part ways, both the community and the program. And ever since then there really hasn't been any reconciliation. Although now it seems to be better. It also depends on the leaders of the community. It depends on the leaders of the community to establish communication with whoever is in charge here [at the site] and in the community.

The current and two former directors of the site I interviewed argued that the relationship was still very close and that the program was as concerned with the community's well-being as it was with the archaeological remains. However, it appears, based on my observations, that the program tends to use the idea of community development as a vehicle through which to carry out its own agenda. The *comuneros* are encouraged to do what the program wants, but always under the guise of its being in the *comuna*'s own interests. This was particularly obvious at a community meeting I attended at which the program director asked for a *minga* on a weekend to clean the pyramids for the upcoming meeting of shamans. The director felt within his rights to ask this from the community, even though the program had been given additional funds for this event and the community was excluded from the meeting.

The *comuneros* are aware of this uneven exchange and offer their help with their own agendas in mind. The elected *comuna* government maneuvers to ingratiate itself with the program and socially and politically benefits, as when, for example, the former president was hired as site guard. The program is also instrumental in providing transportation, influence with the larger bureaucracy, and economic contributions to the local community, such as money for building the new church. The site does not really offer any direct service to the community, but, overall, some *comuneros* and the local government gain an enormous amount of prestige, which at some point may be translated into economic gain.

For Salcedo (1985: 103–105) the difficulties between the *comuna* and the program have two roots. The first is the social differences between the mestizo urban staff and the mestizo rural peasant community. Because all of the decision-making power is held by the white/mestizo staff located in Quito, the two groups exhibit contrasting mentalities and sociocultural and economic forms. The second is the program's portrayal of social development as an abstraction, when the *comuneros* need tangibly better economic and social conditions.

Finally, there is a mystical or mythical feeling in the *comuna* about the pyramids at Cochasquí. Stories about unexplained events in the area around the site abound, many of which were recounted to me by the staff and *comuneros*, and others that I experienced firsthand. Most of these stories deal with one of the following elements: *la yumba* (a white blonde woman), *la sirena* (a mermaid), balls of fire, hidden treasures, *el cuiche* (a local devil figure), volcanic lakes, and UFOs. The local people always refer to the site as the area of the pyramids or of the crosses (Chicaiza in Salcedo 1985: 68): "What we know of these mounds is that they were made by the Incas and the Caras. But before, the mounds were called the 'crosses,' I could not tell you why, but that is what they were called. Now everybody just calls them *tolas* [mounds]." Although it is unclear why they would use this name, it might be because of the T-shape of the pyramids or construction of crosses in the area to protect against the "haunting," visions, and unexplained events associated with the pyramids. This practice of setting up crosses in natural haunted areas is fairly widespread in Ecuador, for example, on the Santa Elena peninsula.

A haunting occurred during the full moon in March, 1997. A group of new-age practitioners and a shaman had permission from the director to spend the night at the site to chant and perform cleansing rituals. They were snorting—quite painfully—herbs and pseudo-hallucinogenic liquids. The driver and two of the site guards, who arrived late, mistakenly believed that the activities were being carried out on pyramid 14. They were adamant about having heard voices and seen people on the pyramid, only to find nobody there once they made it to the top. In typical macho fashion, they did not make much of the matter and silently made their way back to the camp. When one of them felt his jacket being pulled, however, he and his two companions ran in fright to the main building of the site as fast as they could. They were found there panting and terrified. Although more "unexplainable" events occurred that evening, the most meaningful element for me was to see how these three men, who were usually so adamant about their courage and masculinity, refused to be left alone for the rest of the night.

COCHASQUÍ IN THE NATIONAL IMAGINATION

On February 27, [1613], the Indians acted out scenes of the history of the country and of the life of Huayna Capac: "The armies of the last Queen of Quito and the Incas walked into the plaza . . . they acted out the combat . . . the scene ended with the death of the Queen of Cochasquí and an imitation of the manner in which the Indians sang their victory." These few elements allow us to identify the depth of the enactment, with the history described by Montesinos, of the love affair between Huayna Capac with the Queen Quilago, whose realm was located on the north side of the Quisque [Pisque] River, that is, Cochasquí (Jijón y Caamaño 1997: 36).

This particular event, narrated by Don Diego Urbán de la Vega and commented on by Jijón y Caamaño, took place in Quito, in 1613, as part of the Audiencia's festivities celebrating the birth of the Prince of

Asturias, Baltasar Carlos Felipe of Austria. The ritualized enactment of the armed struggle against the Incas, which implies the love affair between the Queen of Cochasquí (who, it is also implied, is the Queen of Quito) and the ruling Inca, Huayna Capac, synthesizes two of the elements that relate Cochasquí to the national imagination. To this day, Cochasquí's resistance to the Incas and Quilago's love affair with Huayna Capac are highlighted in the guided tours of the site.

This enactment of an event that took place over 350 years ago impresses upon us the pivotal place of Cochasquí in the larger historical discourse of what was initially the Real Audiencia de Quito and later became the Ecuadorian nation. What seems most relevant about Cochasquí and its female ruler is not necessarily the element of historical truth so much as the fact that these histories merit continual retelling—especially since they were not simply written down, but were played out in a ritualized drama in the polity's capital in 1613 or repeated today in the setting of Cochasquí's pyramids.

Both of these events contain elements that allow for the subtle representation of the site and its pre-Hispanic inhabitants in a national light. Within the description of Quilago's amorous involvement with Huayna Capac and her ultimate downfall when her plan to murder the Inca ("prepararle una celada") is betrayed by her subjects is engraved a whole narrative of origin and legitimization for the emerging Ecuadorian nation (Pullas de la Cruz 1997: 12): "Where the Incas wanted to conquer them, they wanted to gain control of the great forts, but they could not, there were great battles and with Quilago at their head they were able to stop the Incas. The Inca is embarrassed by this strong woman, this forceful woman who made herself be obeyed. Telling the absolute truth and speaking like a 'historian' [*cronista*] they say that she prepared a trap in her room, but was betrayed by her own subjects, who told Huayna Capac, and she falls in the trap herself and the Incas gain absolute control."

In this description, Quilago and Huayna Capac are portrayed as the founding couple of an ancestral Ecuadorian heritage. This is possible in spite of, and probably because of, Huayna Capac's ambiguous role as leader of the enemy Inca army and father of the soon-to-be-last ruling Inca, Atahualpa (Pareja Diezcanseco 1990; L.N.S. N.d.). This Ecuadorian ancestry is associated in the tours with Cochasquí, its inhabitants, pyramids, museum, and festivals. This national association is never questioned or deemed lacking in empirical evidence; rather, the linkage between the site and an ancestral Ecuadorianness is actively represented and presented as natural.

The second element, the site's communal resistance to the onslaught of the Inca conquest, is also subject to representation as a national phenomenon (Vinicio, guide, February 2, 1997):

> It was a matriarchy, we call it a matriarchy when there is a kingdom of women, and in Cochasquí we have the Quilago, the Princess Quilago; in the area of Malchinguí, the general Marango. Who would have thought that these people, or that this culture, that this Quilago was going to unite forces with the Marangos, with the people of Cayambe. . . . The Incas scale the northern part of the Pisque River, from the Pisque on, there is a great flow of blood, with people falling from both sides, where both Incan and Quiteño forces die, where the weapons are found, like the stones.

The resistance to the Inca Empire is narrated as a preamble to the nation's fierce struggle against foreign domination, represented in this instance by the Incas, later, by the Spanish, and most recently, by the ongoing struggle with Peru for territory. The Inca invasion allows Cochasquí to be represented as the national community heroically defending itself against a larger, ruthless enemy. It is also this narrative of unequal power structures that excuses the nation's continuing defeats at the hands of foreign aggressors (not the least problematic in the national consciousness being the 1941 military loss that gave Peru almost half of Ecuador's national territory) (see Silva 1995). The displacement that the Incas suffer in the narrative (discussed in more detail below), as they are first hailed as the natural enemies of Cochasquí and then as Ecuador's ancestors, expresses the ambiguity of a historical discourse that is ultimately concerned with national appropriations more than with historical congruency (see, e.g., Pullas de la Cruz 1997; see Salomon 1990 for discussion of a similar process among the Cañaris). It is also important to note that this historical ambiguity, far from being an anomaly, is an essential element of any historical discourse (Alonso 1988; Foucault 1991).

It is safe to state that the meanings and implications of and the motivation for the ritualized enactment in 1613 were probably very different from contemporary reasons. Yet there is something about Cochasquí and many of these particular histories that is useful in the nation's portrayal of itself (see Moreno Yáñez 1981). There are many elements present in the program's recounting of Cochasquí's history, a history that the nation strategically attributes to itself.

NATURALIZING ECUADOR

Cochasquí as Ecuador's Hidden History

We are proud of being Ecuadorians.

—L. B., TOURIST, AUGUST 16, 1995

Several themes emerged in tourists' responses to my questions about what they thought of Cochasquí. Most visitors hail Cochasquí as a site of national importance. To the foreigners, Cochasquí is a place where "[the Ecuadorian] people can find out about their own history and appreciate the patrimony they have" (C., April 8, 1997). The site seems to represent another Ecuador that is hidden under the country's contemporary governmental corruption and underdevelopment. In the foreign visitor's mind, it is a place of dignity that, unlike other contemporary elements of the country, should make Ecuadorians proud of who they are. At Cochasquí the visitor can "feel the things that existed, there is a living testimony of history" (S., May 2, 1997).

After visiting Cochasquí, many foreigners leave with a positive image of Ecuador that is more in tune with what they want the country to be: "[I left the site] reaffirmed in my ideas about the [Ecuadorian] nationality" (C., March 29, 1997). This need is also addressed in the program's guided tours, during which the guides strive to provide a picture of what Ecuador "is really like," were it not hampered by the ancient and modern forms of conquest and domination.

For Ecuadorians, Cochasquí is a place where they can express their national pride: "Because it is necessary to give our existence and nationality the value it deserves" (A., July 20, 1995). Cochasquí represents a part of history that was taken from them, that was hidden from view and literally buried: "It teaches us to return to what is ours" (E., March 27, 1997). The site of Cochasquí "informs us about our culture and keeps alive our traditions" (E., April 9, 1997).

This site is a living symbol of the tragedy of the Spanish conquest, the rape of Ecuador, and the rewriting of its history. The "development of our people [*el pueblo*] was very prosperous until it was terminated by the Spanish conquest; everybody knows that the development of our culture was excellent before the [Spanish] conquest" (E., April 9, 1997). To the Ecuadorian visitors, Cochasquí is emblematic of another Ecuador, an Ecuador hidden under years of colonial exploitation and genocide.

To these visitors, the site is a triumph of indigenous effort and resistance, and therefore is undoubtedly a site not only of Indian, but of "Ecuadorian," pride.

For Ecuadorian visitors, Cochasquí is a place where they can find out about a history they do not know, their "own history," since "[our] history is important and a lot of us don't know it" (I., August 14, 1997). The roots of what Ecuador is are there: "The site is a place where you can go and feel our roots" (H., July 20, 1995). But these roots are hidden almost everywhere else in the country and, to some degree, even at Cochasquí. That is why the site should continue to display the true Ecuador, its roots: "[The site] must continue forward for an authentic Ecuador" (B. J., December 28, 1995).

The unfulfilled promise of discovery of authenticity is essential to Cochasquí's allure and is one of the reasons many visitors say they return to the site, bringing others with them each time they come back. The site is frequently revisited, even though there have been no new excavations or research in the area since 1962. The sensation of renewal and promise there is so strong that it ultimately comes to feel like a privilege to live in this land which is Ecuador: "Today I prayed to the ancient Gods [Apachita] that they allow me to live in this land" (S. B., July 27, 1995).

These reactions establish a tie between the thousand-year-old pyramids and mound constructions at Cochasquí and the modern Ecuadorian nation-state of fewer than two hundred years of age. The contemporary nation-state becomes the inheritor of this mythical Ecuador. For many visitors, the site displays the roots of what Ecuadorians are today, and those roots need to be discovered and displayed with pride, just as the program is doing, because "this is the history of our country, which needs to be made known" (N. H., n.d.). In this sense, Cochasquí *is* Ecuador.

Reactions to the site allow us to glimpse the process through which the past is rendered as a factual essence. Alonso (1988: 44–44) defines this process as one of naturalization, in which dynamic actors, discourses, and practices are rendered as natural essences or things. This naturalization is accomplished by "the transformations effected on subordinated histories by turning re-presentations into 'raw facts' which cannot be contested" (Alonso 1988: 45).

In this manner, different mechanisms, such as narrative structure, content, and voice, are utilized to naturalize the work (and power) of reinterpretation and re-presentation (Alonso 1988). In these instances, the particular historical discourses present at Cochasquí are subsumed

74

under the narrative appropriation of the nation-state and its inherent legitimization.

Pristine Authenticity: An Ecuador before Ecuador Existed

In the guided tours, the pre-Columbian occupants of the sites are referred to as "our ancestors," thus laying claim to a mestizo heritage under which every Ecuadorian is a descendant of an Indian past (Jacinto, guide, February 8, 1997; my emphasis):

> [Cochasquí] as an astronomical observatory, where *our* ancestors, in these pyramids, especially the ones that are exposed, used them to carry out calendrical calculations or to observe the constellations, or, let's say, seasons of the year. Therefore *our* ancestors had already determined here the zero point. The true zero point is here. That *our* ancestors already knew it, they already knew that the earth was round. And they already knew that this is where the sun passed by [the site is six minutes off the equator] and according to that they could do astronomical readings. Therefore Cochasquí, for *our* culture, meant "middle of the lake," "*cochas*" means "water," and "*qui*," half. And this is precisely the center of the equinox, the pyramids.

All Ecuadorians, especially visitors to the site, are thrust into a genealogical tie with "our" Indian past. This claim to Indian heritage goes unquestioned, and as such the pyramids are the remains of what "our ancestors" constructed before the multiple conquests of the territory. Thus, the site at Cochasquí is seen as representing an authentic Ecuadorian culture, one that recurring struggles and, above all, constant loss of territory have obscured.

The Indian and local traditions that are celebrated at the site also contribute to its interpretation as the holder of autochthonous cultural tradition. During the biggest festivities at the site, such as the Inti Raymi (Festival of the Sun), many Indian communities come to perform traditional dances and rituals. The Inti Raymi is an Inca festival that traditionally falls on the summer solstice (around June 21) and commemorates the longest day of natural sunlight in the year. The Inti Raymi, as the paramount religious celebration of the Inca Empire, was very much a sign of cultural domination over the conquered Andean *ayllus* (local regional kinship structures). However, this initial cultural (and political) signification is no longer the only (or even the most important) one

75

expressed in the contemporary Andean celebrations of the Inti Raymi (Whitten 1981).

The celebration of the Inti Raymi has taken on a pan-Andean existence, being celebrated in many Andean communities, but with local adaptations. One of the most interesting modern characteristics of this celebration is the mixture of the Inti Raymi with the Catholic Feast of Saint Peter (which falls within the same week, June 29). Indians most probably used this Inca and Catholic symbiosis during colonial times to continue to celebrate Andean tradition under the eye of Catholic hegemony (Isbell 1985; Silverblatt 1987; Weismantel 1992), much like other followers of non-normative religious practices, such as santería, candomblé, and voodoo.

At Cochasquí the festivities usually vary from year to year. Unfortunately, even though there was lots of planning and talk about having the program organize a major Inti Raymi celebration at the site, this did not occur while I was working there in 1997. Instead, there were smaller celebrations carried out by independent groups of shamans and tourists. Based on interviews with staff members about previous celebrations, the following picture emerged. Previous Inti Raymi celebrations traditionally included speeches by high-ranking politicians and officials of the Consejo Provincial. This usually gave way to performances and dances in honor of the sun by invited Indian communities. There also tended to be an enormous amount of *chicha* (a beer made from corn) and other types of liquor, which contributed to an overall feeling of belonging and excitement.

At this moment, the Indians hold center stage at Cochasquí and are portrayed as the true inheritors of the site. The rest of the tourists, foreign and Ecuadorian, are spectators and celebrate the survival of their Indian cultures. I would suggest that it is also at this moment that the Indians' presence is co-opted by the nation-state and that their ancestral claim is undeniable proof of the Ecuadorianness of the site. If the site is truly Indian, as proved by the Indians' claims in their dances and rituals, and Ecuadorians are all descendants of that Indian heritage, then the site itself is their heritage. The site represents a pristine Ecuadorianness lost through the ages. This representation directly, and not surprisingly, justifies and legitimates the present-day nation-state.

Other festivities, such as the world championship of *cabes* (giant tops), meetings of shamans, and weddings celebrated at the site, produce a very similar impact. At all of these events, there is a nostalgic desire to arrive at a primordial source of identity. In the first wedding ceremony ever held at the site, celebrated on the summer solstice of 1997 on pyramid no. 14, there was an incantation to the indigenous genealogy of the Ecuadorian bride through a fictitious matrilineal line that gave her the right to marry her foreign (Russian) husband in this land that was rightfully hers. This appeal to the native is more telling if one takes into consideration the fact that the bride had no direct ties with any contemporary Indian community and had not even lived in the country for over a decade. Both she and her husband (they were legally married in the United States) had flown in for a weeklong vacation from Miami, where they lived, to get married at Cochasquí. She chose Cochasquí to justify her living outside of the country and marrying outside of the national fold.

As a guest at the wedding, I sensed the inherent quality of ritual activities held at Cochasquí, that is, an urgency to establish and connect to a national sense of belonging. The bride came back to reclaim her Ecuadorianness, to "invent" it, and her getting married at Cochasquí accomplished that. The wedding service was full of symbolic appeals to the Caras, Incas, Cañaris, and natural deities like the wind, the sun, the moon, and the earth, without any actual concern for historical or geographical truths. There is no archaeological or historical evidence for the existence of the Caras, and the sites were repeatedly pointed to in the wrong direction, for example, Quito to the north, when it is actually to the southeast.

The wedding expressed the need to constantly reaffirm a symbolic truth that wove all of these indigenous elements into a common fabric and allowed those present to claim the site as Ecuadorian. This symbolic commonality allowed us all to participate as Ecuadorians and permitted us to see ourselves as the natural inheritors of the site. Echoing Foucault (in J. Miller 1993: 250), the symbolic truth at Cochasquí is not and does not necessarily have to be true, but that does not make it any less real or lessen its impact on performers and spectators alike.

In the national appropriation of traditional festivities or symbols, there is an ongoing process of "departicularization." Historical symbols and practices are severed from their initial localities and concrete meanings and represented in a more generalized fashion, making them the property of everyone and no one at the same time (Alonso 1988: 45). It is through this process of departicularization that national (i.e., ethnic and racial) differences are smoothed out and the "other" appropriated, making it possible for the past to be "invested with new meanings which reproduce a hegemonic national ideology and the relations of domination it configures and legitimates" (Alonso 1988: 45).

A similar effect resulted from the international shaman celebrations held at the site in July 1997. The indigenous affiliation of many of the shamans, evidenced in their knowledge of traditional healing and their external characteristics (dress, language, etc.), appealed enormously to the tourists. The line of cars waiting to enter the site extended to the Pan-American Highway, a full eight kilometers away, meaning a record number of visitors to the site. There was such an enormous number of people (in the thousands) that the staff gave up supervision, allowing the tourists to wander unaccompanied throughout the site. Shamans set up small structures (*kioskos*) toward the lower part of the site, and people visited as many of them as they wished. Most of the shamanistic rituals were related to divination, or "reading," of the person's health and over-all well-being, including ensuring good luck and positive economic pros-pects. If needed, the shaman bathed and cleansed "patients" in public. People participated in different ritualistic activities, even ones that de-manded partial nudity, such as bathing in water and other organic ele-ments in the cold outdoors.

In many ways, this appeal to a mysterious element at the site is also part of and expressed in the tours: "And we have [pyramid] no. 14, the one with the longest ramp; the ramp is 250 meters long. On top of this, we are told that this place is full of energy, it is a magnetic place, because in this place they would come together to perform their rituals and cer-emonies. Therefore, it is a very important place. But for all this energy, they would take advantage of the equinoxes and the solstices to carry out this activity of 'receiving' the energy" (Jacinto, guide, February 8, 1997).

> You are visiting a site of peace, of happiness, you are receiving positive energy.
>
> —Virgilio, guide, February 2, 1997

The engagement and presence of indigenous shaman healers, readers, and spiritual counselors at the site provided an element which enticed the national population. As expressed by one of the tourists: "One feels the presence of the prehistoric spirits, as if they were here" (S. E., Janu-ary 4, 1997).

This esoteric truth does not seem to be independent of the sense of mystery in which most of the Ecuadorian nationals hold the indigenous past. It is related to the mystery with which a primordial Ecuadorian entity supports itself. This is why at Cochasquí, one "can feel all the energy of our ancestors" (T., July 17, 1995). Tourists see Cochasquí as a "mysterious site, [where] we can feel our roots" (T., July 20, 1995). "Roots" in this case means evidence of an ancient Ecuadorian identity of which we have only remnants exposed in these indigenous celebrations and their products. The Indian rituals are appropriated through our bodies and, ultimately and unbeknownst to us, relate us to the body of the Ecuadorian nation-state (this is discussed in more detail in chapter 3).

What is both interesting and telling is that this co-optation of Indian celebrations and traditions so far has gone uncontested at the site. The powerful Indian movement, represented in a national forum by the CONAIE, has not had any impact on the celebrations or the cultural ownership of the site. Until now all the indigenous communities have claimed their own Indian heritage at the site, but not ownership of the site itself. The absence of specific cultural ownership, therefore, does not challenge the Ecuadorian spectators' own claims because there is no politically organized or culturally recognized indigenous group in the area that is directly linked to the site. I would argue that the absence of a strong, specifically Indian affiliation at the site permits Cochasquí's national appropriation to go uncontested and be more viable.

THE PRODUCTION OF AN OFFICIAL COCHASQUÍ

I imagine that every historian is similarly affected when he begins to record the events of some period and wishes to portray them sincerely. Where is the center of events, the common standpoint around which they revolve and which gives them cohesion? In order that something like cohesion, something like causality, that some kind of meaning might ensue and that it can in some way be narrated, the historian must invent units, a hero, a nation, an idea, and he must allow to happen to this invented unit what has in reality happened to the nameless.

— HERMANN HESSE (1994)

The Programa Cochasquí's voice is the privileged one when it comes to determining what is socially significant in historical terms at Cochasquí. The program and its staff have the final word about what is expressed to the public; however, the program is not the only voice. Other major groups—the local *comuneros,* the anthropologists and archaeologists, the tourists and visitors—are struggling for representation and recognition, that is, power, at the site. None of these groups are univocal or monolingual. Each of these groups represents more heterogeneous and dynamic voices than would initially appear to be the case. Just as the different archaeological publications do not agree on the nature of findings at Cochasquí, neither do the local *comuneros* agree about what Cochasquí is or what it means to them: for some, the site is very important while for others, it holds no value whatsoever.

The challenge, then, becomes how to understand the nature and production of history from such a myriad of voices and the different and, at times, contradictory descriptions and interpretations of a large number of actions and events at the site. What makes the understanding of this phenomenon more challenging is the fact that, although different versions are present and expounded, only one of them is hailed as the right one, or, more precisely, as the official one. The Programa Cochasquí has appropriated this claim for itself. The program stands alone and unquestioned in its right to determine what is historically accurate for the site, even when its version is obtained through the same sources everyone else uses. That is, the program's version, expounded by the guides, is asserted to be valid, even when it has no greater claim to objectivity than the other versions expressed at the site and outlined in chapter 1.

How, then, does the program accomplish this? What mechanisms allow it to proclaim itself the holder of historical truth? In the next chapter, I will describe three of the techniques the program uses to impose its authority through the elaboration of a "history that always encourages subjective recognitions and attributes a form of reconciliation to all the displacements of the past" (Foucault 1993: 152) and several of the other mechanisms of official appropriation present at Cochasquí.

THREE

NATIONAL MECHANISMS OF APPROPRIATION

History, Territory, Gender, and Race at Cochasquí

~

*As a result of the [archaeological] research carried out by
Jijón y Caamaño, Uhle, Estrada, Bell, Meggers and Evans,
Mayer, Lathrap, Oberem, Porras, Holm, Zevallos, and many
more, it is now possible, taking into account some important
voids, to project ourselves [as Ecuadorians] ten thousand
years back, to start history at the beginning.*

—PLUTARCO NARANJO (1985)

THE LOGIC OF OFFICIAL HISTORIES

Official Scripts 1: The Programa Cochasquí as Synthesizer

This chapter continues to analyze the elements and techniques involved
in the national appropriation of Cochasquí, assessing how Ecuadorian
nationality can be stretched back for several millennia. In this regard,
the Programa Cochasquí's contribution is central, as it claims to incorporate the different archaeological versions of Cochasquí and thus offers
itself as a synthesizer of historical truth. For this endeavor, it uses archaeology and its mantle of truth and objectivity to obtain even greater
legitimization, in this instance, scientific. The program therefore presents
itself as an objective synthesizer with no real interest in manipulating the
truth. Its only interest lies in obtaining the truth (as if truth exists independent of anything else) to further strengthen the site's claim to authentic Ecuadorian heritage. What hidden agenda could such a noble purpose hide?

Not surprisingly, however, the program does not merely synthesize information or obtain the "truth" about Cochasquí; rather, it creates or constructs truth, just as any of the other historical versions do, picking and choosing. It claims not to select only what it wants to hear, but what it assumes to be truth based on its own rigorous definition of what the truth is.

This form of historical production, under the guise of synthesis, is evident in the Programa Cochasquí's dismissal of historical elements that are potentially disruptive and, coincidentally, do not meet the program's criteria for historical truth. It is also present in the program's minimal exploration of possible human sacrifice at the site. The over six hundred skulls Max Uhle found in his excavation of pyramid no. 9 are explained away as being simply executed prisoners of war whose skulls were trophies:

> When all that research is done, they conclude that it is a result of the massacre, the war that they had with the Incas. They [the Incas] put them here; as you have heard, it is from the sacrifices, from the description of our ancestors. Most important, this culture did not sacrifice people, but it was the Incas, there is a theory that it was the Incas who most probably sacrificed the local people. But not our culture. They sacrificed animals, but since they only found skulls and not the rest of the bodies, and that is why I refer to the war brought about with the Inca invasion. And that is why this place is defined as a ceremonial center.
>
> —Jacinto, guide, February 2, 1997
>
> And inside those corridors they found skulls, that is, during the times of the owners of the Hacienda Cochasquí, they found 560 skulls. The age of the skulls [at the time of their death] is around twenty-five to thirty years old; they were young. There are hypotheses, theories that say those skulls could be war trophies put in the pyramid during their religious ceremonies. . . . There are several investigations, many of which say that they were human sacrifices. Others say that they didn't sacrifice, because we believe more that these were peaceful cultures, that they didn't carry out human sacrifices, right. There are some canals where supposedly flowed the blood of the virgins [sacrificed] in the religious ceremonies, and it was precisely those skulls that they took to a museum in Quito. That museum burns down completely and that is the end of the skulls.
>
> —Vicente, guide, February 2, 1997

This explanation overlooks the disturbing possibility that "our ancestors" (how the guides refer to the original inhabitants of the site) practiced human sacrifice, of foreigners or members of their own community. By claiming that these skulls belonged to enemies, the guides can justify the beheadings and cleanse the past of any "savage" or "primitive" behavior, which is unjustifiable and almost inexplicable in contemporary terms. Since the tour seeks to make Ecuadorian visitors proud of their ancestors, human sacrifice is an element that the program can easily do without.

Glossing over the skull offerings, however, also makes the site's history much more attractive: by making the original inhabitants mysterious and forbidding, the guides can arouse greater interest in them. By censoring any discussion of ritual violence, the Programa Cochasquí has "installed rather an apparatus for producing an ever greater quantity of discourse about [it]" (Foucault 1990: 23). This form of treating such a delicate subject ensures that no one is alienated from Cochasquí's history by a distasteful interpretation and assures a positive and morbid fascination with a mysterious and exciting past. Ultimately, this treatment results in the most economical form of benefit from a possibly disruptive historical element.

Another example of the program's selective construction of Cochasquí's history is the guides' description of the Inca conquest. The Incas are not presented simply as another conquering Indian community, but as a foreign conqueror. They are equated with contemporary Peru, the pre-Columbian struggle to the contemporary one between Ecuador and Peru (Gallardo 1995). One guide told me that Peruvian tourists, offended by his remarks, once abandoned the tour. Yet for him there was nothing he could do about it: "It was not my fault, that is just how history is." The Incas, in this instance, are interpreted as nothing other than Ecuador's mortal enemies. Therefore, not coincidentally, the visitor's pride in the Ecuadorian nation is boosted by the description of Cochasquí's valiant defense of what will eventually become the "national territory":

We have narratives that state that this culture was governed by a woman, by a princess called Quilago, but this woman was "matriarchized" ["matriarcada"], that she fought against the Inca invasion. Therefore, this culture has had a formidable struggle. But after the struggle with the Caranquis, pardon me, with the Cañaris, comes Huayna Capac and he conquers this culture. But this culture had a formidable struggle for seventeen or twenty years, not where we are visiting, but, rather, on the shores of the Pisque River. That is where this culture had constructed its fort to stop this invasion. However, since the Incas came with a very big army, history confirms for us that this culture was conquered, that they [the Incas] moved on to the north, conquered the Province of Imbabura, the Caranquis, and fought in the Lake of Yaguarcocha, that is why Yaguarcocha means "lake of blood," because that is where the massacre occurred.

—Jacinto, guide, February 8, 1997

An alternative understanding of Cochasquí and the Incas as being prenational (in contemporary terms) entities and existing three centuries before the modern nation-states of Ecuador and Peru is never presented. It is through this process of idealization that "the past is cleaned up, rendered palatable and made the embodiment of nationalist values" (Alonso 1988: 45). Unsettling elements such as ritual killing and conquest are tidied up and serve either to increase the mystery of the site as another intriguing curiosity or to foster support for a xenophobic national and ethnic pride.

Official Script 2: The Programa Cochasquí's Historical Range

The program's (i.e., the official) version of Cochasquí's history is freer to incorporate changes and adapt to different sources of historical facts. In this regard, Cochasquí's official history is much more accommodating than the other versions, precisely because it attempts to present itself as more democratic and historically accurate or truthful. Cochasquí's official history can incorporate these differences because it is being produced and expresses itself at both an individual and a communal level. At an individual level, the guides are free to adapt the history to the particular audience they are addressing, which ranges from five-year-old kindergartners to full-fledged shamans. Cochasquí is fascinating because it has something for everybody.

It is no surprise, therefore, that Cochasquí's official history can accommodate stories about UFO encounters, energy flows, and shamanistic rituals. Some accounts claim that members of the staff (including the director) have seen or heard inexplicable lights, strong energy sensations, Indian ghosts, strange sounds, and other fearful encounters that have made them run from the site. The mystery and firsthand knowledge expressed in the accounts enhance their authority:

The mermaid was supposed to be a she-devil who presumably knew how to play the guitar. Apparently, she was always where there were few people, in hidden places and where you don't hear anything. With the music she supposedly attracted people and then she'd disappear.

—Salcedo 1985: 117

One day I got close to the pyramids, because there was a lot of noise and I thought there were people. And there I saw that there were some naked men and there were some women with long hair. They were the *yumbas* [spirits that present themselves as beautiful women to seduce men]. I got scared. And then when they saw me they let me go and they were very mad.

—Salcedo 1985: 117

In the pyramids which were called the crosses, they say that they used to see a shiny ball come down from the highest point to the flatter area and then it would disappear. Meanwhile, they would try to find it, but they wouldn't find anything. Other times, they would say that the ball would illuminate the sky when it would be coming down. They also would see it in the morning when the sun would be rising with its radiant rays while the mounds of Cochasquí would become orange and yellow.

—Pullas de la Cruz 1997: 66

These accounts are accepted because they rely on the individual authority of the official guides and staff of the program. Anything they say is immediately accepted as truth and incorporated into the site's history, although with different constraints. The most important constraint is not expounding anything in direct opposition to the official history of the site; inconsequential matters are tolerated, not oppositional ones. Another condition is that the audience must believe the explanations. Therefore, program staff has an enormous amount of leeway in the production of the site's historical truth.

This individual authority works, on the one hand, because it can easily be incorporated into the program's hidden agenda, and, on the other, because it can just as easily be denied as an individual's opinion. This is similar to the manner in which repressive institutions blame individuals for the institution's violent behavior, all the while defending the honor and dignity of the institution (e.g., the "dirty war" in Argentina and Chile). The Programa Cochasquí's staff has authority and wields power, but, just like all the other players in the historical drama, their power is not unlimited.

Even the general truths, however, as communal representative of the program expressed in either written materials (site pamphlets) or museum exhibitions, are not any more rigid than the other elements of the official version of the site's history. The site was at one time housed in the War Museum, which, during much of the 1980s, was incorporated into the program's official tour of Cochasquí. The War Museum, built under the initiative of the second director of the site, Dr. Alfredo Costa-les, housed weapons and artifacts of war, not limited to Cochasquí or even Ecuadorian cultures. In the early 1990s, this museum was disman-tled because the new director (Ramiro Mantilla) did not feel it was ap-propriate any longer. Along with the museum, a sign containing a prayer to an Andean deity at the entrance to the site and the Apachita (the pre-Columbian crossroads deity) were removed. The staff or tourists might have protested the removal of these elements, but, ultimately, their dis-appearance did not bring into question the authority of the official his-tory. Their use said nothing (or possibly all) about what sustained the official discourse.

The official discourse operates as if it has a life of its own, indepen-dent of its content. It needs content to exist, but the nature of this con-tent is of only secondary importance. Thus, the War Museum might have been an integral part of the program's history at one moment, but its re-moval was not essential to the program's existence. When one compo-nent is removed, some other element replaces it. For example, the hut-like building that used to house the War Museum is now a small, round auditorium that houses meetings of shamans and accommodates over-night visitors who are participating in rituals at the site.

The program's history relies on a greater authority than simple his-torical facts. This explains why the shifting or changing of these "facts" does not have a major impact on the official discourse's claim to au-thoritativeness; greater authority is conferred by the state's and the na-tion's implicit support of the Programa Cochasquí's discourse.

Official Script 3:
The Programa Cochasquí's Relationship with the State

The official history at Cochasquí relies on more than its content or con-stituent historical elements. The official version can muster social ele-ments, such as state support and national clout, to legitimize the pro-gram's historical truth. Ultimately, these descriptions allow the Programa Cochasquí to appropriate the empirical evidence it is trying to interpret and hail it as proof of the program's own historical validity.

The program has greater economic resources and more social status and social capital than the other groups at the site with which to legiti-mize itself. Its social capital is obtained simply because it has the back-ing of a governmental institution, the Consejo Provincial de Pichincha. The Programa Cochasquí's claim to historical objectivity (via state backing) is enough to move it far above the other historical versions competing for legitimization.

Thus, it is the state, or its absence, as Abrams (1988: 58) notes, that helps legitimize the program's version of the site's history. The absence of formal state representatives at the site only assures that every person involved in the program becomes the state, or its spokesperson, and that individual opinions become one with the program and, ultimately, with the state itself. This scenario brings us back to the question of the program's claiming not to have a hidden agenda, when in fact its agenda is very subtle and essential: the maintenance and legitimization of the Ecuadorian nation-state.

Cochasquí's official history supports the notion of Ecuadorian nationhood, and, finally, it is this intention that becomes its system of truth. Accordingly, the state exercises its power to legitimize and maintain the program's existence and official history. However, this state support is extended only to ensure its own reproduction; if the program fails to follow the nation's agenda, support will be withdrawn or made inoperative. That is, no overarching figure will give meaning to the stories told by the guides at Cochasquí; in fact, Cochasquí's history will have no national meaning. This is why the legitimization of the nation-state—the trumpeting of the nation—is the system of truth through which the program tests all facts. This is the Programa Cochasquí's most rigorous demand and serves to regulate the official discourse, to make the propping up of the nation the program's most subtle and unspoken means of survival.

The relationship between historical production and nation-state formation is essential and, in many ways, much more intimate than has traditionally been understood (e.g., Chatterjee 1986; Patterson and Schmidt 1995; B. Williams 1991). Neither of these phenomena can exist without the other, and the presence of one necessarily implies the presence of the other. Thus, the state must claim a history, in this instance, the Programa Cochasquí's version, and once it has done so, all other versions are defeated, and any competing one (including mine) can anticipate victory only by becoming the new hegemonic/state/official version of history. All histories must "overcome the rulers through their own rules" (Foucault 1993: 151).

The nation-state, like all hegemonic discourses, including Cochasquí's official history, does not enjoy opposition and seeks to meet it with deadly force. It is therefore not the competing versions that significantly affect the hegemonic discourse, even if they win, as much as it is the latter's neutralizing the contesting version's most nonunifying demands and appropriating them into its own version of the truth. The factual elements are not a real empirical constraint on the appropriation process, which facilitates the process.

Cochasquí's official history, as we have seen, can have a War Museum as an integral part or not, but it must always have some element that fills it or "makes it up." This is part of the process by which hegemonic constructions constantly usurp, appropriate, and integrate what were initially counter-hegemonic discourses (Chatterjee 1986; Foucault 1991, 1993; Patterson and Schmidt 1995; Silverblatt 1988; I. Vargas 1995; B. Williams 1991; Wylie 1995).

This guarantees, as I observed repeatedly on the guided tours, that very few people go away unhappy with what they have seen at the site, no matter their national, cultural, ethnic, racial, class, gender, generation, or sexual-preference background. They leave happier because "they have found out about their roots and origin, and now more than ever they believe that we are descendants of fabulous people" (E., April 12, 1997). Or they believe that the visit was "excellent" and the guide was "very impressive" (E., March 29, 1997). Everybody is offered an individualized history of sorts produced by the rapport between the guides and the visiting group, a history which implicitly legitimizes and is integrated into the Ecuadorian nation-state's discourse.

The techniques of historical production discussed here are the main ones, but they are not the only ones used to produce the official history of Cochasquí—that is, to actually present the site as an important archaeological site. It is also how the site becomes a symbol of itself, how its empirical elements are used to represent the program's own truth. More specifically, at Cochasquí this reality is further symbolized by the representations of the empirical evidence, in this case, the pyramids. At times, the llamas and shoe-type pots, as seen on the logos and T-shirts sold at the site, also serve this purpose. However, the pyramids are the most imbued with the meaning the program projects:

> The bigger the material mass, the more easily it entraps us: mass graves and pyramids bring history closer while they make us feel small. . . . [T]hey embody the ambiguities of history. They give us the power to touch it, but not that to hold it firmly in our hands—hence the mystery of their battered walls. We suspect that their concreteness hides secrets so deep that no revelation may fully dissipate their silences. We imagine the lives under the mortar, but how do we recognize the end of a bottomless silence?
>
> —Trouillot 1995: 29–30

Once the tour is over, the pyramids have been inculcated with the program's specific meaning and they can be referred to as evidence that everything that was said is true. Therefore, the pyramids themselves become the evidence of what they stand for, which could be the burial place of the Inca Atahualpa's mother or the center of energy flow and UFO activity, proving that what they stand for changes not only every decade, but every single day, in every single tour, right in front of our eyes.

THE NATIONAL LOGIC OF HERITAGE AND TERRITORY

The Incas and Their/Our Heritage

The site of Cochasquí also signifies an ambiguous relationship with the Incas, territorial sovereignty, and complex gender and racial dynamics. One of the main concerns of the guided tours is to establish Cochasquí as a pre-Inca site (Programa Cochasquí 1991: 8): "The urban center of Cochasquí is one of the most important pieces of evidence for a pre-Incaic civilization in the Province of Pichincha, its settlement pattern different from the ones in Mesoamerica and others in the Andes; it is deteriorating for many reasons, which is why its conservation and preservation require immediate attention." The pre-Incaic origin of these pyramids is constantly emphasized, as is the statement that the Incas, like the Spaniards, were invaders and, as such, subjugated and enslaved the local population (Pullas de la Cruz 1997: 11): "Well, this people or this culture to which we legally belong as Ecuadorians corresponds to the Quitu-Cara culture, which we know to be pre-Inca, that is, before the conquest of the Incas, a people who supported a harsh struggle against the Incas. They have calculated that this struggle lasted seventeen to twenty years, that they did not allow themselves to be easily dominated, even though we know they were peaceful people."

Great emphasis is also placed on the two decades–long resistance, under the leadership of a woman, Princess/Queen Quilago, to the invaders from the south. It was only through her marriage to their ruler, Huayna Capac, that the Incas were able to conquer and subjugate her people (Guillermo, guide, February 15, 1997): "It is said that the Inca conquest was possible because of treason, with the marriage of Tupac Yupanqui [i.e., Huayna Capac] to a female chief of the area. It was through this marriage that the conquest of the Inca became possible, since during all this time they could not conquer the area."

In this particular version, the Incas are not part of Ecuadorian heritage, but, rather, represent foreign invaders who, throughout history, have seized territory and left the country reduced to one-third its size in 1829 (Efrén Reyes 1967; Villacrés Moscoso 1967). It is therefore no coincidence that the Incas had their homeland in present-day Peru, Ecuador's neighboring antagonist since its emergence as a nation in 1829. The worst episode occurred in 1941, when Ecuador lost over half of its Amazonian territory; the most recent intrusion was in 1995, which led to a diplomatic dialogue with Peru (Espinosa 1995).

The Incas' equation with Peru therefore makes it possible to see Cochasquí as Ecuador, as "our own culture." At Cochasquí, the local communities—the ancestors—defended themselves against the Inca (read Peruvian) invasion, which makes it clear that Peru's contemporary incursions into Ecuador's territory are by no means new, but have occurred since ancient times. This is also made clear in an incident volunteered by one of the guides. According to him, a group of Peruvian tourists abandoned the tour because they were angered by his explanation of the site's resistance to the Inca conquest. To him, their reaction expressed their inability to accept their historical legacy of conquest and oppression of Ecuadorians. As he saw it, they were unwilling to accept the truth, in this case, his or the site's truth. Although saddened, he had no remorse: "It was not my fault; that is just how history is" (Jacinto, personal communication).

But the Incas are not portrayed only as the enemy. In many instances, they are depicted as Ecuadorian or, rather, Ecuadorians are represented as their descendants. This is an ongoing theme within the nation's discourse of claiming Inca sites such as Inga Pirca and Tomebamba (the Inca name for present-day Cuenca) or Inca figures like Atahualpa and Rumiñahui as eminently Ecuadorian (García González 1997: 177): "With the victory in Quipaipán, Atahualpa not only maintained control of the Kingdom of Quito, but also became the only ruler of the Inca Kingdom. Therefore, he took command of the Inca imperial capital [in Peru] of Cuzco, where he officially proclaimed himself the emperor of the Tahuantinsuyu. In this manner, the two portions into which the Inca kingdom had been divided with Huayna Capac's death became whole again, under the sovereign government of the Quiteño Atahualpa." This favorable presentation of the Incas also exists at Cochasquí, which makes it possible for Ecuadorians to be equated with the Incas and make their history an Ecuadorian history.

This reversal occurs at Cochasquí primarily when the Spanish conquest comes into play: the Spaniards become Ecuador's enemies, and the Incas, who saw their end at the hands of the Spaniards, are equated with Ecuador and its destruction. It might be true that the Incas are the enemy, but, ultimately, they are almost family and the Spanish are the supreme foes in this history (Jacinto, guide, February 2, 1997): "because this was a very advanced culture, very intelligent, that unfortunately, tragically, was destroyed because of this problem of the Spanish conquest and [religious] conversion in the area.

The Incas are subtly identified with Ecuador also through the celebration of the Inti Raymi. The display of autochthonous elements, such as costumes, language, music, food, and *chicha,* implies acceptance of an Inca festivity as a celebration of Cochasquí's heritage and, therefore, of Ecuador's.

The Incas are also tacitly equated to the builders of the mounds in the official site museum, where Inca pottery, specifically, *aríbalos* (traditional Inca jars), is displayed. Preceramic and colonial artifacts, which are also present in the area, are not exhibited. The *aríbalos* are presented as belonging to "other" cultures and as being found at the site as a product of regional trade. It is quite telling that, with rare exceptions (one or two guides), on all the tours I observed, the Inca origin of the *aríbalos* was not mentioned (Marcela, guide, February 12, 1997): "This ceramic is only for the caciques and the people. . . . That is, this ceramic is very different. It is from another culture, for example, it is the Panzaleo culture, a culture in the Tungurahua and Cotopaxi Province, a different province. But we find this pottery at the site because they bartered for it. The coca came from the jungle. They exchanged products."

In yet another subtle way, the Incas are identified with Ecuador in references to the Royal Inca Road, which connected Otavalo to Quito and passed by Cochasquí. In these references, the Incas are no longer the conquering enemy, but another of the ancestral communities of the site. Their accomplishments are intertwined with those of the local inhabitants of Cochasquí. Since this road figures prominently in the Spanish chroniclers' description of the site, the Incas are more easily integrated into Cochasquí's history:

And then on the left you can see the historical road where you came up, but you can no longer see the road. You can see it only in the higher mountains, on the banks of the Pisque River; you are going to see that in the south, there is still a lot left of the roadway of our ancestors. But in this area, since they have already built highways for cars, it has been destroyed. There are no remnants left. In our culture's time, the straight road was called *el chaquiñan,* because of the *enacachila,* where the *chaqui* [Inca Road relay messengers] used to pass, carrying the mail and other messages.

—Jacinto, guide, February 8, 1997

From my observations of the guides and my own experience as a tour guide at Cochasquí, there is an urgent need to tell the truth about Cochasquí's ("our," "Ecuador's") history. A visit to the site is supposed to right Ecuador's historical wrongs or inadequacies. This is effective as long as the tourists are willing to undergo this "ordeal of truth"; Jacinto's Peruvian tourists were not willing.

But the truth is far from straightforward or self-evident. What starts out as a quest to put the Incas in their rightful place as enemies of the nation is upturned within the narrative itself, and they end up being us, or we become them, their descendants. The historical discourse at Cochasquí has an internal logic independent of the guides' initially logical intentions. But the historical truth is told, no matter how hard it may be for Peruvians and Ecuadorians alike to hear it. Nobody appears to be spared the historical truth at Cochasquí.

THE NATIONAL LOGIC OF TERRITORIALITY

Territoriality is also an essential element in the Ecuadorianization of Cochasquí. As the Incas are equated with Peru because they have occupied present-day Peru's geographical space, so is Cochasquí equated with Ecuador (Vicente, guide, February 2, 1997): "Because our people have always been attacked by the Cuzqueños, by Peru, yes, even from the time of the Incas, that is why up to now we are always screwed up, that is the reason why . . . , oh well." The fact that Cochasquí is located in the heartland of the northern frontier of present-day Ecuador is enough evidence to proclaim the cultural and national continuity of the site's heritage:

If we go a couple of kilometers east of Quito until we reach the zone of the Inga site, we are already where they discovered the material evidence of the oldest Ecuadorian inhabitants, who lived around thirty thousand years ago; and if we go toward the north visiting the forts of Rumicucho, Quito Loma, Cangahua, Pambamarca, Cayambe, Ayora, and the pyramids of the archaeological complex of Cochasquí, we can recognize a great part

of what was the Kingdom of Quito, origin of the Ecuadorian nation, composed of a great confederacy of peoples.
—Provincial prefect Landázuri Romo, in Programa Cochasquí 1991: 5

Cochasquí's overall discourse of territoriality provides another way of tying the site to the nation. The history of the site, as told to the visitors, is a story of struggle and subjugation, resistance and conquest, survival. Here, "the ancestors," authentic Ecuadorians, met the onslaught of foreign invaders. First there were the Incas, and then the Spaniards. But no matter what, Ecuadorians (and therefore they) have survived to tell the story. Cochasquí represents the resilience of a nation that survives no matter how adverse the conditions. But the question to ask is whether it really does survive, especially within the historical discourse itself?

The story produced at Cochasquí has strong parallels to what Silva (1995) proposes as one of the nation's central myths: territorial ungovernability. No matter how grand the resistance shown at Cochasquí, what comes across is the local inhabitants' essential inability to control their own territory. It is the foreign groups, Incas and Spaniards, that are able to conquer, dominate, and take total control of the region. Cochasquí's inhabitants can never successfully defend themselves from foreign conquest in the historical narratives; therefore, they never really achieve total control of the territory.

The territorial discourse at Cochasquí has a subtle way of enriching the nation's sense of self. As we have seen, it takes pride in Cochasquí's resistance. In this sense, the outcome of the struggle does not matter; what matters is the courage and will to struggle against foreign domination (Guillermo, guide, February 8, 1997): "As we must know, the Inca conquest in this part of the country was characterized by a war that lasted fifteen to seventeen years, approximately. The end result was the Incas conquering the territory, with the most bloody part of the struggle in the north, in the Lake of Yaguarcocha, or the lake of blood."

Once again, the parallels between this description and the general sentiment concerning Ecuador's defeats at the hands of its stronger southern neighbor, Peru, are quite striking. Ecuador has always been defeated by Peru, but somehow this is overlooked and the courage and resilience of the nation's spirit as embodied in its troops is instead emphasized:

The institutions in which the current chiefs of the armed forces were trained were taught by former veterans of the year 1941. From them they learned the bitter experience of having to fight an enemy ten times stronger and better equipped, as well as the lesson that war is won initially in times of peace by preparing and maintaining the armed forces.

—Gallardo 1995: 8

That unity and solidarity were symbolized in one name: Tiwintsa, the humble military dispatch that resisted the Peruvian attacks throughout the conflict and enraged the Peruvian president Alberto Fujimori.

—Espinosa 1995: 59

The nation's ideal is also embedded in the territorial discourse by virtue of the outcome of the story. It is the Spaniards who ultimately gained control of the territory and a control over the region that surpassed even the Incas'. The narration of the Spanish conquest solidifies the current racial (white/mestizo) control of the nation-state, since this is the racial composition attributed to the Spaniards (Jacinto, guide, February 8, 1997): "Therefore, after that [the civil war between Inca siblings Atahualpa and Huascar] it was much easier for the Spanish conquest. Unfortunately, from that moment on, we have lost our origin, our roots. Everybody says it has given us a white color, but no, that's not why. . . or they say we now have beards, or I am Spanish, right. They insult the Indians, Indians so and so." It is only the white population that ultimately gains autonomous control of the site of Cochasquí and the whole region, just as in contemporary Ecuador (see Silva 1995). The racial undertone of the conquest story at Cochasquí justifies the current racial hierarchy of the Ecuadorian nation-state and legitimizes the white/mestizo sociopolitical control of the country. In this manner, the racial and ethnic composition of the nation subtly benefits from both a territorial discourse that is supposedly exclusively about Cochasquí and its history.

THE NATIONAL LOGIC OF GENDER AND RACE

Quilago, Queen of Cochasquí and the Nation

One of the most provocative gendered elements of Cochasquí's official history is the pervasive narrative of the last leader of the pre-Columbian polity, Queen or Princess Quilago. Her importance is recognized in several ways, including the naming of the local museum after her and the association of her image with the site's resistance against the Incas: "Before, I mentioned that this area was populated by the Quitos-Caras. In military terms, they were governed by the Princess Quilago, who resisted the Inca invasion for seventeen years. It is after this period that the

Incas are able to conquer these territories, since they used not to live in this area" (Marcela, guide, March 26, 1998).

Quilago is described not only as the political leader of the Cochasquí polity, but, more surprisingly, also as the military leader who led the resistance, successful for over a decade, against the Inca invaders. Female leadership is startling because in modern-day Ecuador women are generally relegated to domestic roles and not considered fit for political or military office. Only recently have a significant number of women been allowed to join the police force, mainly as transit police, and to do part-time military service. This inherent sexism was also probably one of the main reasons why the country's first and only female vice president was not allowed to succeed President Abdalá Bucaram when he was ousted in February of 1997. So how is it that an image of an all-powerful woman who valiantly defended her territory against foreign (read Peruvian) invasion is presented to the public and is made believable under the sexist hierarchy that permeates present-day Ecuador?

The origin of the history of Quilago is unclear, and there are very few written sources. Spanish chroniclers (Cieza de León 1986: 212; Montesinos 1957: 107) mention this female leader in their depiction of the region's resistance to Inca expansion. This initial mention is ultimately made confusing by the fact that in Quechua all elite and high-ranking women were called "*quilagos.*" (Oberem and Wurster 1989). However, Uhle (1933) proposed that the *quilago* of Cochasquí was also the *quilago,* queen, of Quito and therefore Atahualpa's mother. This belief in Quilago as mother of one of the recognized Inca heirs led to a state-sponsored search for her remains at the site in the 1930s (*El Día* 1930).

This initial search for Quilago's body was an attempt to link her with the ancestral Ecuadorian nation, since Atahualpa is traditionally hailed as the Ecuadorian heir of both the Ancient Kingdom of Quito and the Incas. Atahualpa's Ecuadorianness is established by his birth in the ancient territory of what today is Ecuador (although a significant and respected group of scholars provide evidence of the contrary, that is, that Atahualpa was most probably born in Cuzco) and by descent, through his Quiteño lineage (L.N.S. N.d.; Navas Jiménez 1994). There is a vested interest at the site in making Quilago an icon of the nation and representative of the motherland (*la madre patria*), as has happened in different national movements around the world (Mosse 1985; A. Parker et al. 1992).

It was this national ideal that led to direct state intervention and the presence of the national military force during the excavation of Quilago's remains at Cochasquí (*El Día* 1930). The state's interest in this enterprise is obvious if one remembers that the issue of multiple *quilagos* was never brought up. Even Velasco's notion of the existence of an in-digenous Quiteño nation (Ancient Kingdom of Quito) has no empirical support and is fraught with historical inconsistencies (Jijón y Caamaño 1918b; Salazar 1995b). Quilago presents an instance of the Ecuadorian nation-state's search for a primordial Ecuadorian identity—a national identity which would benefit only from its ties with a heroic and indige-nous mother figure for the nation.

The necessity of having a mother figure also seems to be implied in the narrative of the love affair between Quilago and the conquering Inca, in this case, Huayna Capac. This tale of love and vengeance is quite am-biguous, as we can see in its description by the guides:

> When the Incas had conquered the area, there are several hypotheses that are formulated, for example, they say Huayna Capac came here for liai-sons with Quilago, some say this. Others say that the Incas were not even here. But ultimately the Incas conquered them.
> —Vicente, guide, February 2, 1997

> And therefore she is betrayed by her close aides and they "gossip" the in-formation to Huayna Capac so that she falls in the trap of the Incas and then come the white people, the Spaniard savages, that destroy these peo-ple, and later this area is abandoned.
> —Pullas de la Cruz 1997: 12–13

Inca imperial policies demanded the complete submission or death of the military leaders, which is probably what sealed Quilago's fate (Murra 1989). What seems to have been constructed at Cochasquí is a symbi-otic origin myth that provides for a founding couple to give birth to the Ecuadorian nation. The myth is symbiotic because, even though it main-tains some typical Andean origin-myth structure (see Isbell 1985; Urton 1990), its forced marriage and genealogical reasoning follow ascension rules more European or Western than Andean (Silverblatt 1987).

The conquering Incas may provide the father figure in this origin myth, but it is Cochasquí who, in the person of Quilago, provides the pivotal mother figure—a figure who is at once as forceful as she is nurturing. It is Quilago who resists the Inca's military and personal advances and only through force becomes his partner. Even then, she'd rather die in an attempt to kill him than live as his wife. This is the imagery from which Ecuadorianness is created at Cochasquí, from a raping of the nation by foreign invaders. The forceful figure of the resistant Indian mother is what gives Ecuadorians the dignity and resolve to carry on.

Quilago's Indianness is essential for providing the nation with the primordial aura of authenticity. It is in the Indian past, Ecuador's Indian past, that Ecuadorians can start to make sense of the embattled present of territorial loss and political corruption (Silva 1995). The history of Quilago as narrated by the guides at Cochasquí and included in the site's official history is very much the opposite of the story of the Malinche metaphor elaborated in Mexico and juxtaposed all over the Americas (Cypess 1991; Mallon 1996). This is not the cunning woman who sells out to the foreign invaders, but a woman who resists the aggressor (militarily and sexually) until she is forced into a social/sexual reproductive relationship.

One could argue that this symbolism intensifies after her death and through the retelling of "her-story" in Cochasquí's official "his-story." Quilago, like La Malinche, takes on certain traditionally male characteristics, but it is the mixture of these with her mothering abilities that endows her with the nurturing quality needed to provide for the Ecuadorian nation.

In appreciating Quilago's history partly as an origin myth, we can understand why such a dominant female figure is not only presented, but also so vividly accepted by all, especially Ecuadorian men and women who live within a sexist hierarchy of female subordination. This is not any woman we are talking about; this is Quilago, the symbol of the nation, who is being described. Quilago is not a symbol of woman's potential or a call to women's liberation, and therefore a disrupter of contemporary gender relationships; she is a marker of the nation's motherhood and primordial origins, and therefore she is a mechanism, contradictory at times, but ultimately useful, for maintaining the oppressive gender status quo.

But even though Quilago is packaged to be more about the nation or woman's role in the nation than about womanhood per se, one notices the excited looks on many women's faces as this story is being told, the demanding glare of wives at their husbands and the demand of some female tourists to "know more about Quilago, Queen of Cochasquí, to imagine that there was here a special woman" (L. R., April 16, 1997). Therefore, even though Cochasquí's history of Quilago cannot extricate itself from the national discourse of gender in which it is produced, it still provides both hegemonic and alternative readings of gender relations. However, we must remember that alternative versions are essential opposites of any successful hegemonizing discourse (Foucault 1980, 1991; Mallon 1995). Therefore, even though there is an official version of gender relations in Cochasquí's Quilago, one that strongly involves the nation, as is always the case with historical reconstructions at the site, more than one interpretation is perceived and actively deployed by tourists and staff alike.

OF INDIANS AND WHITES/MESTIZOS: COCHASQUÍ'S HEALING HISTORY OF THE RACIAL SELF

Afterward came the problem of the conflict between the two Incas, the two brothers, right, Huayna Capac and Yupanqui, because of the problem of the Tahuantinsuyu [the characters are confused with Atahualpa and Huascar]. Therefore, after that was why it was so easy for the Spanish to conquer us. Unfortunately, after that time, ever since the Spanish conquest, we have lost our origin, our roots. Everybody says they have given us a white color, right, but it is not because . . . [he laughs] or a beard, right. Or some say, "I am Spaniard." They insult the Indians, Indians so and so, but they [the Indians] say, "At least we know our roots." Because you [the tourists] no longer have any roots, have no origins. Those who have no origins are called *huayrapamushcas,* that is what the Indians call them, *huayrapamushcas,* which means sons of nothing, sons of the wind. Good, if you have any questions, if not we can continue.

—Jacinto, guide, February 8, 1997

The racial and ethnic discourse at Cochasquí is multilayered and, as with all the other elements, it is dynamic and ever-changing. But behind the shifting shadows there seems to be a complex discourse of racial healing. The site is a place where one can make amends with history and with the Indian legacy of the nation.

The hour-long tour is a painstaking excursion around the Indian community that lived at Cochasquí, but also around the indigenous communities that populated the space of what is now Ecuador before the Spanish conquest. The site reminds tourists about a past they never knew or that they have supposedly erased, about the Indian population that lived millennia ago and that informs the Ecuadorian nation. At Cochasquí tourists return to the past to revisit what they have chosen to ignore. The guide's voice serves as small notes pasted on things that have been forgotten by the inhabitants of Macondo (García Márquez 1971). But the things we learn are not only about the Indian past, they are also about us, since the Indian past informs who we are. Through the tour we start recognizing and remembering more and more things about ourselves. The acknowledgment of the past is therefore about recognition of repressed memories and a change of heart.

There is a transformative urgency in the guide's description of us, of our divided identities. There has to be a reaction to the guide's words, a change, an effect caused by the historical truth being offered. We should no longer be capable of seeing ourselves as better than our Indian ancestors, superior to our Indian siblings. This is especially true since we have learned that we are their descendants, that they were capable of great things and suffered at the hands of the Spaniards (the non-Indians).

This initial contradiction hints at a resolution. Our nascent self, disparaged and wounded in the genocide of Andean history, is bandaged by the recognition of our other self, the Indian past, which we have neglected and forgotten for so long. But things are, or at least could be, different now. The visit to Cochasquí has allowed us to reconcile ourselves with our past, a part of our historical selves we have long neglected. The hour-long trek is a sign of our redemptive intentions; it is a peregrination of archaeological and historical healing and understanding (see Silberman 1995). We learn about the Indian past, which is part of our own past, and about ourselves.

In this manner, the biggest racial and ethnic differences between Indians, mestizos, and whites are obliterated at Cochasquí. The racial, ethnic, and class differences so apparent in every aspect of the visit to the site—like vehicles used to get to the site, the clothes people wear, the accents, cultural mannerisms—are resolved, hidden from view, readily denied, allowing for a peaceful departure. The tour guide represents a holistic national history which actively incorporates the Indian past. The visitors' fresh understanding of Ecuadorian history renews their sense of self and allows them to live more easily in a setting of racial, ethnic, and class oppression and contradictions.

In an interesting way, Cochasquí's story of a search for the past, literally digging for the truth and lost memory, is a cover-up and a forgetting. Just like any of the national histories, the racial and ethnic discourse at Cochasquí strategically selects those elements that are suitable to its promulgation of the nation. The narrative at Cochasquí ultimately allows for a subtle erasure of the blatant racial contradictions of Indian and Afro-Ecuadorian oppression in which all Ecuadorians are immersed, and from which whites and whites/mestizos benefit the most. It is also not surprising that the two latter racial categories are the ones that make up most of the visitors at the site.

The tour is not a lie so much as a history of itself, that is, a story constructed for the site about itself and for its own existence and survival. This history is itself readily appropriated by the nation-state's racial discourse, which, after all, is (or tries to convince us it is) the origin of history itself.

In this sense, at Cochasquí we can see at least two major sexual and racial discourses being represented and acted upon. One, which is the one most visible to the public, is a politically correct narrative of gender and racial equality as represented in the image of Queen Quilago and in the recognition of the historical worth of Ecuador's Indian ancestors. This same discourse is essential if Cochasquí is to continue to receive the public support it needs to get financial support from the Consejo Provincial. However, there seems to be another discourse subsumed under all these elements, a discourse of an unequivocal gender and racial hierarchy. This hierarchy is expressed in the form of white/mestizo male domination of women and weaker males as an expression of the power relations inherent at the site, relations which are representative of the nation-state. It is the patriarchal structure of the male Ecuadorian state (*el Estado*) which is astutely and appropriately hidden under the nurturing guise and feminine image of the motherland (*la Patria*) and the nation (*la Nación*) (see chapter 4).

MECHANISMS OF APPROPRIATION: PARTICIPATING IN AND GAZING AT THE PAST

Cochasquí, as we have seen, represents many things for the nation: Ecuador's hidden history; a seed of resistance to foreign intervention; a pristine place of authentic traditions; and a place of racial healing. But how is it that the nation is capable of producing itself in the narrative of this ancient site?

Neither the discourse of Cochasquí nor that of the nation-state is unique in meaning, nor are they completely independent of each other and of other grand discourses. These discourses benefit from a complexity of meanings and representation that makes their deconstruction utopian. Only their transformation is possible. As multiple and complex organisms, their resilience is demonstrated in their enormous capacity to integrate what seem to be contradictory elements into a coherent structure. This transformative capacity only elevates their layering of meaning and their capacity to integrate even more contradictory elements and to produce new hegemonic discourses.

It is this complex layering of meaning that allows Cochasquí to be readily incorporated into the national narrative. Single elements, such as the Incas, have multiple layers of signification, all of which can, and are, arranged as multiple strands around the discourse of the nation. As is vividly described in the ritualized enactment of the events of 1613, the Incas are hailed both as foreign invaders (who kill the queen of Cochasquí/Quito) and as the founders of the nation. The multiple meanings produced by the different constitutive elements of Cochasquí are not an obstacle, but, instead, seem to facilitate their appropriation into a similarly complex discourse, that of the Ecuadorian nation-state.

At Cochasquí there seem to be at least two mechanisms through which the nation-state makes the site's story its own: gazing, and physical participation. These devices relate the elements of Cochasquí to our sense of self-care (J. Miller 1993). In doing so, the historical elements are integrated into our bodies before they are incorporated into the larger social body of the nation-state. The two techniques of appropriation that I outline in this section are closely linked to the research into understanding the forms of internalized domination (e.g., Freire 1992; Memmi 1991; Ribeiro 1988). This particular concern has led not only to understanding power in a much more pervasive and totalizing manner (Foucault 1980) and, even more important, to understanding its centrality when imposed on the body (see, e.g., Taussig 1992b).

Merleau-Ponty (1963 and 1964) forwards significant theories about the complexity of the internalized domination of our existence through the mechanism of our body. This is further elaborated by De Certeau's (1984) problematization of "everyday practices" and their subtle associations with the structures of state domination (Joseph and Nugent 1994)—forms of domination that for Foucault (1993) result from the shift of power coming from above the social body (e.g., from monarchies) to power inscribing itself within the body per se (e.g., social democracies). This represents an individualization of power that makes it harder to struggle against because "what makes power hold good, what makes it accepted, is simply the fact that it doesn't only weigh on us as a force that says no, but that it traverses and produces things, it induces pleasure, forms knowledge, produces discourse. It needs to be considered as a productive network which runs through the whole social body, much more than as a negative instance whose function is repression" (Foucault 1980: 119).

This concern with internalized domination expressed and articulated in our bodies is not foreign to Andean historicity. Classen (1993: 145), for example, is concerned with how the different Inca rituals "sought to internalize the Inca social order in the bodies of individuals" in such a manner that "the bodies of the Incas and their subjects were thus not only inserted within the structure of the Inca state, they manifested that structure within themselves." I argue that this process can also be observed concretely at Cochasquí, in the manner in which looking/gazing and participating in the different rituals (such as visiting the site) actively contributes to the site's nationalization and further serves to legitimize the Ecuadorian nation-state's forms of oppression.

Gazing at the Past

The first mechanism of appropriation is the act of gazing. To look at the other is a powerful act which allows the onlooker to appropriate what is being observed and to incorporate it into his or her own sense of logic (Bronfen 1996; Gómez-Peña 1996; Minh-Ha 1997; Pratt 1992; Saleci and Zizek 1996; Zizek 1996). The gaze of the other at Cochasquí, in all of the site's constitutive elements, is actively and readily translated in our bodies and minds into the nation's multiple meanings and regimen of truth. This active gazing is particularly relevant in moments such as the celebration of the Inti Raymi, when the "other," in this instance, modern Indian communities, takes center stage and personifies the site.

The gaze of tourists and visitors immediately brings the ritual enactment or act into their realm of experience, which is none other than the one constructed within the nation-state's discourse of what Ecuador is. It is the experience of Ecuadorianness and its multiple interpretations that contribute to the reading of the spectacle they are being offered. As one tourist remarked to me, visiting the site "allows me to love my country and my nationality even more" (M. V., January 24, 1997). In this manner, the "other's" act is actively incorporated, through the onlooker, an individual, into an Ecuadorian, and therefore a national, way of seeing and being.

Gazing is relevant not only during special ritual enactments or celebrations, but also throughout the visit to the site. Tourists are constantly looking at the site, at the pyramids, artifacts, llamas, museum, and so on, and are actively encouraged by the miniature models and guides to imagine what the site was like in earlier times (L. B., January 18, 1998): "[The guide] has informed me about the period and encourages me to imagine the life of the inhabitants of this period." That imagining provides us with a representation that is readily translatable to our own experience and allows us not only to conceptualize the site as it operated in other historical moments but, more important, also to make sense of Cochasquí in the national discourse as interpreted within ourselves."

This gaze is particularly powerful because the site itself is constructed in such a way as to be looked and stared at. It is a life-sized display of the "past," and, as such, we are encouraged to actively consume it through our eyes and imagination.

The program relies on the tourists' gaze and imagination to justify its managing of the site:

> Yes, because it is one thing when they tell you about it or when you read about it, and it's a completely different thing when you are present at the actual place where the events took place.
> —G. A., February 4, 1998

> Because the books are different from the actual natural and original place.
> —M. B., February 14, 1998

> [The visit] has made me more sensitive [to history].
> —G. G., February 22, 1998

This is why the project encourages the site to be gazed at, appropriated, and therefore understood in the program's own terms. This gazing is crucial for the understanding of the site, but, more important and unwittingly, for the appropriation of its history and the invention of a national past.

Participating in the Past

The second means of appropriation is the gazer's participation in the display of what Cochasquí is. It is through the onlooker's participation, specifically, their physical movement at the site, that they make its history theirs and, therefore, the nation's. This is also clearly expressed in the ritual enactment of the site's history in 1613 and is still very much present in the tour. The physical exertion required to visit the site is essential in allowing tourists to feel the site, what Silberman (1995: 258–261) describes as the pilgrimage to national sites. The pilgrimage, requiring sweat and exhaustion, allows the onlooker to get an idea of what the site was like and becomes one of its symbols. As the tourists themselves note:

> Theory is not the same as taking in these cultures with one's senses.
> —F. M., February 21, 1998

> To actually be present at the same site where the Caranquis lived.
> —B. C., February 2, 1998

The process of identification is also present in the shamanistic and other rituals carried out at the site. The enthusiastic support of these activities by both the Programa Cochasquí and the tourists (a former program director viewed them as living remnants of the past) points to the importance of active participation in allowing one truly to understand Cochasquí and what it was like. Participation in these rituals, in the form of baths, prayers, incantations, walks, or meditations, allows visitors to imagine what Cochasquí was like. It is also through taking part that the multiple meanings of the site become incorporated into the participants' sense of being, literally, into their physical experience, thereby serving as a living metaphor for the body of the nation-state—as some tourists expressed their feelings to me: "To transmit and live our past in some form" (M. V., January 24, 1998); "to be an actual product of our ancestors" (T., N.d.).

Whether someone is participating in a wedding ceremony or simply trekking along the site's trail, his or her body is helping make sense of the site and appropriating its meanings. This participation allows the site's meaning to be translated into that of the nation-state, but only because the connection has been made through the body. The site's meanings are intertwined with those already structured within the participant by previous experience of the Ecuadorian nation-state and its imagined national past: "It is so different to live our own [national] reality from just hearing about it" (A. S., n.d.).

For both modes of appropriation, that is, the gaze and physical participation, we are the nation-state's instrument of translation. It is in our gaze, in our body, and our sense of self that the translation is performed, that the historical truth is inscribed (see Butler 1993). Just as certain plants, such as maize, have "figured out" a way of making us responsible for their sexual and social reproduction and can no longer survive without our help, the nation also seems to rely entirely on us for its reproduction. This is an interesting solution, since, ultimately, it is for us that the nation needs this history; it is for our own conversion that the nation-state is eager to appropriate Cochasquí's history.

In this sense, we are both the instruments of domination and the dominated self. It is almost as if we bring domination on ourselves. But this is not entirely accurate, because we are never outside the domination process; we are at the center of it. As Foucault notes, power is not only or even mainly strategically placed outside of us; rather, it is wired in our center, which allows forms of domination to be even more subtle and pervasive (1980:39): "In thinking of the mechanism of power, I am thinking rather of its capillary form of existence, the point where power reaches into the very grain of individuals, touches their bodies and inserts itself into their actions and attitudes, their discourses, learning processes and everyday lives." In caring for ourselves, in logically structuring our self's experience, we are unknowingly, unwittingly, and relentlessly activating mechanisms of appropriation and domination that work on us and that contribute and connect to explicit, violent forms of coercive domination.

Thus, the appropriation of Cochasquí's history into a wider web of meanings in the national sphere can be performed through the individual (Butler 1997a, 1997b). The gaze and physical participation which stem from care of one's self, from the need to make sense of one's experience, ultimately activate the nation's construction and appropriation of historical truths within the visitor. The nation survives in the visitors' daily activities and thoughts about their existence, and through their actions appropriates and rewrites other narratives about itself in their experience (De Certeau 1984; Sayer 1994; Taussig 1992b). These two mechanisms enable the official history to become the nation's narrative of itself and to be incorporated into personal experience of the site. These mechanisms, therefore, make it seem as if Cochasquí is exclusively related to Ecuador's national past, and, more significant, that it always has been and always will be.

~

FOUR

BETWEEN FOUCAULT
AND A NAKED MAN

*Racing Class, Sex, and
Gender to the Nation's Past*

~

*That female power is invisible, elusive, and holds
a great potential for violence has contributed greatly
to the stubborn resilience of native Andean culture. In the
centuries following the Spanish Conquest, women of the high
puna—less accessible than men to tax collectors and
missionaries—were instrumental in preserving indigenous
religions and culture. Women have also played a prominent role
in the Andes' long history of peasant rebellions.*

—CATHERINE J. ALLEN (1988)

BETWEEN MARX AND A NAKED WOMAN:
NATIONAL HEGEMONY AND THE
CONTEMPORARY FRACTURED SUBJECT

In 1976 Ecuadorian poet Jorge Enrique Adoum published his first novel, *entre Marx y una mujer desnuda* (between Marx and a naked woman), narrating the life of an anguished Ecuadorian character caught in the absurdity of his (neocolonized) existence. Adoum, expressing a wish to break from the stylistic prescriptions of the genre and the main character's life limits, referred to the novel as a "texto con personajes" (text with characters). The novel—using sidebars, bracketed information, prologues in the middle of the book, unfinished sentences—narrates the permanent fracture of the character's life. In this chapter, I use Adoum's work to gain insight into the role played by the fractured subject in Ecuador's hegemonic project.

entre Marx y una mujer desnuda has had a dramatic impact on the Ecuadorian scene, forming, as it does, part of a prestigious literary tradition that surpasses any other intellectual tradition in the country. This is not surprising, since most Latin American intellectuals understand that the continent's exceptional literature provides one of its few competitive "goods" for global export (Fuentes 1988). However, the novel also refers to a specific Ecuadorian reality that makes the book a popular vehicle for assessing the country's political and historical juncture at the end of the twentieth century. The 1970s saw a return to military rule, reinforcing many of the authoritarian strands of Ecuador's postcolonial existence, although military rule, particularly under Gen. Guillermo Rodríguez Lara, was fraught with contradictions. Unlike Southern Cone military dictators, Ecuador's military leaders took a much more left-leaning political stance, nationalizing the country's booming oil industry and elaborating a nationally homogenizing rhetoric of *mestizaje.*

Ecuador's military dictatorship followed the lead of previous Andean military dictatorships in which the army was interested in sustaining populist ideals rather than serving as political puppets of the ruling elite. However, these same "progressive" military dictators accrued "development" debts that soon crippled the economy. The military's transition out of political power in 1979 was due as much to its inability to maintain a sound economy (including the need to begin debt repayment) as to the democratizing demands of Jimmy Carter's administration.

It was during this period of political turmoil that Adoum's novel was published. The novel, along with other works (e.g., Cueva 1981, 1986; Tinajero 1982, 1986), highlights the paradoxical time in which Ecuadorian society was caught: a progressive dictatorship, a booming economy in debt, the attraction of U.S. culture and the shame of Indian heritage, and a new postcolonial global identity created by membership in international oil export associations and rising oil prices.

These political contradictions were inherent in the emotional incongruity expressed in the novel. The central character is described as existing in a contradictory and ambiguous state: trying to decide whether to stay in the country or go abroad; loving a married woman who does not love him; belonging to a personally divisive socialist movement; living in a country that cannot (and does not) take care of him; and, worst of all, not knowing if he is actually alive or just somebody's (the narrator's or another country's) incomplete dream (Adoum 1976: 196):

"Probably now you understand (why the best conversations with my friends take place when they are not around) that you had no right to get upset when you asked me: 'But what the fuck do you want to do with your life,' and I sincerely answered: 'Nothing.' Because am I not just a character that is not able to conclude his destiny and that either. . . ."

Not surprisingly, this perplexing novel and its ambivalent protagonist captured the nation's literary imagination and became, in the mid-1990s, the second successful full-length Ecuadorian commercial film. The novel poses questions about the national character and a poorly understood Ecuadorianness. It succeeds because of how it asks these questions. The book's broader impact was a result of its lived-in, fractured feeling rather than being a purely scholarly or academic assessment of Ecuadorian reality. After all, Ecuador's national heritage had been thoroughly discussed in other works (Benítez Vinueza 1986; Cervone and Rivera 1999; Donoso Pareja 2000) and even by Adoum himself in the span of his fifty years of intellectual production (Adoum 2000). The novel identifies a national subject that is splintered at all levels, including the historical levels of identity and legacy that had been subsumed by the nation's official recording of the past. The question it poses is quite simple: If Ecuador's national identity is well grounded, why is the "I" (as an Ecuadorian subject) fraught with confusion, contradiction, anguish, and misunderstanding? Adoum's willingness and even ability to pose such a question in a meaningful, dramatic way is probably the work's greatest contribution.

The patriarchal figure of Marx and the heterosexual image of a naked woman serve as the two pillars on which to sustain the enormous chaos and confusion in the book. Were the main character completely fractured there would be no way even to start the novel, but Marx and a naked woman serve as solid ground at either end to support the anguished Ecuadorian subject. In this sense, at one level, an explicit political reality is afforded by the paternal image of Marx as a charismatic leader and progressive dictator (echoes of Fidel Castro). At another level, a more cultural and structural reality is expressed through the feminine image of a naked woman, which provides the underlying nurturing social and sexual component. I argue that these two images constitute the parameters of the intrinsic hegemonic project of the Ecuadorian nation. Thus, Adoum's novel reflects not the absence of a national hegemonic project, but the characters' existence in the project's midst, in its actual transformation. As Joseph and Nugent (1994) state, hegemony is a constant reformulation and transformation, and it is this anguished process of contradictions, officialization, and counter-hegemonic devices that is described in the novel. Therefore, the characters do not exist outside the hegemonic project as much as they (and their lives) result from being caught in the very middle of hegemonic production. To a large degree, the novel thrusts us into the bowels of national authority, into the very center of its "hellish" state production (Taussig 1992a)—a disturbing experience, since we usually see ourselves only as unwilling spectators.

With this shift comes the sudden realization that dominance is at the very center of our own historical identity production (Foucault 1980). The nation's hegemonic production, its state project in the making, is fixed on culturally meaningful definitions of class, gender, race, and sexuality. Even Marx's critique of the capitalist state, with its class (and race) connotation and thought to be essentially counter-hegemonic, actually nourishes and upholds the hegemonic project as it constantly struggles against it (Wylie 1995). Meanwhile, on the other side, the sexualized and gendered image of a "naked woman" (the counter-hegemonic image of hedonism provided by a Catholic guilt-ridden sexuality) also sustains the hegemonic project. Marx and the heterosexual female image provide the two sides of the project's trappings.

National hegemony is expressed in Adoum's novel as a never-ending articulation that utilizes our own historically defined class and race identities and the fuel of our own gendered selves and sexual desires to define the national setting—the limits of who we are and how we see our (national) selves. Adoum's greatest contribution is not breaking this pervasive national project, but, rather, giving us an understanding of the contradictory logic of its inner workings: the national project succeeds because of our willingness to believe ourselves free of it and because of our appearance, which at heart we know not to be true (see Baldwin 1984, 1988a, 1988b; Sayer 1994).

The following analysis of the fractured production of national identities assesses history's role. Following Adoum and Foucault (1980), I do not look to define liberated spaces as much as contradictory instances that better focus the hegemonic project in its national articulation and that serve to highlight our role in its political production. My analysis, therefore, may not provide the key to liberation, but it will increase our understanding of what hegemony is and of our investment in its reproduction. It is in this regard that the notion of strategic marginality (elaborated by feminist scholars of color) insightfully exposes the ambivalent composition of hegemony (see Mallon 1996: 173). One of my objectives is to use Adoum's female image as an analytical category: instead of a naked woman as an object of desire, she becomes a sexual subject. As one of the nation's fractured subjects, women desire rather than simply producing desire in others. As well, they posses a vibrant and vital sexuality that goes beyond being a mere object of desire and receiver of violence from other gendered subjects.

I would also like to utilize a second image—the fractured homosexual subject—as another way in which a strategic marginality can inform our understanding of national hegemony. I shall discuss the notion of the homosexual and highlight the essential (and hidden) role of homosexual desire in Ecuadorian historical representation and hegemonic production.

I shall use the images of these two fractured subjects (or strategic marginalities)—a naked woman at Cochasquí and a homosexual representation of the past among the *enchaquirados* (members of a pre-Hispanic religious male harem)—to assess the multiple processes inherent in hegemonic production. As the chapter title suggests, Foucault's work (based on, but not simply reproducing, Marx's) serves as the other parameter of this analysis. The following discussion therefore looks to further elucidate the dynamic state project in its evolutionary relationship with the cultural reconfiguration of race, class, and gender in this period of advanced capitalism (Hall 1997). At the same time, I look to understand historical representation not as a means of total liberation but as small levels of transgression (Foucault 1998) which will (and must) be contained again, thereby providing a greater level of political awareness and social consciousness each time. Specifically, I assess the analytical power of strategic marginalities in two pre-Hispanic contexts: at the site of Cochasquí, and in the historical production of the *enchaquirados*. My analysis will more specifically address how these powerful fractured identities are historically produced and constituted as politically and culturally meaningful in the national hegemonic project.

SEX AND THE NATION

Research in the 1990s (Domínguez 1996; Foucault 1990; A. Parker et al. 1992) emphasized the manner in which gender, class, and race are intertwined in national discourse. This interrelatedness is so profound that, as Cornel West (1994: 120) knows "it is virtually impossible to talk candidly about race without talking about sex." Stoler's (1996) research on the colonized class subject also highlights the impossibility of treating sex as an independent category; rather, she recognizes its elements in a complex racial discourse. For Stoler, the capitalist colonial enterprise "subjected" the colonized populations and the colonizers at home in the metropolis and abroad in the colonies as well, reinforcing class structures in both settings. This subjection, or creation of a knowable subject for the West (see Butler 1993, 1997b; Foucault 1991), was very much done as a reflection of sexualized (i.e., concerning females, perverts, etc.) and racialized/class-stratified (i.e., concerning colonized populations) others. In this manner, the colonizing/civilizing mission "shaped the sexual and racial coordinates, the boundaries at the core of what bourgeois morality and respectability were to exclude and contain" (Stoler 1996: 209).

Mosse (1985) analyzes in detail how present notions of Western morality and respectability come into play from the seventeenth century on in Western Europe, specifically, in Germany and Britain. An essential sense of respectability was present in Europe's middle-class support of a national agenda in which sexuality played a vital part. Mosse's argument springs from the anthropological understanding that "manner and morals, as well as sexual norms, are part of a historical process; what one regards as normal or abnormal behavior, sexual or otherwise, is a product of historical development, not universal law" (1985: 3). More important, probably, is that the absence of more such studies signifies a failure to apply Marx's belief that systems of thought are always historically contingent on bourgeois morality itself (Mosse 1985: 185). Mosse's work is also important because it contributes to an already growing academic interest in normative identities (e.g., the issue of whiteness [Babb 1998; M. Hill 1997]). The explicit engagement with European subjects (Foucault 1988, 1990), instead of exclusively with only the oppressed or colonized other, allows for a wider understanding of the dynamics at work in different post(neo)colonial settings.

This particular argument has been further elaborated by Andrew Parker et al. in their study of nationalisms and sexualities in different cultural settings. Their contribution offers a more complex reading of the national enterprise—a reading in which the nation is both genderized and based on an excluded other:

National identity is determined not on the basis of its own intrinsic properties but as a function of what it (presumably) is not. Implying some element of alterity for its definition, a nation is ineluctably shaped by what it opposes. Hence, on the one hand, the nation's insatiable need to administer difference through violent acts of segregation, censorship, economic coercion, physical torture, police brutality. And hence, on the other, the nation's insatiable need for representational labor to supplement its founding ambivalence, the lack of self-presence in its origin or in its essence.
    —Andrew Parker et al. 1992: 5

Therefore, it is not surprising to find bourgeois notions of sexuality and race to be volatile symbols at the center of the debate about national identity (Murray and Handler 1996; A. Parker et al. 1992). The newfound understanding of the inextricable linkages of race, class, and sex is one of the many contributions of the scholarship produced by women of color (Anzaldúa 1987, 1990; Fusco 1994, 1995; Hooks 1994; Lorde 1997; Mohanty and Alexander 1997; Mohanty, Russo, and Torres 1991, to mention a few). Other feminist scholarship (e.g., Enloe 1990) has also been instrumental in pointing out that tourism and tourist sites are linked to complex discourses that implicate nations' unspoken gender roles and racial norms. As national showcases, archeological sites, in many cases, more than any other tourist sites, represent the nation's image of its gendered and racial self to all visitors. These representations are actively contested and reformulated in settings in which a greater number of visitors are asked to actively imagine and confront these representations. As a display of the nation's past, Cochasquí offers an image of the social practices of the country's prehistory. In doing so, it provides even more elements that struggle and help reformulate the nation's own class, racial, and gendered normalizing truths.

Like other postcolonial settings (see Dávila 1997; Franco 1992), Ecuador has developed a racial discourse in which all sex and gender discussion are immersed, formulated, and inextricably linked. As I argue here, racial and gendered negotiation at Cochasquí is not free of strong class and ethnic implications and, thus, of pervasive and subtle discourses relating it to the Ecuadorian nation-state. Key in these discussions is an understanding of the actual (almost individual) deployment of the different sexual and racial identities and practices. This is not to deny that there is a quite powerful coercive state ideology and regulatory class system, which is imposing a sexually racialized norm. Rather, this coercion does not explain everything; the state's coercive power does not predict the dynamic series of individual and social acts.

The discussion of sex and gender looks to question "the putative agent of regulation, rather than to assume the normalizing nation/state as a constant" (Schein 1996: 199). The fact that we do not simply do what the state tells us to do has interesting implications both for understanding how is it that we construct our (sexual/racial/national) self and for the impact the state has on structuring coercive state regulations—regulations which are established through the reformulation of the nation's representation of its sexual and racial norms. These norms are themselves activated as cultural representations which, when analyzed, can help us elucidate antagonistic practices, signals of resistance, and homogenizing appropriations, all bound in one (A. Parker et al. 1992).

Ecuadorian women have a long-standing tradition of struggle, including the occupation of the IMF offices in Quito in 2001 (Acción Ecológica 2001; Pinto 2001). Their struggle has resulted in concrete victories such as securing the right to vote at the beginning of the twentieth century and the passage of the Law against Violence to Women and the Family in 1995 (Muratorio 1998). It is this same feminist consciousness that induced several women's groups to rally around Ecuadorian Lorena Bobbitt when she visited the country and to hail her as a national hero for cutting off her husband's penis. Bobbitt's act was invested with symbolic political importance as Ecuadorian men and women identified with her. As then-president Abdalá Bucaram noted, it wasn't any penis that she cut off, it was a "[North] American" one. President Bucaram's remark immediately evokes the complex relationship between sexuality and nationalism (A. Parker et al. 1992) in Ecuador. In this context, the United States becomes the male aggressor which has been castrated by the submissive female partner in the sexual liaison.

This misogynist and homophobic model is very much inscribed within the gender hierarchy of Ecuador, where not only females, but homosexuals as well, are actively portrayed as the inferior and negative representation of what Ecuador is not. As the national political rhetoric implies, references to homosexuality are powerful tools for maintaining a heterosexist, male, white, and upper-class definition of the Ecuadorian nation (Andrade 1995, 1997; Cifuentes 1999; Lamas et al. 1998). This violent heterosexist/homophobic structure is affirmed in the random killings of transgendered individuals, layoffs of persons infected with the HIV virus, and the fact that until 1997 homosexual acts between men were legally recognized as criminal (even between consenting adults) and punishable by a mandatory eight-year prison sentence. However, this explicitly homophobic structure, as a result of local and global mechanisms, is starting to be publicly contested (Benavides 1998).

Scholars are also beginning to engage the patriarchal and white representation of an Ecuadorian national identity. The two most visible contributors in this regard are Muratorio (1994, 1998) and Andrade (1995, 1997). Muratorio deconstructs the manner in which the Indian, particularly the Amazonian Indian woman, is portrayed nationally to sustain a hegemonic image of whiteness. Andrade's work explores Ecuadorian maleness as a gender category that has been instrumental in maintaining unequal sexual, class, and racial relations. It is in this context of internal inequality that the following histories have been reproduced and are represented. My contention is that these "stories" illustrate how Ecuadorians of different backgrounds and national sentiments contribute to the production and transformation of identity systems of unequal hegemonic articulation.

SEXUAL JOKES AND RACIAL MYTHS AT COCHASQUÍ

The sexual jokes and stereotypes elaborated by the staff at Cochasquí provide an insight into gender relations and the hierarchy at the site. They also provide an approach into many of the reigning gender and sexual discourses pervasive within the much larger setting of the Ecuadorian nation-state. These sexual jokes and assumptions do not speak only about sex and gender; they also have strong racial and ethnic, class and national implications. This allows one to understand how different identity markers are conflated to constitute powerful social discourses— discourses that become imperative for structuring the way we think about and see our own sexual and gendered selves and our surroundings (Domínguez 1996). This joking allows us to see how we are free to construct our own sexual classification, yet are very much constrained by the jokes and other agents, including institutional ones (Beriss 1996).

The two groups most often singled out at the site for sexual and social ridicule are women and homosexuals. Significantly, both of these groups are underrepresented among the staff, and openly gay persons are also visibly absent among visitors at the site. Only three women—less than one-fifth of the total staff—worked at the site while I was there: an archaeologist, a sociologist, and the tour guide chief. However, by the end of my fieldwork, only the archaeologist was still going up to the site regularly, as the other two had to stay at the office in Quito for medical reasons. There were no openly gay people working at the site, and I knew of only one gay man and his lover visiting and sleeping at the site, and this only because he was the provincial prefect's nephew.

All three of the women who worked at the site either held university degrees or had postsecondary education; only the *consejero* and the director among the men had a university degree. All but one of the remaining male staff members had only a primary school education. But even their higher social standing did not spare these women from being the subject of sexual jokes and innuendoes. These "jokes" ranged from being slapped on their buttocks to being constantly harassed about their sexual practices. Their education could not save them or was not as important as their inferior sexual positioning.

The archaeologist was the only one who repeatedly countered the attacks on her sexual activity. She also "joked" back, for example, by trying to give the men hickeys so they would get in trouble with their wives. However, the archaeologist's capacity to interact with the men at such an explicitly sexual level was attributed to the fact that she was a *mona* (monkey)—that is, someone from the coast, in this case, Guayaquil. She was the only *mona* at the site. All the other women from the coast, including the program secretary, who worked at the Consejo Provincial in Quito (where the program had its main office), were also represented as being very sexually provocative. They were constantly celebrated for their unwillingness to put up with harassment ("No se dejan ver la cara de cojudas") and for benefiting from their sexual exploits by receiving money, status, and better job opportunities. These women's geographical genealogy was used to explain their daring and aggressive behavior.

Coastal women are cherished and sought after in the highlands for supposedly having an extrovert nature, a no-nonsense attitude toward sex, and, not the least important, voluptuous bodies. As a graffito in Quito claimed: "To make love in Quito is not a sin, it is a miracle." (Graffiti are a very widespread popular expression in Quito; see Ron 1995.) *Monas* are idealized as women who do not worry very much about virginity or premarital sex. Not surprisingly, they are portrayed as voracious and extremely voluptuous sexual beings; pictures of them feature inordinately large buttocks and hips, a stereotype also used to depict Afro-Ecuadorian women (see Muteba Rahier 1998).

The response of both men and women to the archaeologist's defense of herself and her sexuality links gender attitudes to sexual attitudes and, even more important, to a specific physical and racial (i.e., quasi-genetic) element. It was supposedly her fiery nature, bestowed by birth, that allowed her to be so explicit about sexual themes and to use foul language, which is not typical or appropriate for Ecuadorian women. There is a racial reason behind the attribution of her manner of defending and representing herself, a reason that endows all coastal women, Cochasquí's archaeologist included, with "an attitude" that seems to be attributed especially to women who question and contest their traditionally subordinate position. This is a point specifically elaborated by Hooks (1990, 1994) and West (1994) for African American women in the United States, who tend to be represented, like coastal and Afro-Ecuadorian women, not only as outspoken, fiery, and attitude prone, but also as particularly sexually enticing and exotic (see also Morrison 1993).

In the archaeologist's behavior we see an individual form of gender deployment, a form that seems to deviate from the national sex/gender norm. We also detect an implicit and wider racial reasoning, which seems to contradict the norm (that all women are sexually submissive), but actually allows this particular deployment to be integrated into the nation-state's sexual/gender norm. The race-related reasoning that looks to explain away the archaeologist's behavior, like that of all *monas*, sanitizes it and allows it to be incorporated into the mainstream and normalizing picture of all Ecuadorian women as sexually passive and inhibited. It neutralizes a contradictory element and further completes the view that unequal gender relations are natural. The gender norm is secure once the exception has been satisfactorily accounted for, even though over half of the female population in the country comprises coastal and Afro-Ecuadorian women.

The Ecuadorian nation-state's sex/gender norm—the white heterosexual male—would not be complete without the constant homosexual jokes and ridicule of gay, particularly male, sexual practices (Benavides 1998; see also Andrade 1995, 1997). All the men at Cochasquí joke about each other's sexual performance and accuse each other of having homosexual "tendencies" or "inclinations." The constant jokes, for example, the feminizing of male names, brings "manhood" into question. These jokes have to be rebutted immediately, and successfully, otherwise, gender identity and reputation are destroyed, because homosexual references do not only imply sexual preference as much as they question moral character.

It is also clear at Cochasquí that homosexual jokes have a very strong hierarchical structure, which allows those with higher status (defined by their post, seniority, age, class, gender, and race) to question others' sexuality and character (see Lancaster 1996 for a similar process in Nicaragua). This is clearly visible during the big festivities and other unofficial occasions, where all the staff got together. I witnessed the director subtly select the people to be harassed or ridiculed. It was apparent that homosexual jokes were a control mechanism that made it very clear who was in charge at the site. This type of behavior, however, was exhibited not only by the director, but also by all the other staff members. As with the jokes about women, homosexual jokes, mostly but not exclusively about men, exposed forms of sexual deployment within the larger national constraints of normalizing discourses.

The homosexual jokes or ridiculing at Cochasquí are not unique to the site. Homophobic images and language are pervasive throughout the Ecuadorian nation-state and vital in the maintenance of the gender and national status quo in many instances (Benavides 1998). As a result of its pivotal place in the general discourse of national identity and, at the same time, as evidence of the reigning heteronormative, homophobic slurs and homosexual images pervade the national political scene (Andrade 1995). Homophobic slurs play an essential role in politicians' efforts to construct a masculine, heterosexist identity that fits the modern representation of the nation. Both male and female politicians construct an overly aggressive and powerful masculine identity built on selective readings of the country's pre-Hispanic past. They make continual references to the warlike nature of the Indian communities and Indian heroes, for example, the Manteños-Huancavilcas and Rumiñahui, etc., who resisted both the Inca and the Spanish invasions. This selective reading of history ignores the complex narratives offered about pre-Hispanic sexual practices—some of which refer to explicit homosexual activity among Indian communities such as the *enchaquirados*—to construct a white heterosexual identity in tune with current discourses of the Ecuadorian nation-state (Muratorio 1994; Stutzman 1981).

Politicians' masculine identity, however, is not based exclusively on an association with a selective representation of the Indian past; it is also constructed of direct attacks on opponents' masculine identity (see accounts of Assad Bucaram's and Abdalá Bucaram's infamous sexual political rhetoric in Macas Ambuludí and Ramiro Miño 1997). Ultimately, homosexual references, just like the racial construction of *monas,* are useful for explaining away unsettling contradictions that question the white and heterosexual construction of Ecuador's national identity. This essentially stabilizing recourse explains Ecuador's traditional reticence to decriminalize consensual sexual activity between men, which was finally accomplished in January 1998.

These particular narratives illustrate individual forms of sexual deployment and their resulting racial and class effects within the reality of a greater national norm and its local variants. As in the national arena, the sexual/gendered hegemony at Cochasquí doesn't work because everybody blindly follows the rules (Domínguez 1996; Schein 1996), but because this hegemonic construction incorporates varied sexual practices and gendered truths and transforms them, and itself, into a more palatable reality (Alonso 1988). This ambivalent and contradictory reality then presents itself convincingly as a static entity. The sexual narratives at Cochasquí are useful for understanding how strategic marginalities relate to hegemonic constructions, national propriety, and racial myths (Beriss 1996; Mallon 1996).

FEMALE SEXUALITY AND NATIONAL IDENTITY

Another sexually charged event I heard about at the site centered on a young local woman, Rosenda, who lived alone with her mother in the *comuna*. She also spent significant time away from the community, working for the flower companies in the neighboring towns. The story has powerful hegemonic implications for bringing women with a "problematic" sexual agenda in line with the national fold. Rosenda was defined as "crazy" because her sexual behavior did not conform to that of a typical rural mestiza woman belonging to a low-class community such as the *comuna* of Cochasquí. Thus, the "truth" of the story is not its most relevant element, since the narrative holds enormous social power to instruct racial, class, and sexual norms.

As the story was told to me, one evening Rosenda and six men were drinking and partying together. Different accounts told to me by the driver and different staff members claim that, after everybody was drunk, Rosenda consciously (and this voluntary aspect was emphasized) proposed sex with all the men, except one, the eldest. It seems that she was taken up on her proposal and had sex with all of them, including the one she had initially excluded. The accounts declared that no simultaneous sexual activity occurred—which excluded any possibility of male homosexual interaction. Afterward, she was abandoned in the woods, where the incident took place, and her clothes were thrown away by the men. One of the site's local workers reappeared to take her home, since she had been given permission to leave her home under his supervision.

It was only after everybody at the site knew the story that local workers (all men) were willing to publicly discuss and comment on it. Their main reaction was disgust, rejection, and self-righteousness. I wondered aloud to one of the workers about his reaction had he been involved, and he looked me straight in the eye and said he would not have had sex with her; instead, he "would have put a handful of sand up her vagina and left her there." This painful and cruel image made it evident that she had committed a major transgression in his eyes.

But what was the nature of her sin? What was so horribly shocking about the sexual act being described that it merited punishment? Why was Rosenda immediately convicted and "punished"? Why did no one wonder about the veracity of the story or even whether some sort of co-ercion or even rape might have taken place? Finally, what of the possi-bility that this story was fabricated to make Rosenda into a monstrous (i.e., unnatural) being for behaving so differently from the other local women?

These questions can be partly answered by considering Cochasquí as a place of sexual invention (Butler 1993) and considering how stories at the site reflect an obsession with the plausible construction of non-traditional sexual space. Spatial specificity and atemporal structure have made the site's offices and housing a splendid setting for the private ren-dezvous of some of the staff members. The site would seem to offer a common sexual meeting ground (reflected in sexually charged banter) between all the members of the staff. The staff is kept in line by explicit and implicit national hierarchical norms. These structures demand that the highest-ranking official (i.e., the class and racial element), the con-sejero, and the directors have the greatest amount of sexual freedom, followed by the nonlocal staff, the local staff, and, finally, the comune-ros. Yet this relaxed environment (i.e., invented space) is also intersected by a normative structure reflecting the site's ambivalent hegemonic pro-duction. That structure expresses very clear gender norms, within which it is the males who fill the role of predator and submit women to their desires, not the other way around. In this story, Rosenda, as a woman and a member of the comuna, dramatically subverted both gender and class/race norms.

In another story brought to light after the previous incident became known, Rosenda was described as having been with three men at differ-ent times during the same day. Once again, leaving aside the accuracy of the story, what is interesting is how it highlights the main problem as be-ing Rosenda's challenge of men's authority. The men should have been the aggressor and seducer. It was only later that they found out that they had been tricked (and had not tricked Rosenda, as they thought)—a mistake for which the other men in the group ridiculed them. But here, at least, the façade of their superiority as males had been respected, and their gendered integrity and dignity, although battered, were still very much intact.

Even though this story highlights men, and not women, as having ex-tramarital affairs, the incident shattered the site's men's sense of what was proper and their image of women as innocent beings who are se-duced and conquered by men. It questioned their identity as natural sex-ual aggressors. It made them the passive, and therefore the inferior, ele-ment in the sexual exchange. The men were shocked, turned off, repulsed by Rosenda's use of her sexuality. Their responses to the story implied that there was something terribly shocking in her flagrant use and enjoyment of sex.

These incidents depict Rosenda as the aggressor, when official gender categories allow her to be portrayed only as the fragile female unwillingly seduced and fooled. However, this male resentment was also shared by the men who claimed to have engaged in sex with her. What else would explain their anger? They threw away her clothes and left her naked in the cold highland woods. It would seem that this was done despite their just having had sex with her, and maybe because of it.

The men's attitude reflects Cochasquí's local response to a national sense of gendered/sexual relations characterized by male superiority and aggression, the condemnation of explicitly sexual females, and, an apparent contradiction, the fantasy construction of a sexually voracious female or femme fatale (See Mosse 1985; A. Parker et al. 1992, for insights into these phenomena as Western). This national ideology is best exemplified by Ecuadorian writer José de la Cuadra's short story, "La Tigra" (1973), about a sexually compulsive and aggressive woman. "La Tigra" (the tigress) is negatively portrayed because of her voracious sexual appetite and daily sexual "use" of men. Not surprisingly, she is punished by the end of the narrative. Significantly, "La Tigra" was the first Ecuadorian literary text to be made into a successful commercial film in the country.

In this national context, the hostile reaction to Rosenda's sexual escapades becomes quite understandable. The story is shocking because it features the wrong person as protagonist, that is, a person with the incorrect gender, class, and race characteristics. This is the reason why Rosenda (not the men) is considered immoral. I heard several stories of multiple-partner sex at Cochasquí, but whereas the rest of them had men as the central figures, this one did not. Rosenda's story is doubly disturbing because it upset the sexual norms and race and class hierarchies that were implicitly instituted at the site as part of the Ecuadorian nation. Rosenda, as a woman and a member of the racially inferior and lower-class local community, had overstepped the bounds of "moral behavior" (as culturally defined) in the most explicit and public of ways. A woman, especially one of her race (a rural mestiza) and class (peasant), could not, and should not, wield the enormous power evidenced in the role of sexual aggressor. The men's reaction to this incident reveals that she had no right, in their eyes, to (re)present herself the way she did.

This narrative showcases the varied manner in which people at Cochasquí construct their own social ranking against nationally sanctioned gendered/sexual discourses. Rosenda's story is a female-gendered form of sexual invention that reflects a particular construction of sexual practice—a form of sexual disposition that does not fit into the implicit gendered norm of Cochasquí and the nation. It also reflects the almost inherent set of multiple meanings hiding behind the ambivalent hegemonic structure which masks itself as static, predictable, and an easy target for simplified forms of militant activism. The fact that I never heard any of the women at Cochasquí (except one whose husband was one of the six men involved and who also shared with Rosenda one of the male staff members as her lover) condemn or defend Rosenda argues for a more varied set of alternative discourses than a static hegemonic construction would allow us to appreciate.

But perhaps more telling in this story is the oppression of a rural/mestizo identity as represented by Rosenda (and reflecting a direct Indian legacy) at the hands of a powerful state constituted of whites/mestizos. These sexual stories contribute to the state's articulation of the Indian past as a way to further the state's oppressive national agenda. As the previous chapters show, the state continually incorporates and produces histories that heighten the Indian past but diminish their contribution and legacy. The Indian past is tolerated as an essential part of Ecuador's construction of authority, and all contradictions are used to further this homogeneous national program.

ALTERNATIVE HISTORIES AND SEXUALITIES IN LATIN AMERICA

Despite some evidence from my own fieldwork,
I had not thought much about the connections between
nationalism and sexuality. But I was jarred into considering
those connections by a little gray-haired lady standing on
the sidewalk holding up a sign that read: "If you're Gay
and Irish, your parents must be English."

—DAVID BERISS (1996)

Since the 1970s there has been a significant and concerted effort to evaluate alternative forms of sexuality and gendered construction in terms of the reigning normative heterosexual interpretation of Latin American societies (see Lancaster 1986; Murray 1980, 1987; R. Parker 1986). These studies have provided a much more complex picture of sexual desire and gender roles in Latin America. They have also provided a much more textured understanding of the reigning heterosexual norm on the continent as not devoid of contradictions and multiple alternative sexualities (Gutmann 1994; Prieur 1998). This has contributed to our analysis of cultural hegemony and its need for alternative interpretations in the dynamic process of historical officialization (see Wylie 1995).

These Latin American case studies, however, are indebted to two research agendas—feminism and third-gender studies—that, although elaborated outside the continent, have strongly influenced various scholars to broaden the questions they are asking about sexual agency and gender construction. The initial feminist breakthrough was not lost on academic disciplines like anthropology, which saw in gender a powerful analytical category that, although previously acknowledged (Mead 1949), had not been realized to its full potential. Gender studies in anthropology (Brettell and Sargent 1997; del Valle 1993; Fausto-Sterling 1992; Gero and Conkey 1990; Moore 1988) benefited not only from feminism, but also from a resurgence in analysis of gender categorization and sexual classification among Native American populations. These third-gender studies (see Lang 1998; Roscoe 1998; Nanda's [1990] research on hijras) rapidly expanded the theoretical constraints initially placed on the normalization of sex (see Foucault 1990) and the political implications of gender constructions.

Both feminism and Native American transgendered studies have enriched a burgeoning field of research closely linked with the contemporary gay social movement. They have targeted both Latin Americans and their Latino descendants in the United States. Provocative in this regard is the ongoing Latino literary production since the 1990s in the United States (e.g., by Castillo 1992, 1996; Díaz 1997; García 1992; Gómez-Peña 1991, 1994; D. Taylor 1998; Xavier 1999). These contemporary "gay" narratives (see Manrique 1992, 1997; Martínez 1992, 1998) are interesting in the way in which they separate themselves from the traditional homosexual canon of Latin American writers (see Arenas 1991, 1993; Leyland and Lacey 1983; Mistral 1998; Puig 1986; Sarduy 1997) by not situating themselves exclusively in the rich Latin American literary tradition, but also within a U.S.-based gay rights movement and transgendered identity. This transgendered Latino literature also brings up questions of cultural authenticity and the role played by other hegemonizing racial and economic discourses that have traditionally produced social exclusion in the continent, but now are imbued with a more liberated sexual program (see Benavides 2001; Bustos-Aguilar 1995).

Significantly enough, this "new" Latino literary boom has seen a greater emphasis on transgendered narratives, including the publication of several literary anthologies on gay themes (e.g., Bergmann and Smith 1995; Cortez 1999; Guerra 1999; Manrique and Dorris 1999; Molloy and Irwin 1998; Patton and Sánchez-Eppler 2000), including ones that tackle taboo subjects in the Latin American intellectual world, such as mothers and masculinity. In *Muy Macho: Latino Men Confront Their Manhood* (R. González 1996) and *Las Mamis: Favorite Latino Authors Remember Their Mothers* (Santiago and Davidow 2000), the authors tackle personal issues previously outside the normative realm of Latino literary and intellectual discussion. In the former, contributors analyze an engendered historical heritage that has both defined and limited their self-expression. An ambiguous macho legacy, expressed in years of silence and of performing the socially accepted masculine role, has left a mark on these men's lives, alienating them from their cultural past and artistic present.

Las Mamis, interestingly enough, fails to reach the heights of critical self- and social examination that many of the contributors to *Muy Macho* attain when analyzing their fathers and masculine heritage. In some cases, authors are reticent because they would not be able to face their mothers and family after writing about them, or they could not face questioning *la familia*, since it holds such a pivotal place in their lives (Davidow 2000: viii–ix). As a result of this shortcoming, the work carried out by Anzaldúa (1987, 1990; Anzaldúa and Keating 2000), among other Chicana and Latina scholars (e.g., Alarcón 1990; Alarcón, Moraga, and Castillo 1993; Moraga 1997; Moraga and Anzaldúa 1983) on the impact of sexual constraints imposed by family and their relationship with the greater cultural hegemonic project stand out even more as pathbreaking and thought-provoking accomplishments.

Possibly also as a result of the difficulty of critically addressing concerns of family and motherhood, masculinity has become one of the most productive areas in Latin American sexual and gender research. For example, Mirandé's (1997) analysis of male gender identity in *Hombres y Machos: Masculinity and Latino Culture,* Carrier's (1995) *De los Otros: Intimacy and Homosexuality among Mexican Men,* and Gutmann's (1996) *The Meanings of Macho: Being a Man in Mexico City* analyze this question of gender from different personal, theoretical, and geographical positions. Mirandé incorporates himself and his family into his study of the role of transnational migration in the historical transformation of a male/macho identity. Gutmann and Carrier conduct more traditional anthropological studies of manhood and gender in the Mexican capital, relating gender and sexuality to larger questions of cultural dynamics and political hegemony.

It is precisely this "traditional" anthropological stance that has been questioned by many Third World researchers as, contradictorily enough, contributing to the domination rather than the liberation of the communities serving as objects of study. For these postcolonial scholars, the imperial structure is the same; only the contents have changed. Instead of religious conversion, sexual liberation is the new gospel of contemporary global developmental discourse (see Benavides 2001; Bustos-Aguilar 1995; Manalansan and Cruz-Malavé 2002). Bustos-Aguilar (1995) incisively uses lyrics from a Willie Chirino salsa song—"Mister don't touch the banana, the banana belong to Changó"—to question this radical new sexual-liberation gospel as yet another form of (neo)colonial sexualized discourse concerning the racialized other (see Stoler 1996). Despite this "native" critique (see Kulik and Wilson 1995; Lewin and Leap 1996 for the initial response to this approach), recent academic contributions have furthered research on transgendered identities and alternative sexual histories in Latin America.

Some of the most relevant examples of these nationally based anthropological studies are Kulik's (1998) *Travesti: Sex, Gender, and Culture among Brazilian Transgendered Prostitutes;* Parker's (1991) *Bodies, Pleasures, and Passions: Sexual Culture in Contemporary Brazil;* and Prieur's (1998) *Mema's House, Mexico City: On Transvestites, Queens and Machos.* Lancaster's (1996) *Life Is Hard: Machismo, Danger, and the Intimacy of Power in Nicaragua* is by far the most influential and exhaustive in its anthropological critique. Lancaster analyzes homosexual desire subtly articulated with the process of national hegemonic production. Rather than simply defining specific gender constraints, he outlines a powerful sexual discourse of "being a *cochón*" in Nicaragua that is quite different from North American homosexual discourse, or even from the particular top-aggressive/bottom-passive discourse elaborated by several anthropologists for Latin America. *Life Is Hard* outlines a more subtle and contradictory sexual ideology that uses national fears to reinforce unequal and hierarchical gender roles that are reproduced alongside racial and class inequalities.

Lancaster's (1996) nuanced theoretical analysis of sexual practice and gender identity is a particularly rich starting point for reexamining sexuality and gender in Latin America. His complex understanding of gender, race, and class has also made its way into analyses of Latin

America's colonial past (Adorno 1993; Burns 1999; Greenblatt 1993; Gutiérrez 1991; see also Martínez-Alier 1974; Spalding 1970, 1982, 1984). However, analyses of colonial times that prioritize homosexual desire and practice or tightly weave homosexuality into the larger heteronormative Portuguese and Spanish Catholic sexual discourse are yet to appear.

HISTORICIZING THE *ENCHAQUIRADOS*

The *enchaquirados* (a harem of young male religious and sexual servants) are described by the same ethnohistorical accounts that have been used to reconstruct Guayaquil's Andean colonial history (e.g., Benzoni 1995; Cieza [1553] 1971, 1986; Guamán Poma de Ayala [1613] 1980; Montesinos [1644] 1920). These accounts, however, have been consistently scrutinized to reconstruct Ecuador's history (in, e.g., Ayala Mora 1983; Efrén Reyes 1967; Pareja Diezcanseco 1990) and have been used to produce and legitimize a particular heteronormative national discourse. Not surprisingly, the proponents of this discourse have relied on the supposed objectivity of the official history to support their claims and have denied the inherent circularity in the hermeneutical process of representation which always "obscur[es] the conditions of its own creation, [and] cover[s] its own tracks" (Hale 1996: 2; see also Alonso 1988; Taussig 1992b).

I hope to address the question of sexual representation and to point out the problems with the historical interpretation of Guayaquil's indigenous heritage. In no way am I assuming that my interpretation is more accurate than others; instead, I hope it spurs an assessment of the interpretive base of all historical representations, especially those that believe they express absolute objectivity, taking into account the social and personal motivations inherent in all historical discourse (Alonso 1988). As Foucault (1993: 139) so eloquently expresses it in "Nietzsche, Genealogy and History," "Genealogy is gray, meticulous and patiently documentary. It operates on a field of entangled and confused parchments, on documents that have been scratched over and recopied many times."

In this sense, it really is not a question of proving the existence of a transgendered past; after all, the "evidence" has always been there. The more relevant question concerns how this "evidence" has been excluded or, more accurately, represented in an effort to question heteronormative history used to fuel and sustain this hegemonic ideology. There is no doubt that Guayaquil's official histories and even most, if not all, of its alternative ones exclude the *enchaquirados*.

Present-day Guayaquil is located inland from the Santa Elena Peninsula, in the Guayas Gulf. There is some disagreement about the pre-Hispanic population of the general area where the city now stands. The most commonly held belief is that the Manteño-Huancavilca polity inhabited this region; therefore, it is this group that is referred to as the city's indigenous ancestors (Holm 1986; Martínez Estrada N. d.). However, based on the ethnohistorical accounts of the chroniclers, historians are not as certain about the ethnic affiliation of the pre-Hispanic communities of the area (Aspiazu Carbo 1970; Carrera Andrade 1957; see Muse 1991 for a provocative reconstruction of pre-Hispanic communities in the area).

According to the Spanish chroniclers, these groups engaged in idolatry, dealt with the devil, sacrificed both animals and humans, and, quite significantly, performed sodomy. Paramount in this sexual practice was a group of young men recognized for their ritualized homosexual activity and their ritual attire of *chaquiras* (shell beads) and gold ornaments (Cieza de León 1986: 199–200):

> And in other regards, for the devil to have them in his chains of sin, it is accurately maintained that in their oracles and temples where they were given the answers to their questions, it was assumed that it was necessary for their service that some boys from a very young age live at the temples, so that at certain moments and when there were sacrifices and holy feasts, the lord and other principals performed with them the damned sin of sodomy. And so that you understand what you are reading, how some among them still maintain this diabolical ritual: I will narrate a story that was given to me in the city of the kings by Fray Domingo de Santo Tomás, which I have in my powers and goes like this:

> *And that is that each temple or primary* adoratorio *has one or two men, or more, depending on the idol. They have been dressed as women from childhood, and they speak as such; and in their treatment, clothes, and everything else, they imitate women. These men engage in carnal union as a sign of sanctity and religion, during their feast and holy days, especially with the lords and other principals. I know because I have punished two. The ones who, when I have told them of the evil they were committing and the ugliness of the sin they were doing, an-*

swered: that they were not at fault because, since the moment of their birth, they had been placed there by their caciques, to use with them this damned and nefarious vice, and to be the priests and keepers of the temple. So what I gathered from this is that the devil was thus in charge in these lands: that he has not been content with making them fall into such a grand sin: but he has also made them believe that such a vice was a form of sanctity and religion, and in such a manner has enslaved them more.

This was given to me by Fray Domingo, known by all, and known for being a friend of the truth.

Fernández de Oviedo describes the *enchaquirados* in the following manner ([1535] 1959, vol. 4: 221: "These lands of Puerto Viejo are flat and with very few hills, and the sun beats on them a lot and they are somewhat sickly. Most of the Indians who inhabit the coast are abominable sodomites, doing this with boys, and they have the boys very well beaded [*enchaquirados*] and adorned with lots of gold jewelry. They treat their women very badly. They use small shirts, and their shame is exposed."

This also seems to be what the Inca Garcilaso de la Vega (1998: 390) is referring to when he says that "the naturals of Manta and of the region, particularly the ones along the coast (but not those from inland, who are called *serranos*), practiced sodomy more in the open and with less shame than any other; that is, than all the other nations that until now have been noted for this vice."

Very little is known about these young men, although they hardly seem to have been an exception. Similar religious structures are described for both Central Peru (Cieza de León 1986) and Mesoamerica (de las Casas 1982: 70). When we take into account the boys' adornment in *chaquiras* and gold, we can assume that they were held in some regard by the community, especially since the *chaquiras* were considered priceless artifacts by these coastal groups. The *chaquiras* are described in several of the accounts, among them this one by Fernández de Oviedo ([1535] 1959, vol. 4: 122): "They had red shells like the ones they have in chaquira *id est sartales,* like the ones in the Canary Islands that are sold to the king of Portugal to ransom Guinea: and for this the Indians give all their gold and silver and clothes that they bring as ransom."

In another of Cieza de León's descriptions, he seems to hint at the emotional importance of some of these young men when he describes the traditional practice of burying the chief's most intimate companions with him ([1553] 1971: 204, my emphasis): "If he is lord or principal, they put two or three of the most preferred and beautiful of his women, and other of the most precious jewels, and with the food and the pitchers of their maize wine, however much they want. . . . This custom of burying their dead with their weapons, their treasure, and many provisions was widespread in these lands that we have discovered; *and in many provinces they would also bury live women and boys.*"

Several other accounts also seem to suggest the value of the young boys' service to their lords, to the point that many of them were also buried along with their wives in the lord's grave:

> One or two of his women would bury themselves with him the ones that he loved the most and because of this, sometimes there were fights between them, and so the deceased would leave this decided upon before his death, *and in the same manner, they would bury with him two or three young boys in his service,* putting in the grave all the gold and silver vessels that they had.
>
> —Zárate [1555] 1995: 33, my emphasis

> It was the custom to put the weapons with the deceased in his grave, and his treasure, and a lot of work went into maintaining this in these lands that have been discovered. *And in many provinces they would also include live women and boys.* . . . And they claimed as truth that they buried with the deceased their most beloved women, and their most private servitors [*servidores*] and servants [*sirvientes*] . . . and in these valleys it is very common to bury the dead with their riches and most important things, *and many women and servants of the most intimate ones that the lord had while being alive.*
>
> —Cieza de León 1986: 166, 194 and 197, my emphasis

Other homosexual activities are described by many of the chroniclers who visited these coastal groups:

> But as these people were evil and full of vices, notwithstanding that among them there were many women, and some of them extremely beautiful, most of them engaged (which has been certified to me) publicly and in the open in the nefarious sin [*pecado nefando*] of sodomy, in which it is said that they glorified themselves in the extreme. It is true that during the last years, Captain Pacheco and Captain Olmos, who are now in Spain, harshly punished the Indians who committed the above-mentioned sin, admonishing them about how God was displeased, and they were so remorse-

ful that now very little or none of this sin is practiced, or any of the other bad customs that they had, nor do they make use of other abuses of their religions.

—Cieza de León [1553] 1971: 198

This last account both acknowledges the widespread practice of sodomy among the Manteños-Huancavilcas and Cieza's reticence in discussing the practice in detail.

In other accounts, such as that of Fray Reginaldo de Lizárraga, the use of homosexual activity to create a sense of "otherness" is particularly explicit. Distance is not only afforded from the Spaniards, but is also instrumental in segregating the different Indian communities. In this account, in which Lizárraga seems to have confused the two groups, his descriptions of the acts of sodomy have not only civilizing and racializing undertones:

> There lived in this city and its districts two nations of Indians, one called Guamcavillcas [sic], well-disposed people and white, clean in their dress and good-looking; the other ones are called Chonos, blacks, and not as sociable as the Guamcavillcas; both of them are warring people; their weapons, bows and arrows. The Chonos have the bad reputation of engaging in the nefarious vice of sodomy; they have their hair on end and the tops of their heads are completely bald, which is why the rest of the Indians ridicule them; calling them Chono dogs *cocotados* [shaved], as we will later say.
>
> —Lizárraga [1605] 1968: 66

Benzoni seems to share this moral and racializing tone when he describes the vassals of the cacique of Manta as "ugly, dirty sodomites, full of all evils" (1995: 110).

There is no mistaking the Spaniards' negative moral judgment of sodomy among the Manteños-Huancavilcas. In every instance, the chroniclers predict divine wrath in retribution for the unnatural and diabolical act of sodomy:

> It is accepted as truth by the Spaniards, after seeing these signs, considering that these people were given to the vice against nature, divine justice banned them from the earth, sending an angel for this effect, as he did in Sodom and in other parts
>
> —Zárate [1555] 1995: 35–36

And so they say that being all of them involved in their damned sodomy, fire came from the sky, frightening and scary, making great noise. From the center came a shimmering angel, with a grand, blinding sword with which, with a single blow, all of them were killed and a fire consumed them, and that all that was left was some bones and skulls, which, to make them remember the punishment, God desired that they survive without being totally consumed by the fire. . . .

— Cieza de León [1553] 1971: 206

The narrative about giants in this area is another interesting element in the description of ritualized male homosexuality among these coastal groups. It is very likely that this narrative was fueled by the discovery of mastodon bones. The presence of these giants is noted by all the major chroniclers, who describe them as predatory, first in terms of food and supplies, but later in terms of sexual satisfaction. The accounts suggest that Indian women were killed by the sexual advances of these giants, which is why they turned to having sex among themselves. One striking characteristic in the descriptions is that the giants are all said to be men; the absence of female giants never warrants an explanation:

Added to this is the account that the Indians themselves give, particularly those along the coast by Puerto Viejo, who say that giants had come there from the south in large rafts, but since they had not brought women with them, they died out.

— Cobo 1983: 95

Some years having passed and these giants still being in these parts: since they did not have women: and the Indian women did not fit them because of their size, or because it was a common vice among them on the counsel and support of the devil himself, they used with one another the nefarious sin of sodomy, so horrendous and with grave consequences; which they used and carried out publicly and in the open, without fear of God and very little shame. And all the Indians [*naturales*] stated that God our Lord, not being pleased by ignoring such horrible sin, sent them a punishment in accordance with the ugliness of the sin.

— Cieza de León [1553] 1971: 206

Likewise, the spies told how very large and tall men had arrived at the cape which today we call Santa Elena, and that they were ruling that land from Puerto Viejo, and that the natives were fleeing from them because they used their bodies so evilly. And in my opinion, it was not that they fled from the sin, for they themselves had it also, but that they fled from the danger of the instrument with which the giants took their lives. But so great were the excesses of these giants that divine justice took their punishment upon itself, and it punished then in an instant, sending fire from heaven which suddenly consumed them. (Montesinos [1644] 1920: 41)

GUAYAQUIL: THE LOCAL CONTEXT OF RACE, CLASS, AND REGIONALISM

Ecuador's mestizo population has historically distanced itself from the Indian population and even from the name *cholos,* given them as they were assimilated (Espinosa Apolo 1996; Puga and Jurado 1992). This distancing trend, inherited from Spain, has been invigorated by a new global order in which whiteness still constitutes itself as a marker of civilization (Acosta et al. 1997). However, now England and the United States, not Spain and the rest of Europe, are the markers of civilizing culture. This racial construction (Stutzman 1981) has been the prevalent reality of the ethnic formation of the white/mestizo elite players in Guayaquil's economy. This ethnic formation inspired a progressive liberal revolution (1895–1905) at the turn of the century which linked the nation to an international capitalist economy and introduced its lower classes to a proletarian existence (Ayala Mora 1983, 1986).

This particular form of ethnic competition, which in five centuries has allowed a significant number of mestizos to, if not belong, at least to closely identify with the elite white population, has not developed without difficulty and provocative social experimentation. The most central to our discussion of the *enchaquirados* is their historically ambiguous relationship with an Indian heritage. This relationship is ontologically implied in multiple ways within contemporary Indian communities, but perhaps much more subtly in the representation of an Indian past that is shared by the contemporary Indian and white/mestizo population of Guayaquil. This Indian past is not exclusively about a racial legacy, but about a class and sexual one, mainly because this racial legacy depends on the sexual reproduction of common ancestors and on the mechanisms of social reproduction and contemporary representation that each group has put into place to ensure its historical continuity and legitimization (de la Torre Espinosa 1996; Stoler 1996).

This form of historical ambiguity and its corresponding ideological and identity framework are particularly inescapable because they refer to the haunting question of cultural authenticity (Quintero López 1983; Quintero and Silva 1991). An essential contradiction is constantly replayed in the reclaiming of Indian heritage: support of the legitimization of a much-needed historical authenticity, but ethnic differentiation from the European colonizers. However, European legacy demands a racial division from Indian ancestors and, to some degree, from themselves or their image of themselves (see Fanon 1966; Freire 1992, for other postcolonial contexts). Thus, there is an internal incompatibility between striving to be and conducting oneself as white, of Spanish descent, and claiming, or struggling to claim, Indian ancestry while desperately needing to distinguish oneself as superior to the contemporary Indian population.

In Guayaquil this particular historical representation has resulted in a widespread form of regionalism, directed particularly against the highland population (Maiguashca 1994). On the coast the *serranos* (as highland people are pejoratively called) represent the backwardness, hypocrisy, "Indianness" of the country. The highlanders hold the coastal population in low esteem, referring to them as *monos* (monkeys) because they are popularly held to be cunning, good imitators, and always eager to con someone for their own benefit, economic or otherwise. These regional representations mimic the colonial geographical legacy: whereas the coastal Indian groups assimilated immediately into the colonial structure—"imitating" or "mimicking" the colonizers—highland Indian groups have not only maintained an Indian identity for the last five centuries of colonial and neocolonial domination, but, along with the Amazonian groups, have also been able to form the strongest social movements since the 1990s through groups such as the CONAIE and Pachakutik Nuevo País.

Coastal regionalism is most fiercely supported by residents of Guayaquil (Guayaquileños). This fierceness could be interpreted as another distancing mechanism—one that helps Guayaquileños deny any Indian component in their current existence, but not necessarily in their heritage. This connection is made even clearer by the fact that most of the visible Indian migrants to the city, many of whom are part of the market economy, are of highland extraction and are phenotypically, linguistically, and in their mode of dress distinct from the mestizo Guayaquileño population. For Guayaquileños, *serranos* represent more clearly the Indian past toward which Guayaquileños have such ambivalent feelings—of longing for ancestral recognition, yet fear and hatred of racial rejection. The latter is profoundly present in the rejection of Rosenda's (and all Indian) sexuality. The pervasiveness of the city's regionalism is also a marker of its administrative separation from the nation's capital and centralized political control, which has been cause of resentment throughout the territories' colonial and republican existence.

Regionalism, however, points not only to this political resentment, but also, and maybe even more, to a deeper sense of internal colonialism and self-loathing (see Mariátegui 1955; Zea 1991: 32, for further discussion). The hatred of highlanders seems to reflect Guayaquil's ambivalent feelings toward itself and its Indian past, especially since many Guayaquileños have a highland ancestry themselves. Regionalism is a sign of the difficulty of effectively factoring in the elements of historical construction that may prove detrimental to the progressive Western ideal that Guayaquil adopted almost five centuries ago. This anti-Indian construct is an essential component of what Guayaquil and Guayaquileños are today.

We can also see in this discourse of regionalism the reason why the *enchaquirados*' legacy has so often been ignored and misconstrued. In the modern construction of Guayaquil's historical identity there is very little room for any Indian element, especially a "problematic" sexual one. Therefore, it is impossible to claim the misrepresentation of the *enchaquirados* as a sign of biased or bad scholarship; rather, it is an essential emblem of the much larger regional racial discourse that underlies Guayaquil's contemporary and historical representation of itself.

It is this same historical ambiguity that makes the city's and the region's representation of the Indian past a contested issue, because, or even when, historical reconstructions of the Indian past in Guayaquil have been presented as fact, as historically objective. Thus, most educational institutions, historical texts, and Guayaquileños assume that the original Indian population was the ancient and extinct Huancavilcas (Martínez Estrada N.d.; Navas Jiménez 1994; Pareja Diezcanseco 1990). The Huancavilcas are presented as a community of fierce warriors who resisted and rejected the Inca conquest and fought to the bitter end against the Spanish conquistadors. This image of fierce resistance is enshrined in the most popular explanation of the origin of the city's name: "Guayaquil" is supposed to have come from the name of the leader of the Huancavilcas, Guayas, and his wife, Quil, who resisted the Spanish to their death.

This particular origin myth is quite similar to the race/gender problematics presented in other American settings, for example, La Malinche in Mexico and mestizas in Peru (De la Cadena 2000; Mallon 1996). Like politicians in these other regions, contemporary politicians in Ecuador understand the lucrative potential of relating to an ancient myth and historical heritage. Ecuadorian politicians, educators, and other public figures invoke a heritage of great resistance with precise gendered and sexual specifications (see Radcliffe and Westwood 1996). In this past, being from Guayaquil means and demands having courage, physical strength, and moral superiority. It is this particular brand of machismo, with its gendered behavior and implicit heterosexuality, which is reinforced in Guayaquil's normative behavior. The ethnohistorical accounts about the Manteños-Huancavilcas and other pre-Hispanic communities in the area provide an opportunity to place Guayaquil's regional construction of its sexual past in context. The pervasiveness of a transgendered community in the nonurban setting of Ecuador's Santa Elena peninsula, particularly in the town of La Libertad, has much to offer in terms of assessing the nature of sexual identity in general and in terms of resistance, accommodation, and daily existence in the face of capitalist cultural dynamics.

This somewhat triumphant tone of recognition of a possibly local gay identity (at La Libertad), however, is only half of the picture. The other half is afforded by five centuries of religious and moral ideology that has shaped and constituted transgendered identities in Ecuador and throughout Latin America. Thus, it is likely that Catholicism has contradictorily enabled transgendered communities in Ecuador. One must ask how Latin American Catholicism's sexually repressive ideology has contributed to rather than merely repressed the expression of queer Latin American identities. This is a particularly complex subject in light of the church's explicit condemnation of homosexual activity and contribution to a secular homophobic ideology that has significantly ostracized transgendered communities.

To complicate matters further, the church's homophobic ideology has been reinforced in a racial ideology of white/mestizo control of public policy, national images, political representations, and a discourse of regionalism. In Ecuador this racialized control has meant the almost complete erasure and outright denial of a different or alternative pre-Hispanic sexual practice in favor of that advocated by the Catholic Church.

This binary opposition (between conservative morality and sexual liberation), however, does not fully explain the complex involvement and centrality of religion and sex in the construction of contemporary Latin American sexual identity. There is no doubt that the church's homophobic dicta have not been satisfied; the large transgendered communities along Ecuador's coast are a testament to that. But was the annihilation of sodomites ever the church's ultimate objective? After all, as Foucault's (1988, 1994) work so explicitly maintains, deviants are essential if we are interested in normalizing any form of social or sexual behavior. I would suggest that more subtle forms of domination were being instituted during the colony, forms in which both pre-Hispanic and Spanish religious beliefs were equally captured. Both the church and the Indian communities could be seen as intersections within greater webs of hegemonic constraints. These constraints are still represented by the "moral debate" over sexuality in Latin America, what Roseberry (1994) and Thompson (1978) refer to as the "field of force" that is inherent in the contemporary constitution of Latino identity.

This existential debate about Latin American sexuality is also suggested by a myriad of racial, class, and national undertones. The contemporary formulations of Guayaquil's Indian past, with its specific sexual depiction, are highly indebted to both actual descriptions in and the religious tone, morality, and sentiments of the ethnohistorical accounts. The city's dismissal of any public reference to homosexuality speaks to the systematic production by Spain and the church of a sexual discourse devoid of nonheterosexual elements. In this light, the officialization of homophobic historical interpretations is implicitly undertaken in the reification of a regional way of being (*regionalismo*) and class dynamics that marked the city's portrayal of Europe as the civilizing cultural center.

Thus, it is not surprising that the *enchaquirados* have escaped historical notice, because, in the eyes of official historiography, they really did not exist. Julio Estrada's discussion of Cieza de León's presence in the American territory, for example, systematically excludes every mention of homosexuality or sodomy in Cieza's texts, even though they are quoted in the notes (Estrada Ycaza 1987: 243). Estrada even argues against the existence of these "unmentioned" sins by blaming Cieza de León and other chroniclers for attributing unspeakable acts to Indian communities that failed to fit within their agenda. Estrada thus accuses the chroniclers of doing what he is doing in his text, and what thereby falls into the inescapable dilemma of any consciously committed historian (Alonso 1988).

Julio Estrada's historical analysis is also key because it expresses the class and racial dynamics inherent in Guayaquil's representation of its past. His membership in one of the city's most traditional elite families and his role as head of the Historical Archive of Guayas for years indicates the intersection of class and racial interests in the production of the city's history. This intersection is not so much the result of an explicit program of domination by the white/mestizo elite as it is a more disputed regional articulation of a racial and national discourse initially expounded by the first European migrants to the area. It is this particular racializing and nationalistic program that has been consistently implemented and dynamically normalized by generations of Guayaquileños.

At the same time, this hegemonic discourse has inherent national sexual and gendered patterns that have been normalized in the last five centuries. Even when other historians, like Emilio Estrada (1958) and Jorge Marcos (1986a), mention a disturbing homosexual existence, this counter-hegemonic description has not been able to bring into question the reigning heteronormative discourse. It is regionalism's civilizing behavior and good manners (*buenas costumbres*) that constrain and contribute to a national history without any significant positive homosexual images.

The transgendered community has not suffered from this heteronormative existence as much as it has actively been produced and engaged by it in Guayaquil. In this sense, gendered Ecuadorians are active in the demise of their transgendered identity and, through this repression, constitute themselves as a historical subject with the voice and authority to represent themselves, the city, and the historical legacy of the *enchaquirados* (see Butler 1997a, 1997b). It is through this transgendered submission that historical agency is afforded, allowing an alternative interpretation of the *enchaquirados*' legacy and historical representation.

The discussion of the *enchaquirados* and sexual stories and jokes at Cochasquí illustrates two things. The first and most obvious element is the complexity of gender/sexual, class, and racial constructs and the impossibility of treating them as independent variables. These sociopersonal variables are essential elements of the nation-state and, as such, are implicated in the relevant historical discourses surrounding the nation and the construction of a national identity. The second and most important point is how different pre-Hispanic discourses construct particular forms, alternative or not, of sexual/racial deployment and, in doing so, contribute to the nation's normalizing discourse. However, even though at times these different discourses achieve alternative practices of the gendered and racial discourse, they have relatively little power over the final outcome or impact. As I have pointed out, the contradiction between alternative constructions of hegemonic production is essential in the constitution of all national histories. This is a problem I turn to again in the Conclusion. It is also for this reason that I believe Foucault's (homo)sexual inquiry helps investigate the nation's hegemonic production and supersedes but does not deny Marx's class analysis. This is also why I believe situating Ecuador "between Foucault and a naked man" further contributes and enhances Adoum's (1976) initial assessment of national hegemonic production in Ecuador.

FIVE

ALTERNATIVE HISTORIES
The Indian Movement's
Encounter with Hegemony

Our political priority is to decolonize history.

—LUIS MALDONADO (1992)

THE CONTEXT FOR ALTERNATIVE
GLOBALIZATIONS: THE NATIONAL POLITICS
OF AN ALTERNATIVE INDIAN PAST

Beginning in the 1970s the indigenous peoples of many Latin American countries began to engage in a new level of discourse that demanded a shift in the conceptualization of traditional Indian identity and offered a more self-critical definition of themselves (Varese and Kearney 1995). This movement is referred to as *"indianismo"* (Indianism) to differentiate it from the *"indigenismo"* (indigenism) ideology of earlier decades. The Indianist trend was related to globalization processes affecting the world in general, particularly what Escobar (1995) calls the postdevelopmental phase of history. Postdevelopment economies are based on flexible manufacturing and service industries organized on a global scale to take advantage of the most competitive sources of labor and markets. Not surprisingly, workers in these economies receive low wages, no benefits, and no job security—all factors which contribute to a growing informal economy.

Transnational corporations that make the international arena their economic playground are a key component of postdevelopment economies. They retrieve raw materials and labor from Third World nations, the least-explored regions of the world. It was precisely these marginalized regions into which the indigenous populations were pushed during the initial development period of the 1950s and the 1960s. This new transnational influx into regions like the Amazon made many indigenous groups into "development refugees." With nowhere to retreat, indigenous groups were more willing than ever to go on the offensive and assert their rights. The lack of options led to the founding of the Federación Shuar in the Ecuadorian Amazon, one of the first locally organized groups in the country and on the continent (Becker 1992; Maiguashca 1992; Selverston 1994).

Transnational corporations are highly influential in the modern economies of Latin America, but they are not the only transnational characteristics present. For instance, many indigenous populations do not live in a single nation-state, but, rather, occupy regions that crosscut two or more countries. The globalization process and the new forms of postmodern capitalism have also produced a long-term migration of Indians into urban centers in their native countries or major industrialized nations like the United States. Even in the United States, more Native Americans live in cities than on the reservation.

Today, the Indian's main antagonist is transnational forces outside the control of the national government. This has forced many indigenous groups to work with First World transnational sectors. These sectors are also responding to similar economic conditions in their own countries and benefit from transnational alliances with groups from around the world. The two most important transnational groups for indigenous populations are environmentalists and human rights organizations. These two international spheres have greatly strengthened the continental ties of the indigenous movements (Maiguashca 1992).

Flexible capital, growth of the informal economy, transnational corporations, and the internationalization of social movements have contributed to the reworking of indigenous identities beyond any traditional or strictly modern categorization. As Varese and Kearney (1995: 219) point out, Indian organizations like the CONAIE, which "were formerly marginalized are now actively engaged in establishing a transnational civil society in an effort to bypass state mediation and to situate themselves in a global civil society while maintaining strong ethnic, cultural, and local loyalties that contest their own nation-state authority and hegemony."

In Ecuador, the June 1990 Indian uprising initiated the national redefinition of the position of the Indian as being in direct conflict with the Ecuadorian state. It brought to the forefront strong demands in many areas, such as land, education, and productive strategies, and ultimately questioned the authority of the state to decide the future of the Indian communities. The uprising also brought into question the uneven distribution of wealth and proposed ways to construct a more democratic and pluralistic society (CONAIE 1989, 1997).

This "alternative" national history is provided by the single most powerful social movement in Ecuador today and largely represented by the Confederación Nacional de Indígenas del Ecuador. The CONAIE has been able to consolidate the collective grievances of the majority of the Indian community. These grievances range from land claims to constitutional amendments. I am mainly interested in the CONAIE's reading of the pre-Hispanic past, which legitimizes its struggle and has contributed to its becoming a viable political force.

The CONAIE's rendering of a national past is always narrated in the first person (1989: 19): "A diverse group of our communities have lived on the American continent for thousands of years, with different forms of economic, social, political, religious, and cultural organization. Some of us integrated this historical process until we formed complex socio-political systems such as the state. Such is the case of the Mayas, Aztecs, and Incas." The CONAIE sees family and reciprocal relations as the most essential form of social organization. For them, even though there was a level of social differentiation during the time of the Incas, this distinction was never pronounced enough to create a social class. The consolidation of the Inca Empire lasted for about a century (the 1400s) and was interrupted by the Spanish conquest. The Incas' presence was most strongly defined in the southern and central Andean regions, with some presence on the coast and none in the Amazon (CONAIE 1989: 20).

The Incas do not represent a break from the traditional Andean way of life in the eyes of the CONAIE, since they were organized along an agrarian form of production. The Incas also contributed to the introduction of better technology for the harvesting of maize: "The great range of productivity reached by the Inca state was a direct result of knowledge of the region and environment, level of technological development, and the ability to organize the work force for production" (CONAIE 1989: 20). They also respected the local gods and *huacas* (mountain deities) while at the same time extending the existing worship of the sun to the state level. The Incas also introduced the forced resettlement of population (*mitimaes*), which contributed enormously to the reconfiguration of the Indian communities (CONAIE 1989: 21).

The Inca presence in the national territory was brutally interrupted by the Spanish conquest: "The Spanish invasion started in 1492 with the presence of adventurers and colonizers who dedicated themselves to the looting and robbery of the land from the very beginning. In this way, the economic and political domination of our peoples started with the most inhumane forms of exploitation and repression in the name of the Spanish crown and church" (CONAIE 1989: 21). The CONAIE's alternative to the official history found in textbooks is striking for both its benevolent portrayal of the Inca occupation and the understanding of Velasco's Kingdom of Quito as an outright fallacy (Pakari 1994).

The CONAIE's two most important counter-hegemonic claims are its demand for territorial self-determination for each Indian nationality and for a multinational state. The demand for territorial self-determination relates to both an understanding of the land—nationalism—and economic development. As Karakras (1990: 5, 20) explains: "We are peoples, we are nationalities, we have our own national processes. . . . The Indian peoples are interested in making the proclamation of autodetermination a reality and in taking their historical destiny into our own hands."

The land is seen as an integral part of Indian culture and essential for constructing an independent livelihood, just as a mother is essential for the nurturing of her children. This is why the CONAIE presents its claim for the land as an integral part of its demands and reaffirms that the land "is the indispensable condition for life, for the existence of a people and its development. Without this basic element, it is impossible to have the conditions to educate a child, to be in good health, and to reproduce our culture" (Macas 1991: 10–11).

In contrast, the present Ecuadorian state strives to continue its century-long project of constructing a single homogeneous Ecuadorian nationality and to locate all the nation's natural and commercial resources under a central authority that will oversee its development. The Indian proposal is aimed at saving native lands, customs, and environments from outside exploitation, including by the state. It in no way shares the dominant view of capitalist production as the way to prosperity; rather, it sees it as further contributing to the destruction of indigenous land and culture. The CONAIE believes that only communal and autonomous self-government will help each national group and, therefore, the state, improve local conditions (CONAIE 1989).

The CONAIE's demand for a multinational state would entail constitutional changes. According to the CONAIE, this is necessary because each Indian community is a nationality in its own right, with its own culture, heritage, traditions, and language. Constitutional reform would benefit not only the Indian nationalities, but also other oppressed groups, like Afro-Ecuadorians, who would gain from a more pluricultural and democratic state apparatus (CDDH 1996; CONAIE 1989, 1997). The CONAIE proposal is changed from previous Indian stances because it recognizes the reality of the Indian nationalities caught within the Ecuadorian nation-state. It also recognizes the complex makeup of the country and the presence of other ethnic and racial groups. In contrast to its earlier positions, it now appropriates Western concepts to serve Indian interests (Ramón Valarezo 1992). A multinational state also inherently speaks to the right of each nationality to autonomous self-determination (CONAIE 1989, 1997). Such self-determination is understood as permitting legal control over one's own society within the structure of a single, more representative, and democratic state, "that is, you can be of a different nationality but belong to the same state" (Karakras 1990: 23).

Both of the CONAIE's main demands are potentially counter-hegemonic, and it is clear that the state is striving to neutralize each of these radical changes. The National Assembly has reworked the Constitution to present Ecuador as a multicultural state. However, never addressed is the enormous reticence to give up the economic and political power that such wording implies.

THE INDIAN MOVEMENT'S ALTERNATIVE HISTORY: POSTCOLONIAL INDIAN HISTORICITY

The Indian has been a pervasive theme in all national debates (Malo González 1988), in literature (de la Cuadra 1973; León Mera 1989), the social sciences (Jaramillo Alvarado 1988, 1993; Santiana 1966), policy discussion (Garcés 1933; also see Guerrero 1991), and missionary work. The "Indian problem," or, rather, the Indian as a problem, has a tradition as long as the Ecuadorian imagination and in the social entities, for example, the Real Audiencia de Quito and Gran Colombia, that inform this imagination. Politicians (Ayala Mora et al. 1992), social scientists (Santiana 1966), and writers (Icaza 1936, 1981, 1983, 1993; León Mera 1989) have portrayed the Indian as a problem for the country's development. The constitution proposed by Simón Bolívar for the emerging republic of Gran Colombia (a short-lived republican experiment joining Ecuador, Venezuela, and Colombia as a single country) portrayed the Indians as a hindrance to the modernization of the nation, and mechanisms for their "unindianization" were proposed. Later so-

cial research only refined this ethnocentric position by proposing benevolent ways of incorporating the Indian into the national community,
thereby giving way to the indigenism ideology.

Indigenism was a continental movement by whites/mestizos who
blamed the state for the Indians' plight, but saw no solution other than
their incorporation into the national ideal (Icaza 1993). It is only as a result of direct Indian involvement in their political future, that is, Indianism, that a new alternative has been offered to the Indian problem. This
solution presents the nation and the state, rather than the Indian communities, as the problem (CONAIE 1989). The 1990 Indian uprising in Ecuador and national organizations such as the Organización de Pueblos
Indígenas de Pastaza (Organization of Indigenous Nationalities of Pastaza, OPIP), the Confederación de Nacionalidades Indígenas del Ama-
zonas Ecuatoriano (Confederation of the Indigenous Nationalities of the
Ecuadorian Amazon, CONFENAIE), the CONAIE, and Pachakutik
Nuevo País crystallized the Indian legacy. Indigenous political organizing finally made it evident to the rest of the white/mestizo nation that a
different and more active Indian understanding of their own existence
was present.

It is this understanding of the Indian reality, existence, and historical
legacy that I shall discuss as an alternative national history that questions what has traditionally been assumed to be "Ecuadorian" history.
This alternative history is so rich that I shall limit myself to the basic
structure of the alternative reading and its own understanding of its relationship with the pre-Hispanic past.

From the very beginning, the Indian debates (known as Indianism)
dealt with the essential role of history in supporting the power dynamics inherent in any discussion of the Indian community (Karakras 1990;
Macas 1992). This uneven power dynamic is still apparent in the racist and socioeconomically exploitative social relationships between the
state, the major landholders (*latifundistas*), and the Indian communities
(Centro de Estudios y de Difusión Social [Center for Social Study and
Dissemination, CEDIS] 1992). For Maldonado (1992: 152) this means
that "the manipulation and utilization of history started with the European invasion of our continent; that is why the history we know is the
written history, thought of and conceived to protect the interests of
the conquerors and the contemporary dominant classes. The history of
the Indian peoples, of the oppressed peoples, has been hidden, denied,
or presented as acts of vandalism or violence."

There is still very little understanding of the exploitative racial categories created and utilized to dominate both the Indian population—in-

digenous to the continent—and the African population—brought to the continent at the end of the colonial and in the early republican periods. The inhumane conditions under which both populations were forced to live have been explicitly described in fiction (Gallegos Lara, Aguilera Mata, and Gil Gilbert 1970; Icaza 1993), but only rarely in analytical ethnographies and social texts. Extraordinary exceptions are Guerrero's (1991) and Muratorio's (1994) work on the complex production of imagined ethnic and racial categories. There is a pressing need to better understand the social relationships which determined how the nation was to develop after the colonial period. Thus, the "decolonization of history," that is, a more authentic reading of the past, is of utmost urgency in sustaining the new debates and in supporting the territorial and multinationalistic claims of the Indian communities against the powerful nation-state. The nation-state is understood as a racially oppressive entity comprising an elite minority of whites/mestizos and serving their interests to the detriment of those of Indian groups and other minorities that make up the Ecuadorian nation (CONAIE 1997, 1998). This new reading of history to present a nation of racial equality has two major elements.

The first element is a totally new understanding of the concept of history which demands the questioning and, ultimately, the denouncing of history as only a written reality. Like many other postcolonial critiques (e.g., Mamani Condori 1989), this alternative history maintains that the written word, rather than possessing any inherent historical validity, is an oppressive tool used first by the European colonizers and later by the white/mestizo rulers of the Ecuadorian nation-state to conquer, repress, and undermine the Indian and all other minority communities (Allauca 1993). This understanding of the colonial underpinnings of the historical enterprise provides a new way of seeing or relating to what has traditionally been out of the Indians' reach: history itself. This new postcolonial understanding of history has also made it viable for the Indian communities to be incorporated into their own debates, not as passive policy and research objects, but as full historical subjects (CONAIE 1989; Macas 1991). It has also opened a route for incorporating a millennial oral heritage which has been denied any historical authority (see, e.g., Ayala Mora 1983). This new social reality allows the newly founded (in 1990) Academia de las Lenguas Quichua-Castellano to say: "We know about the history of the Indian culture through conversation between parents and children, from our elders, from our ancestors and from the life of the Indian himself, in relation to Mother Nature [the cosmos]). . . . The Indian, without needing letters or writing, knew how to read the elements of Mother Nature and knew that the sun, earth, moon, stars, clouds, water, rain, animals, plants are useful to the life of the Indian" (1993: 11, 18).

It is this particular reality that is emphasized in the many *testimonios* (oral accounts) that have appeared in the last two decades as a result of social struggles and nationwide contests promoted by the different Indian organizations (CEDIS 1992; CONAIE 1988a, 1988b; Federación Indígena Pichincha Runacunapac Riccharimui 1993). This is what José María Allauca is referring to when he writes (1993: 42): "The Indian people do know how to face any problem. There is a history; it just isn't written." He continues (1993: 59): "For example, in what book are you studying in what year the lands that belonged to the Indians passed to the hands of the rich? They memorize the heroes of Ecuador's independence, and the kids are all happy remembering those foreign heroes. Where has the Indian found his independence?"

It is at this juncture that the distinction between the official history and an alternative is made. The alternative history, unlike the official concern with the dates and names of national heroes, is interested in the dialectical process of understanding reality (Allauca 1993: 5): "Those phrases permit us to glimpse the conscience of the people, that their history is different from the official 'history,' that history that privileges dates, places, names instead of trying to understand society's situation in its totality, the deep cause of the historical facts."

It is in this sense that no "true" Indian history has been written. Most of the written accounts to date come from an outside perspective to talk "about" and not "of" the Indian experience (Academia de las Lenguas Quichua-Castellano 1993: 11): "The native population's [Indian] history has not been written; if somebody has written something, it is not complete, it is not exact." Therefore, all claims about a written Indian history could only be a white/mestizo lie promulgated to appropriate the Indian experience and legitimize their oppression. What is presented as Indian history is "many times the history of our own enemies. They never tell the truth" (Allauca 1993: 59).

The second major element in this alternative history is the political dynamics present in its invention. If history is not the simple repetition of homogeneous elements and entities, then its elaboration must also be dramatically different. History no longer entails only an academic pursuit; rather, it is an essential enterprise in the struggle for freedom in which the movement is engaged (CONAIE 1989; Pakari 1994). History is the struggle itself, a constant struggle, untiring and unending, for the last five hundred years, a struggle based on history itself: "The historical continuity of the Indian communities is based on the permanence of their economic, political, cultural, and social organization. These forms of social organization have survived during these five centuries of oppression though varied forms of resistance, struggle, and adaptation to the different historical processes that have contributed to making the original inhabitants of this continent into contemporary historical and political entities (Maldonado 1992: 152).

Their social struggle includes every form of resistance, uprising, and territorial dispute that the Indians have experienced in five centuries of domination: massive uprisings (in 1990), marches (in 1994), and the formation of national organizations, including a political party, Pachakutik Nuevo País. History is made, not passively experienced. And it is this very understanding of the wide implications of the Indians' struggle which demands a reinterpretation, a rereading of accepted and assumed pre-Hispanic Indian figures like Atahualpa, and a discovery of negated, hidden, forgotten, or erased figures like Dolores Cuacuango (Mullo 1993).

By no means are these struggles the only or the best representatives of an Indian alternative history in the making; I have selected them because they are, without doubt, the best publicized and those which have had the greatest effect on other national communities.

HISTORY AS STRUGGLE: INDIAN ORGANIZING AND NATIONAL UPRISINGS

The conquest has not ended. It continues to the present.

—Macas 1991: 5

The Indian uprising of June, 1990, was a demonstration of that awakening and of saying, "Enough!" to the abuse, to the ethnocide, to the lies, to the discrimination.

—Mullo 1993: 31

At the start of the conquest, the Andean region enjoyed great ethnic diversity adapted to three major ecological environments: the coast, the highlands, and the Amazon. These different groups represented a high degree of sociopolitical complexity, ranging from nomadic foragers to complex agricultural communities affiliated with a centralized Inca state (Bruhns 1994; Patterson 1991). The rapid transculturation among the coastal groups made it difficult for these communities to align themselves with any type of ethnic struggle. Today, there are very few self-identified

Indian coastal groups; therefore, the coast is the least-influential region in the Confederación Nacional de Indígenas del Ecuador as a whole (CONAIE 1989).

The Amazon escaped direct colonization from both the Incas and the Europeans for several centuries, although the indirect impact of European epidemics and goods contributed to a rapid depopulation of the area. It is only in the last century, and mainly because of oil and land exploitation, that the future of the Amazonian groups has been directly challenged (Maiguashca 1992).

The process in the highlands was slightly different. On the one hand, there was direct transculturation; on the other, there were coexisting and complex power relations among Spaniards, *criollos,* and Indians. It was mainly through the institutionalization of forced labor, within the setting of the large landholding or hacienda, that conditions and identities were transformed (Almeida et al. 1992; Ayala Mora 1991; Ayala Mora et al. 1992). During both colonial and republican times, Indian uprisings in the highlands occurred in direct response to the uneven distribution and exploitation of land. It is in this same context that the modern struggles for land have occurred (*Nacionalidades Indias* 1994).

During the 1930s these struggles for land were further exacerbated by social movements supported by both the Communist and the Socialist Parties, bringing into play issues of class, worker's rights, union organizing, proletarianization, and cooperatives. It is in this context that organizations such as the Federación Ecuatoriana de Indios (Ecuadorian Indian Federation, FEI) was born, which, however, glossed over the ethnic component of their struggle (Mullo 1993; Tamba 1993). Dolores Cuacuango, an important Indian leader, was the first secretary general of the organization and, along with Luisa Gómez de la Torre and Floresmilo Tamba, organized the first Indian schools to have Indian teachers teaching in Quechua (Tamba 1993: 29).

In 1964 the agrarian reform was put into place as a direct result of the modernization of the Ecuadorian state. The reform aimed at a more democratic distribution of the land. During this time, the leftist influence in the Indian movement decreased, as did the role of the FEI (Ayala Mora 1985b; CONAIE 1989; Hurtado 1981). The Catholic Church became a central player by supporting the Indians' struggle through the creation of the Federación Nacional de Organizaciones Campesinas (National Federation of Campesino Organizations, FENOC), although the ethnic dimension of the struggle for land was again overlooked. The FENOC was closely associated with agrarian reform, and when the latter failed to meet its initial goals, the influence of the organization rapidly dwindled (CONAIE 1989).

By 1972, months before a second agrarian reform was instituted, a new Indian organization appeared, ECUARUNARI, or "the awakening of the Ecuadorian Indian." This group was also influenced by the church's most "progressive" members. It therefore had greater freedom to incorporate ethnic dimensions and slowly to evolve from making strictly economic demands to broader political and cultural critiques of both society and the state (CONAIE 1989).

In 1980 the CONFENAIE drew on resources from both the missionary sector of the Catholic Church and the ecology movement. The Amazonian groups faced totally different problems from those encountered by the highland groups. Increasing oil exploration and the redistribution of land as a result of agrarian reforms and colonizing projects forced these groups to flee farther into the jungle. Their marginalization, pollution, and the destruction of their land as a result of aggressive agricultural and oil production contributed to their rapid politicization (Maiguashca 1992).

In the 1980s ECUARUNARI and CONFENAIE joined to create the Coordinación de las Nacionalidades Indígenas del Ecuador (Central Committee of Indian Nationalities of Ecuador, CONACNIE). In 1986 it became the CONAIE (CONAIE 1989).

The 1990 uprising was a strategic use of force approved by the CONAIE in April of that year to protest the slow pace of the talks on a new agrarian law and to recognize the different Indian nationalities. The provinces of the central highlands and the Amazon were the strongest supporters of the uprising.

On May 28 the colonial church of Santo Domingo in Quito was taken by the Coordinadora Popular (a grassroots organization loosely associated with the CONAIE), which demanded direct talks with the government to force the redistribution of land. The government refused to negotiate, and the eighty people in the church started a hunger strike. On June 4 Indian communities from all over the country started a week-long strike, blocking main roads and the distribution of agricultural products. The country was stunned by the magnitude of the protest and the assertive role that Indians assumed in it. During this week roads were blocked; haciendas were occupied; military personnel, hacienda owners, and police officers were taken hostage; water supplies were cut; and many local authorities were put on "trial" (several landowners were bathed naked in public to symbolically cleanse them of their social sins).

By midweek Rodrigo Borja's Social Democrat government was willing to negotiate (Comisión por la Defensa de los Derechos Humanos [Steering Committee for Human Rights, CDDH] 1996; *KIPU* 1991, 1995; Moreno Yáñez and Figueroa 1992; *Nacionalidades Indias* 1993, 1994, 1996; *Punto de Vista* 1990).

Since the CONAIE's initial uprising in June 1990, the organization has loomed large in the national political arena. The movement's participation in the political events of 1997 was crucial in forming a wide coalition of political parties and social movements to oust the government of Pres. Abdalá Bucaram. The CONAIE's participation was politically complex, since Bucaram had won the presidency with support from impoverished Indian communities and had even created the Ministerio de Asuntos Indígenas (Ministry of Indian Affairs) to support Indian dissidents. However, the movement managed to mount strong opposition without estranging its own grassroots communities or further antagonizing oppositional Indian organizations, for example, the Movimiento Evangélico de Indígenas del Ecuador (Evangelical Indian Movement of Ecuador). More important, Pachakutik Nuevo País and the movement itself figured prominently, as members such as Nina Pakari were elected to the Asamblea Nacional Constituyente (National Assembly) (1997–1998) after Bucaram's departure.

In 2000–2001 the CONAIE moved even more to the forefront as it led the popular resistance to the government's economic policies. The movement was no longer limited to the "traditional" Indian issues of land and sovereignty, but became the government's most dreaded political adversary. In the year 2000 the Indian movement occupied Ecuador's Congress and formed a coalition with its fiercest rival, the military, to oust Pres. Jamil Mahuad. The movement and the military stated that this political maneuver was warranted by the overwhelming popular demand for Mahuad's resignation. Both groups were adamant that Mahuad's vice president, Gustavo Noboa Bejarano, should assume the presidency. President Mahuad's popularity had plummeted when, at the suggestion of the IMF and the World Bank, he removed the sucre from circulation and replaced it with the U.S. dollar. The financial and political impact of this economic policy on the population again propelled the Indian movement to center stage and made the movement the most logical national representative of Ecuador's impoverished citizens.

The movement's representation of Ecuador's poor was extended when in 2001 the Indian movement once again called for a national strike by all Indian communities against the new president, Gustavo Noboa Bejarano. This strike once again centered on the government's economic policies, which were a continuing part of the IMF's and World Bank's structural-adjustment program. The last week of January saw the capital, Quito, occupied by over ten thousand Indians, most of whom were housed in the Catholic (Salesian) Polytechnic University. After days of violent confrontations, which resulted in the deaths of an estimated four demonstrators, including a fourteen-year-old, and brief imprisonment of the head of the CONAIE, the government conceded to the movement's demand (just as the Borja government had done in 1990).

This time the government retracted the economic policies; agreed to freeze gasoline prices for at least one year; agreed to continue subsidizing cooking gas (a de facto price cut of 20 percent); agreed to subsidize bus fares for children, students, and senior citizens; and removed a 3 percent increase in value-added taxes (Solano 2001).

The IMF was also a focus of protest from a variety of women's groups, which occupied the organization's offices in Quito in support of the Indian movement's demands for rejection of the structural-adjustment program (Acción Ecológica 2001; Pinto 2001). The Indian movement's political power was further evidenced when a national strike called by the leftist workers' union, peasant, and student organizations failed to have a major impact until supported by Indian leaders who had already established direct links with Noboa's government (Taxin 2001).

In this changing political picture, Ecuador had four presidents from 1997 to 2001. The Indian movement, far beyond its initial constituency, continued to figure prominently as the most cohesive national organization, not only in opposition to state policies, but also as representative of a diverse group of disenfranchised citizens. In the political struggle, Indians have distinguished themselves as a remarkable foe of the white/mestizo and Western-inspired Ecuadorian governments, in part because of their unique understanding of organizational strategy and history. The Indian movement's struggle places Indians in the position of protagonist in the making of their own history, after five centuries of political repression, social exclusion, and racial discrimination.

RECLAIMING THE PAST: WRITING AN INDIAN HISTORY

Our art, our science, our wisdom are the weapons, the flowers, the fruit that still rest in the thoughts of our *yayas* [ancestors]. In spite of the West's barbarism and now the neocolonialism, imperialism, they have not been able to destroy us completely. They will not be able to destroy us because we are the product of a millenary culture, because before they were our ancestors they were our *yayas,* our *jatucus,* our *taytas* [fathers], our *mamas* [mothers]. We were first. We were always.

—Nina Pakari, in Malo González 1988: 87–88

The new phase of the Indian struggle has allowed the Indian to gain a fresh understanding of the pre-Hispanic past that the Ecuadorian nation-state claims as its own. Indians no longer see themselves as outside of history, but, rather, as full historical figures who, although silenced, have been able to regain conscious participation in history (CDDH 1996; Macas 1991). This knowledge is what allows the CONAIE to write and narrate the pre-Hispanic past firsthand. It is no longer "them," or even their ancestors, but "we," "ourselves," "our" communities that participated in the indigenous social process of the Americas and that were decimated by the Spanish and colonial encounters (CONAIE 1989: 19, emphasis added): "In the territory that corresponds to present-day Ecuador, *we* were living as multiple societies that had different degrees of socio-economic and political complexity (*behetrías,* chiefdoms, etc.). *We* were not isolated communities, *we* were related in terms of commercial, cultural, and kin exchange, etc. *We* maintained contact between the highlands, the coast, and the Amazon and, in other cases, with others very far away, like communities in Mexico to the north, and Chile to the south."

But writing an Indian history is far from an easy task. Indian history has been silenced for over five centuries (Centro de Educación Popular [CEDEP] 1986). It has been erased, changed, and mutilated in every way possible to alter discursive elements and present the Indian in a negative light. This alteration was first carried out by the white Spaniards and later by the white/mestizo Ecuadorians (Yupanki 1992: 163): "However, the false historiography of our country has hidden all these historical facts because to recognize them would be threatening to society's interest, which oppresses and marginalizes us." History has been so distorted that even important Indian figures, for example, Rumiñahui and Atahualpa, have been subverted to support and represent the oppressive Ecuadorian nation (Maldonado 1992: 153): "The dominant classes have even appropriated or expropriated the history of our peoples, as in the case of Rumiñahui, recognized by the state and its ideology as the father of the Ecuadorian nation."

This ransacking of history takes away from the Indian past. The plunderers have the audacity to use these same stolen elements to legitimize the racist and repressive ideology of the nation-state. This historical genocide is what has forced Indians to reformulate the past in their own terms, to "straighten" history's distortions by proposing an alternative and therefore more realistic historical picture (Pakari 1994). This reformulation has two essential parts. Its first component is to reclaim everything Indian that has been usurped by the nation-state and reinterpret within the new native discourse (Macas 1991; Pakari 1994). The second charge demands the unearthing of the Indian past, which has been buried by the European and Ecuadorian elite to justify its political domination. This requires learning about traditionally hidden events and recognizing unknown figures' historical contributions (Tamba 1993).

These historical tasks are carried out by both individuals and organizations, although it is the CONAIE which has taken upon itself the task of representing the alternative history before the widest possible audience (CONAIE 1989). At the local level, there are conscious efforts to retell history in the simplest way possible for those who have been stripped of their past. Educational pamphlets use cartoonlike drawings to present an alternative picture of the past. In these simple narratives, the Spaniards and the dominant white/mestizo society are unequivocally presented as evil, as bringing torture, pain, havoc, and, ultimately, death to the Indians. The pamphlets also make it clear that the Indians have suffered not only physical injury, but also cultural harm, that the dominant groups have victimized them and then told their story in their own words and blamed the Indian for their own wrongdoing, shortcomings, and cruelty. The pamphlets, according to Indian representatives, are meant to narrate history truthfully and to rescue or regain that sense of self that has been stripped away through the theft of history (Centro de Documentación e Información de los Movimientos Sociales del Ecuador [Center for Documentation and Information on Ecuador's Social Movements, CEDIME] 1987; Campaña Continental 1990; Perugachi 1994).

Alternative Indian narratives also reconstruct the past by presenting it in a poetic way:

> The *ayllus* increased and formed the Tahuantinsuyu. The Tahuantinsuyu gave the royal strength that created and maintains us. Our father, Inti, is the sun and our mother, Allpa Mama, is the earth. We consider ourselves a solar race because our Inti both made us fertile and pushed us to building our towns and homes. The Allpa Mama gives us life, nutrients, cloth and shelter.
>
> —CONAIE 1988b: 6

The laws of the Tahuantinsuyu were AMA LLULLA, AMA QUILLA, AMA SHUA, and respect was given to the beautiful women.
— CONAIE 1988b: 6

The Indians, through these narratives, are able to present a vision of themselves that is more benevolent, caring, and understanding of their situation and plight. It allows them not only to see themselves in a different light, but also to understand the exploitative and oppressive condition in which they have been immersed most of their lives (Chela 1992: 49): "In that way, they took away from us the Inca Atahualpa, the Quipuc, the wise ones, the warriors, all who governed with the Inca. All that we had was taken away by the ones with nice eyes but black hearts like the devil. They still have not tired of killing us, abusing us, but even so, we continue to live, we still exist."

The CONAIE and its national leaders are the most instrumental in putting forward a new Indian history. They are most involved in dispelling ancient myths and replacing them with an authentic history (Pakari 1994: 58): "It hurts in the community, they don't know history . . . that the Caras, the Quitus, but the people don't know, it is painful."

The CONAIE's history presents a generalized first-person account of the Indian communities and the Inca presence in the territory that is now recognized as Ecuador. This history is transmitted to the Indian community mainly through educational pamphlets and magazines and to the national community via journals and conferences. This alternative history presents the ancient Indian polities as organizations based on the family, with no social differentiation or classes and with reciprocal relations as the organizing element. The Incas are seen in a very positive light. They are presented as establishing a system that ensured that everyone was taken care of. And even though the Incas used physical coercion to establish their own socioeconomic organizations, these associations are not viewed as completely foreign to Andean reality — a reality that changed drastically with the Spanish conquest and the exploitative relations established during the colonial period (CONAIE 1989: 20–22).

This renewed Indian consciousness of their struggle, their participation in national politics, and the narration of the past in their own words offer an alternative understanding of Ecuadorian history. It is a history that allows Indian leaders to proclaim that "the Indian people have retaken their cultural historical past, they who throughout history have suffered all types of exploitation and marginalization" (Churuchumbi 1993: 55).

The CONAIE offers the most radical critique of the Ecuadorian nation-state to date. Essential to its analysis is a retelling of national history in terms which incorporate an Indian past traditionally integrated into national readings (e.g., Velasco's account of the Kingdom of Quito) that have served to nullify that past's revolutionary potential. However, the CONAIE seems incapable of protecting itself from hegemonic tendencies that are slowly erasing and homogenizing important Indian differences and identities. In other words, it is in great danger of promoting what is today an alternative version, but, if successful, will become a new national hegemonic discourse (Muratorio 1998: 411). It is also interesting to note that Cochasquí, as well as many other archaeological sites, has so far not been actively included in this reclaiming of the ancient past, even though this has been a recurring theme for the movement, for example, in Cayambe's historical recovery of the pyramids of Puntiachil (*La Hora* 1993b).

THE INDIANS' ALTERNATIVE NATIONAL HISTORY

The narrative content of the alternative national history presented by the CONAIE and the Indian movement is quite different from the history told at Cochasquí, in the print media, and even in official textbooks. The narrative no longer takes place in a long lost past, but in the present, a mythical present constructed from the pre-Hispanic past. The characters are not ancient Indian communities, but the contemporary Indian community, which has become the central character in this alternative national history.

One of the main elements in this alternative narrative is the Indian struggle. The struggle takes center stage and inherits mythical qualities because of its length. It must continue until the exploitation stops or, as the movement's official slogan put it in 1992, "Ni una hacienda más" (Until there is not a single hacienda left). Thus, the construction of an alternative history is part of this struggle. It is a necessary step in the groups' liberation. The struggle itself is both a liberating mechanism and the content of the narrative.

Other narrative elements are the *testimonios*, which project and support the historical struggle. Although each *testimonio* tackles different aspects of the struggle, they all represent part of the larger struggle: *Rafael Perugachi* addresses racial exploitation (1994); *Mi comuna* deals with labor organizing (in CEDEP 1986); and *Entrevista a los ancestros* tackles the issue of religious freedom (in CEDIS 1992). The main characters in all of these *testimonios* are, to some degree, the authors themselves, who speak for the silent majority, which has been oppressed and killed for centuries. The *testimonio* author as a character slowly fades into the backdrop of millenary voices that now speak about an ancient past—not the official, mythical past, but a past that is engulfed by and resurrected within the surviving Indian communities (CEDEP 1986).

At this point, the past reappears as a central element in the narrative content of this alternative history. The CONAIE takes the officializing role of validating the alternative history and, in so doing, seeks to represent the multiple voices and *testimonios* expressed as part of this national narrative. This alternative national history is now being told from the Indians' point of view and is heard for the first time since the inception of the Ecuadorian nation-state.

It is also at this point that the leaders of the CONAIE become central characters in this alternative history. They represent the struggle to reconstruct the past as it actually happened, and not as it has been distorted and narrated by the people who killed history's Indian protagonists. It is this political objective and their ethnic authenticity that allows them to take a first-person approach to the pre-Hispanic past and make it theirs (CONAIE 1989). The Indian communities and the CONAIE leaders have learned the hard way that the past is never about the past. Rather, it is about the present in which they are caught, and they must strive to reconstruct it for their survival.

The Indian movement's understanding of Ecuadorian history is also "alternative" because of its structural or stylistic quality. Many Indian writers are very clear about the need to debunk the official history, especially the one furnished by textbooks and schools. Unlike the official, regimented history, which is concerned with names and dates, the Indians' history is concerned with processes and hidden meaning. Their alternative history is interested in understanding and defining the oppression that has placed the Indian and many other oppressed communities in a subservient position (CEDEP 1986).

The inherent logic of its historical objectives requires this subaltern discourse also to use another structure to express its narrative. Thus, the Indians' portrayal of history is not narrated in a linear fashion, with set names, characters, and plots; rather, it has a more dynamic structure. Its elements and interpretations are less determined by western models (see Wylie 1995), and its very structure is invented as its content is constructed. Instead, any elements that could contribute to decolonizing history are immediately assimilated into this symbiotic discourse. Political struggles, which can range from national uprisings (like the one in June 1990) to labor disputes to *testimonios* to rewritings of pre-Hispanic histories, are seen as essential and transparent elements of the narrative structure. Unlike the rigid description of Velasco's Kingdom of Quito in textbooks, the Indians' account of the past is presented in a freer, more casual style, permitting the incorporation of elements such as community and oral histories that otherwise would be lost and that traditionally have been excluded from official history. According to the CONAIE, this historical exclusion has served to oppress the Indian communities, but they are using these new narratives to struggle against that oppression.

The less-rigid structure and symbiotic nature of the alternative discourse, however, do not preclude constraints and limitations on the narrative. The fluidity of the alternative discourse does not mean anything goes; rather, it implies that the constraints are not the same as those on the official narrative. There is still a level of empirical constraint, and the alternative narrative is not designed to create a "fantastic" history so much as one that does not support the official version. Such a history could easily be dismissed, so the Indians use empirical facts and restructure them in light of new findings about their struggle. This is why Velasco's Kingdom of Quito is easily dismissed (Pakari 1994) and the Inca polity is a rich source of interpretation and meaning (CONAIE 1989).

The commitment to the struggle is another constraint, because the Indians' struggle helps define the structural framework. The alternative version of history, just like the official version, also has clear political objectives. This does not mean that the alternative version is tainted, because all histories (including the official one) work within evidentiary and political constraints (Wylie 1995). It also does not mean that anything will be rejected solely because it goes against the movement's interests; everything, negative elements included, will be interpreted in hopes of gaining a better understanding of the Indians' demise and oppression.

Finally, only Indians or other oppressed groups may contribute to the production of an alternative history. The nature of the struggle and the intimate relationship between political battles and the Indian communities dictates that only an Indian or somebody who racially, ethnically, or culturally identifies himself or herself as an Indian and is recognized as such can affect the alternative discourse. This is why the work of sympathetic scholars such as Galo Ramón Valarezo (1990, 1992) is viewed as supporting the alternative discourse, but is not considered essential to its fabrication. And this is why important ideologues of the movement, such as Nina Pakari, have decided to change their mestizo names and thus their identity to actively engage in the movement (Pakari 1994).

The alternative structure of Indian history is essential for reclaiming the forgotten past, especially as this past was not voluntarily forgotten, but brutally erased. The Indian movement, using a nonacademic style, is proposing a completely different version and understanding of history, one that it hopes will discover the Indians' "own history, a history that has been hidden and stripped away" (lyrics of a popular song from Victor Heredia's *Taki Ongoy*).

The forums used by the Indian movement are more varied and unorthodox than that used by the official version of history. Again, the utilization of different vehicles reflects the opposition represented and expressed by the Indian movement in its contested historical discourse. There is really no limit to or consensus about the media through which to construct a counter-hegemonic discourse. The instrument may vary from written materials to political activity at the local, regional, and national levels. However, the movement is also keenly aware of the role and impact of the media in thwarting or supporting its alternative vision. The movement has therefore tried to collect every bit of print that deals with Indian reality, present or past. Four times a year, the CONAIE publishes a collection, entitled *Kipu*, which includes every newspaper article published in the country during the quarter. The articles range from special segments on the movement's political marches to reports on autochthonous plants and resources. It also publishes special editions when the number of articles is too great, as was the case after the uprising of 1990 and the march of 1994 (*Kipu* 1991, 1995).

It is the CONAIE that assumes the responsibility of representing in written form the whole of the Indian movement. Through its written accounts and documents, it reinterprets national history (CONAIE 1989), the history of the struggle to organize (CONAIE 1988a, 1988b), and the political project that sustains the movement as a whole (CONAIE 1997). Through these writings, the CONAIE not only speaks for the movement, but also constructs a stable framework upon which Indian discourses can be elaborated. Just like the official history expounded in textbooks, the alternative discourse uses the written word to legitimize its content. Once it is written down, the alternative history becomes more difficult to challenge or discredit. The written word is a powerful tool in the Indian movement's effort to forward its version of the past. Individuals, communities, and regional or organizational representatives produce an enormous amount of written material. In addition, oral histories and political projects further the movement's objectives. All of these express different aspects of the alternative historical discourse, ranging from detailed and local elements to national political debates.

The Indian movement also relies on political activity to express its opposition to the state. Many of its political activities are quite ambitious, such as the nationwide marches. This large-scale political organizing involves complex logistical maneuvering, such as turning city parks into campsites for the marchers (*Kipu* 1995). Less-grand political activities include land struggles, labor strikes, and conflicts about environmental concerns. Pachakutik Nuevo País has also been able to muster a great deal of national support with the support of the CONAIE's leadership. The party has won disillusioned voters from the traditionally leftist political parties (the Frente Amplio de Izquierda and the Movimiento Popular Democrático), which failed to bring about the dramatic changes they promised and were negatively affected by the collapse of the Soviet Union. Since 1995 Pachakutik Nuevo País has become the third-largest political party in Congress; has backed the runner-up in a presidential election (a significant feat in a two-round election model); has become the fifth-largest party in the National Assembly, which was created to reform the Constitution and deal with the aftermath of former president Abdalá Bucaram's ouster in February of 1997; has participated in the coup that removed Pres. Jamil Mahuad from power; and has consistently questioned the IMF's structural-adjustment policies (Macas and Ramiro Miño 1997).

HEGEMONIC IMPLICATIONS OF ALTERNATIVE HISTORY

The alternative account of history proposed by the Indian movement is antagonistic. Its objective is to expose the fallacy in the official account of Ecuador's past and debunk it by proposing a new version. Interestingly enough, however, the Indians' challenge hides a hegemonic project similar to the one they are disputing. Their version contains an embryonic element that, by necessity, designates it as a hegemonic history much like the official version, but in a different context (Chatterjee 1986; Wylie 1995).

The Indian movement finds itself walking a political tightrope. One end is its strong opposition to the IMF's and the World Bank's structural-adjustment policies; the other end is its consistent support of the development project being funded and planned by the World Bank. The movement has not yet seriously addressed the contradiction inherent in its acceptance of the World Bank as both the cause of and the solution to the nation's economic woes. The movement continues to work within the bank's economic agenda without admitting that the badly needed development funds originate from the unequal globalization processes that limit and dominate the Third World's economic production.

At the same time, the Indian identity espoused by the movement is in itself partly a result of modern capitalist globalization processes. Only this political and economic reality could justify the Indian movement's being supported by foreign nongovernmental organizations (NGOs) and other First World institutions. This same "Westernization" of Indian identity makes the movement's relationship with its historical enemies, the Catholic Church and the military, much more understandable. After five hundred years of evangelization, the Indians have come full circle and are using the same religious institution that was initially implicated in their ethnocide and genocide throughout the continent.

It is this particular turn of events that allows Indians in Ecuador to rally around an ethnic identity that was the cause (or that was used as such) of their cultural and social demise. Quite significantly, Indians are now able to use their ethnic oppression as cultural capital to obtain funds, political recognition, and other resources from First World nations that were once involved in their cultural destruction. According to Stuart Hall (1997), this resurgence of local and international support of "native" ethnic movements is intimately related to new "old" forms of colonial domination and European discourses of cultural superiority. This repoliticization of the "other," far from being a simple model of ethnic liberation and democracy, relates to transformation of old political alliances between First and Third World nations.

To mistake the Indian movement as representing some pristine cultural authenticity (as the movement, for obvious reasons of economic and cultural survival, would have us do) is to disregard its dangerous underpinnings of capitalist transformation. In this sense, the Indian movement does not represent a more pristine form of cultural authenticity than that defended by other antagonistic groups, including those representing the state, but a modern "reconversion" (to use García-Canclini's [1992a, 1992b, 1993] word) of earlier social symbols and meanings. This reconversion is strongly indebted to Western values, which provide the new symbols and meanings that give the movement its raison d'être, both historically and politically. This reconversion occurs even though the movement, like the state, must insist that it represents an authentic (i.e., natural, pristine) historical struggle independent of "polluting" modern characteristics.

In this complex reality, the Indian movement is the most modern (or even the postmodern) signifier of Ecuador's contemporary political struggle—a struggle that is now also being fought beyond the country's borders. This global context makes the Indian movement's financial support and identity very fragile. If the CONAIE's counter-hegemonic demands are met (and this could occur only after a rearrangement of the global economic order), the movement would soon find itself with no more First World NGOs and development projects to fund it and, perhaps more dramatic, without a global cultural world in which Indians could positively translate or express their identity. It is instructive that it has taken Indian groups this long to find a cultural context that enables their political projects, since it is clear that uprisings and protests are not new.

Since a global economic reordering seems highly unlikely because the IMF, the World Bank, and the First World are not on their own going to invert current socioeconomic relationships, the Indian movement may have to face the inevitability of its own hegemonic reordering. Although the CONAIE consistently defines itself as a tool of greater democratization, it is likely that unequal conditions around the globe will force the co-optation of the organization into a hegemonic enterprise before the state experiences any kind of democratic dissolution. Few scholars, especially anthropologists, for obvious reasons related to their academic disciplines, have been willing to elaborate on the hegemonic constraints of the Indian project. If successful, Ecuador's Indians will finally remove themselves from exploitative conditions, but this will occur at the expense of some other group, perhaps the whites/mestizos, who are unlikely to give up their historically endowed privileges peacefully. History will be central in this struggle, and only the future will allow us to assess which version of the past will be hegemonically successful. The coastal whites/mestizos are the most intransigent in the battle to designate the Indians as worthy representatives of the modern country (*El Universo* 2001). The coastal white/mestizo ideological rhetoric (as expressed in newspaper editorials) is not surprising, since both groups realize that economic conditions pit them against each other as the only viable economic, cultural, and political solution to their fragile situation.

Economic conditions created by issues of race only deepen the hegemonic co-optation of the movement's cultural program. Muratorio (1998) notes how the CONAIE is beginning to constitute itself as a dominant community along Western notions of gender, language, ethnicity, and class. It is not surprising that, as she points out, the movement's leadership positions are mostly occupied by educated Indian men from the larger Quechua- and Spanish-speaking communities. Ironically, the movement's options are limited by both a more democratic global reordering, which would signal its demise, and by its national success, which would create its own form of political and gender domination. As Hall (1997), García Canclini (1993), and Foucault (1991) point out, capitalism and social discourse are reconfigured in quite powerful and truly unpredictable ways.

It might be instructive to highlight an uncharacteristic statement by Foucault that may elucidate the future of the Indian movement and the social agenda it will enable (1991: 173–174): "When I study the mechanisms of power, I try to analyze their specificity: nothing is more foreign to me than the idea of a 'Master' who imposes his own law. Rather than indicating the presence of a 'master,' I worry about comprehending the effective mechanisms of domination; and I do it so that those who are inserted in certain relations of power, who are implicated in them, might escape them through their actions of resistance and rebellion, might transform them in order not to be subjugated any longer." Only the decade between 2000 and 2010 will reveal the political outcome of the Indian movement's encounter with hegemony.

SIX

THE PRINT MEDIA'S CONTRIBUTION TO NATIONAL HISTORY

Who Owns the Past?

*Saint Biritute, how can you be here lying in this position,
abandoned, when we have an altar for you, to adore and treat
you as you deserve?*

— COMUNERO, IN *EL EXPRESO* (1993E)

The print media exert great influence on the composition of the national ethos. Particularly instructive is Anderson's (1983) discussion of the print media and education as central motors to the creation of a sense of cohesion and togetherness in many of the emerging Western European nations in the eighteenth and nineteenth centuries. Although Anderson's model is useful for understanding the development of the modern nation, there is still a significant amount to be learned by studying Third World and postcolonial contexts (Foster 1990; Fox 1990).

The role played by education and the print media in nation building highlights the class and race elements inherent in literacy campaigns and other state-sponsored activities related to literacy. Literacy in Ecuador is quite high—the highest in its history as a republic. There are two main reasons for this. The first is the ambitious literacy campaign (Plan de Alfabetización) instituted at the return of democratic rule to the country in the 1980s after a decade of military dictatorship. This intensive campaign strove to eradicate illiteracy, especially in rural and urban shantytowns, and was one of the many ambitious plans of the newly elected president, Jaime Roldós Aguilera (1979–1981). Even after his untimely and suspicious death in an airplane crash in the Ecuadorian Amazon, the literacy campaign was continued under his vice president, Osvaldo Hurtado Larrea (1981–1984).

Although highly unpopular, Hurtado stayed in office by shrewdly maneuvering political, military, and economic forces. He was therefore able to carry out many of his predecessor's proposals. The literacy campaign offered high school students an alternative to the obligatory senior thesis: a yearlong opportunity to teach adults to read and write. This was the driving force in reducing years of high illiteracy rates.

Literacy rates were also affected by the recognition of both Quechua and Spanish as Ecuador's national languages. Hurtado proposed this change, and Congress ratified it during his term. The decision to incorporate Quechua into the national fold affected the racial heritage of the Ecuadorian nation. A Quechua literacy campaign was initiated in the central and southern Andean provinces, which had a higher concentration of Indians. All of these measures meant that Quechua speakers were no longer officially treated as illiterates.

Newspapers in Ecuador are easily divided into coastal or highland. No single national newspaper can boast the largest readership in both regions. Although Ecuador comprises four large regions, including the Amazon rain forest and the Galápagos archipelago, the battle between the two largest regions—the coast and the highlands—has consistently fueled the country's political history (Deler 1994; Maiguashca 1994; Palomeque 1990, 1994; A. Taylor 1994). This political history has swung between a highland conservative landholding economy in the 1860s, a booming coastal liberal export model in the 1890s, the continuing neoliberal model of agro-exports from the coastal elite, to more centralized and socialist plans from highland groups.

El Universo and *El Comercio* are by far the largest and most important newspapers in the country, as well as the longest running. *El Universo* is the most popular newspaper in the coastal region and advertises itself as the most popular newspaper in the country. It was founded on September 16, 1921, by the late Ismael Pérez Pazmiño, one of the early pillars of journalism in the country and a renowned essayist in his own right. It is based in the port of Guayaquil, the country's largest city, and prints around 300,000 copies daily (Luis Cañarte, personal communication).

El Universo's two closest rivals on the coast are *El Telégrafo* and *El Expreso,* both of which are fairly new, having been around for only about two decades. Although *El Telégrafo* was founded almost a century ago, it ceased publication for two decades, until the late 1980s, when a staff of young urban professionals once again made it a viable enterprise.

The three coastal newspapers represent the most conservative economic forces in the country. Their editorial writers are active supporters of the neoliberal policies of the right-wing political parties, for example, the Partido Social Cristiano (PSC) and the Partido Roldosista Ecuatoriano (PRE). Of the three papers, *El Universo* enjoys the support of the most traditional and elite members of the coastal oligarchy. *El Telégrafo* is supported by the youngest members of the coastal elite, mainly young professionals from traditional families who have been educated in the United States or Europe and have returned to work and live in Ecuador.

In the highlands, *El Comercio* rivals *El Universo* in terms of national importance and, without a doubt, is the largest-selling newspaper in the region, particularly in Quito, where it is published. Its closest rival, *Hoy*, is a very young newspaper, founded in the early 1980s, after the military dictatorship. Both *El Comercio* and *Hoy* are significantly to the left of the coastal newspapers. *El Comercio* represents the traditional elite highland families; *Hoy* is produced by the younger generation of elite professionals. In many ways, these two newspapers re-create the tension between the two leading coastal newspapers.

Hoy is run by a staff of young urban professionals, writers, and social scientists who have broken their political ties with the right-wing elite and offer a more radical reporting of the national condition. *Hoy* is also the most popular leftist newspaper in the country and counts on a significant following among the left-leaning educated elite on the coast. It also has a greater following in the highlands, particularly in Quito, mainly due to traditionally more leftist politics in the capital and in the highlands in general. Many of the writers on *Hoy* are allied with left-of-center political forces in the country, for example, Izquierda Democrática, Democracia Popular, and Pachakutik Nuevo País. Most of these leftist political parties resulted from the restructuring of the now-conservative Liberal Party in the late 1970s (Ayala Mora 1985b, 1986). Not surprisingly, many members of the *Hoy* staff were high-ranking officials during the Izquierda Democrática presidency of Rodrigo Borja (1988–1992).

There are several afternoon papers, *Últimas Noticias* being the most popular. *Últimas Noticias* is published in Quito and run by *El Comercio*. It has a more regional, local, and gossipy tone and tends to run more neighborhood reports. Its coastal counterpart, *El Extra* (published in Guayaquil), is as region and city oriented as *Últimas Noticias;* however, yellow journalism is *El Extra*'s bread and butter, with stories about violent deaths and physical violations and liberal use of the coastal slang known as *coba* (characteristics that make it worthy of ethnographic study in its own right).

SAINT BIRITUTE AND
OBJECTIVE REPORTING OF THE PAST

Newspapers in Ecuador sporadically report on archaeological findings and subjects that relate to the ancient past. Reports and articles range from weekend visits to archaeological sites such as Cochasquí (*El Comercio* 1997a, 1997b) to monthlong series highlighting a different culture each week (*El Universo* 1992a–1992j). There are also reports and articles about ongoing archaeological projects and salvage excavations, interviews with anthropologists and archaeologists (*El Comercio* 1997a), and editorials that discuss the country's national identity and its relationship with history and the pre-Hispanic past.

In general, archaeology-related reports may be classified into nine categories: (1) integrating archaeology and history; (2) describing archaeological findings and cultures; (3) covering salvage archaeology projects or publicizing the need to protect specific sites; (4) museum reports; (5) interviews with archaeologists; (6) issues of national identity; (7) pre-Hispanic festivities and holidays; (8) pre-Hispanic rituals and shaman descriptions; and (9) stories that relate the ancient past with contemporary indigenous communities. Descriptive reports on current archaeological findings and on sites in need of immediate protection are by far the most common. The articles, contrary to what Salazar (1995b) has argued, emphasize the contemporary importance of the archeological past. They describe a past that is neither dead nor unimportant; rather, it is relevant to the founding of the nation. Newspapers in Ecuador are therefore important in the shaping and styling of the nation and in offering the nation a mirror image of itself, although, as I discuss below, the blurring of the reflection is itself always conveniently unmentioned. The central place of newspapers in the national imagination has been highlighted in the debates about nationalism (Hobsbawm 1990).

However, as the coverage of the Saint Biritute controversy demonstrates, the print media's reporting presents a number of opinions and rival interpretations. Rather than blindly responding to the wishes of their owners and the upper class they represent, newspapers seem to reflect the contradictory nature of the social discourses competing for national attention. In this regard, archaeological knowledge, that is, Saint Biritute's resting place, becomes a symbol of the nationwide struggle between the social actors striving to advance their version of historical continuity and national heritage. In some ways, this symbolic struggle resembles the contest at Cochasquí and its multiple interpretations and history. However, in this "multivocal" historical version, the contrasting voices are more consistently publicized and disseminated by the print media, probably because their differences are what ultimately constitutes the historical narrative.

In the following section I shall describe exchanges that appeared in Ecuador's main newspapers during 1993 concerning the rights to an ancient Manteño-Huancavilca monolith known as Saint Biritute. As I collected newspaper articles about Ecuador's pre-Hispanic past, I became intrigued by this story because it presented a good vantage point from which to understand how the print media present the country's archaeological past. This multivocal historical version offers a set of different vested national interests which are neither directly controlled by the state (or its representative government), nor fueled by a permanently antagonistic position. In this sense, the coverage of the Saint Biritute story permits a whole array of opinions absent from other forums. It is because of these characteristics that I am using this story to assess the historical discourse elaborated through, and engaged by, the country's major newspapers.

The Context of the Debate

Monoliths are very common in the cultural complexes of the pre-Hispanic communities of the equatorial Andes (Marcos 1986a; Meggers 1966). They are more common during the period defined as the Período de Integración (Integration Period), especially among the coastal group known as the Manteños-Huancavilcas. The Manteño-Huancavilca culture was initially studied by Emilio Estrada (1957b), followed by another group of academic archaeologists (Marcos 1986b; Norton and Marcos 1982). However, there is still much to be learned about the political and social structure of this polity, including whether they functioned as two separate groups or formed a single cohesive federation. Studies of the neighboring pre-Hispanic Milagro-Quevedo group (e.g., Muse 1991) seem to indicate that these polities might not have been integrated statelike entities, but independent chiefdoms that formed a federation for military or economic reasons.

The ancient polity of the Manteños-Huancavilcas occupied the southern coastal region of contemporary Ecuador, roughly equal to but slightly larger than present-day Guayas Province. Although their political structure is far from being well defined, their use of the same area where present-day Guayaquil is located means Guayaquileños use them to create an indigenous and ethnic ethos.

The intimate relationship between the Manteños-Huancavilcas and the contemporary occupants of Guayaquil is present at many levels. Politicians from all political walks pay homage to a courageous essence inherited from this pre-Hispanic polity that not only fiercely resisted the Incas, but also fought against the Spanish colonizers.

The relationship between Guayaquil and the ancient Manteños-Huancavilcas is also maintained through the use of the monoliths (and other, rarer, totems). During the 1993 reinauguration of the Municipal Museum of Guayaquil, a large totem, over 8.55 meters tall and 1.47 meters in circumference, was selected as the central piece of the new archaeological exhibition hall (*El Universo* N.d.a). This monolith consists of thirty-two (or thirty-nine, depending on the report) sculpted figures, male and female, vertically ordered, with two caimans at the top of the totem, both of which are also vertical and facing in opposite directions (*Expreso* 1993a).

The totem was found by Carlos Zevallos Menéndez in 1936 (or 1934; see *El Telégrafo* 1994). Zevallos was a self-trained archaeologist who was the pivotal figure in the development of coastal archaeology in Ecuador after the tragic and untimely death of Emilio Estrada Icaza in 1965. Among Zevallos's many accomplishments, he trained several Ecuadorian archaeologists who later founded the first independent archaeology program in the country at the Escuela Superior Politécnica del Litoral (ESPOL) in Guayaquil.

The totem in the Municipal Museum of Guayaquil is made out of huasango wood (*Loxopterigium huasango*), which is currently in danger of extinction in Ecuador's rapidly disappearing coastal tropical forest. The naked human figures and their prominent sexual organs were initially interpreted as a vital element in a complex water, fertility, and reproduction ritual. However, during preparations for the museum's opening, this interpretation was challenged, and the totem was declared by museum curators to be a "territorial emblem of the Manteño-Huancavilca nation" because of its likeness to the ancient Manteño-Huancavilca monoliths which served this function (*Expreso* 1993a; *El Telégrafo* 1994). In the words of Argentinean archaeologist Rita Álvarez, one of the curators of the exhibition, "This territorial emblem forms part of the history of Ecuador. We have to incorporate it into its cultural identity, and the citizens must feel proud of what their ancestors accomplished, because history does not begin with the coming of the Spaniards, but goes much farther back" (*El Telégrafo* 1994). The monolith prompted great expectations throughout the world, including a special report by the BBC of London (*El Universo* N.d.a).

Not everyone agreed with the museum curators' explanation. One editorial disagreed with all the information provided by the museum and accused museum staff of stealing Carlos Zevallos Menéndez's analysis (*El Universo* N.d.b). The controversy surrounding this monolith centered on the *comuna* of Sacachún's request to have "Saint Biritute" returned to their town (*El Comercio* 1994; *Meridiano* 1993; *El Telégrafo* 1993b).

Sacachún's Claim

Sacachún is located fifteen kilometers inland from the larger town of Buenos Aires, which is located on Guayaquil's coastal highway. It is described by several newspaper reports as a small town "living in the past":

> It is located on one of the many hills in the area, with a total of thirty houses in the surrounding area, some of them abandoned. There is a small church that is closed most of the time, a school with twelve students, and approximately eighty inhabitants; there are more, almost one thousand according to the people in the area, who live in other towns on the peninsula [of Santa Elena] and in Guayaquil. Sacachún is not even a town, it is a village, completely abandoned.
>
> —*El Universo* (1993c)

> Sacachún, the population that is reclaiming it [the Saint Biritute monolith], is located on a hilltop, just as was practiced by the Manteños-Huancavilcas. It is a very poor *comuna* that is dedicated to agriculture, sheepherding, and lives off the land. It is both socially and productively incorporated into contemporary society, but, spiritually, it maintains the religious aspect of the pre-Hispanic period.
>
> —*El Telégrafo* (1993a)

The conflict began in 1952, when the monolith, Saint Biritute, was taken by force from the small *comuna* of Sacachún by the municipal police under the direct orders of the socialist mayor of Guayaquil, Carlos Guevara Moreno. Saint Biritute had remained in Sacachún since 1869, when the monolith was found on the nearby hill of Las Negras and was brought to the center of town. There are two interesting points here: (1) some sources call the hill *Los Santos* (*El Universo* N.d.a), which is located on the outskirts of the Chongón-Colonche coastal mountain range, approximately sixty-five kilometers west of Guayaquil (*El Comercio* 1994); and (2) the controversy about where the monolith was found parallels the debate about the Virgin of El Quinche, an important colonial icon. This parallel probably expresses many of the region's pre-Hispanic spatial relationships and ethnic conflicts.

After Saint Biritute was taken from Sacachún, it remained on public display for almost forty years on the sidewalk across from Guayaquil's city hall, along with other monoliths in what was known as the Avenue of the Gods (Avenida 10 de Agosto). In 1991 it was given to the Municipal Museum, which is when the *comuneros* made an official request for its return to Sacachún (*El Universo* 1993d).

The *comuneros* claim that they have been struggling to get Saint Biritute back from the moment it was removed from its rightful home. According to one of the *comuneros*, Galo Tigrero, it took several attempts to take Saint Biritute from them (*El Universo* 1993d): "First, some gringos came. They put up some contraptions, but the ancestors didn't let them take him. Afterwards came some priests. I remember so much that they said, they were going to adorn the church, but they also couldn't take him until two weeks later, when some trucks full of police arrived."

On the night the police took Saint Biritute, they placed the monolith on the back of a truck between two mattresses. At the town's insistence, the police took two *comuneros* along so they could see where the monolith was to be taken. However, these men were abandoned a couple of kilometers from the town (Cristolino Lino, in *El Universo* 1993d): "They put Saint Biritute between two mattresses and they took him, no matter how much we protested. They took me and another comrade so that we could accompany them and see that the idol was going to be all right, but they left us stranded. After two weeks, we made it to Guayaquil and nobody would tell us where he was."

The role played by prominent Guayaquileño archaeologist Francisco Huerta Rendón in the removal of Saint Biritute is apparent in the different narratives. Huerta notes that he visited Sacachún several times to, first, observe the famous monolith which he had heard so much about, and, second, to obtain it for the city of Guayaquil. He made the initial attempt by using Monsignor Silvio Luis Haro's authority and offering a couple of statues of Catholic saints as gifts. The visitors were run out of town. Some of the *comuneros* still remember this incident as Saint Biritute's miracle: a shower of rock that fell on their enemies (*El Universo* 1993d).

His initial failure did not deter Huerta, however. He requested help from the municipal authorities. After he recounted the incident to the City Council, the councilmen endorsed Huerta's recommendation to bring the idol to Guayaquil and the monsignor's plea to end pagan rituals. The municipal police were sent to bring the idol from Sacachún. According to Huerta (*El Universo* 1993d): "We did not go on that expedition, but we got the formal promise from the head of the police that no harm would be done to the residents of Sacachún. Fortunately, nothing happened. Some of them—we were told—cried uncontrollably, like when you remove a corpse from the house [Ecuadorian funerals are traditionally held in the deceased's home]."

Huerta described Saint Biritute as the biggest pre-Hispanic anthropomorphic sculpture of huasango wood in Ecuador. Newspaper reports described it as having "a helmetlike head. As with many other monuments in the region, the nose seems to be the only detail on the face that has been sculpted. . . . the right arm rests on its stomach while the left hand is pointing to its massive male genitalia" (*El Comercio* 1993).

Saint Biritute is 2.5 meters tall, but no longer displays the impressive phallus and nose described by Huerta Rendón. Although it is unclear when or how the nose was mutilated and removed, the phallus was castrated in 1952 (some newspaper accounts claim 1949, perhaps because Huerta first visited the town in that year) so that the monolith could be exhibited between the mayor's and the governor's offices on the so-called Avenue of the Gods (*El Telégrafo* 1993a).

The struggle over Saint Biritute is quite complex. The *comuneros'* primary concern is the ritual power of the monolith to assure the well-being of the community. According to the people of Sacachún, Saint Biritute was responsible for producing rain in the area, and they point to the protracted drought since the monolith was taken away (*El Universo* 1993d): "They would finish asking and he would put the things down. He gave us the water so we could eat the fruits, because at that time we did not cut down the trees to make coal, because we used to live off maize and yucca and we made [Panama] hats out of reed, but when the saint left, even the wells dried up."

When the idol did not give the *comuneros* what they requested, a different ritual was performed. One of the strongest *comuneros* was chosen to whip Saint Biritute for not giving Sacachún the much-needed water as all the women stood by and wept for the tortured saint and begged for the punishment to stop (*El Comercio* 1993; *El Universo* N.d.a). The last man selected for this role was Eulogio Tomalá, who beat Saint Biritute so harshly that torrential rains fell. The beating also provoked the idol's wrath, and within a couple of weeks, Tomalá died of an unexplained fever. After that, no one dared hit Saint Biritute again; he was worshiped only through prayers and petitions and was offered copious amounts of food on his feast day, November 2 (Day of the Dead) (*El Comercio* 1993).

There are other claims about the healing powers of Saint Biritute, such as his ability to reinstate a woman's menstrual cycle or to help sterile women have children. But these are typically made by nonlocals such as Francisco Huerta Rendón or Xavier Véliz, former curator of the museum of the ESPOL (*El Universo* 1993d). According to Véliz, his father, historian Ángel Véliz Mendoza, saw "various *cholitos* [pejorative term used for people from the coast] of the peninsula around the monument when it was on the streets of Diez de Agosto and Pedro Carbo. He especially saw a *cholita* who rubbed her sex on that of the idol" (*El Universo* 1993d). This description is consonant with Huerta's account of sterile women rubbing their naked bodies and genitalia against the idol's in order to be cured (*El Universo* N.d.a). However, contemporary residents of Sacachún argue that these practices are not authentic. Women, especially, reject these claims and say that they have never heard of such ritual practices involving Saint Biritute. At the most, they admit to having asked Saint Biritute for help with handling the stress and hardships of having a large family, but not for increasing the size of the family or curing sterility (*El Universo* 1993d).

For Edmundo Aguilar, an anthropologist who has worked in Sacachún, the point is not to argue about the exotic ritual practices of the community, but, instead, about the oral history that it embodies. According to Aguilar, Saint Biritute is the material object of a rich history that is thought to have been lost, which is why "a lot of people say we are devoid of culture. I could demonstrate to them, with a thousand live examples, not only that we have one, but also that it is just around the corner" (*El Comercio* 1993). For Aguilar this culture is to be found in Sacachún, since the importance of Saint Biritute for the community is not an issue of pagan ideology or idolatry, but of its relationship to its past (*El Universo* 1993d): "What the people of Sacachún are interested in is their relationship with their past. Saint Biritute has a special signification for them, because that material artifact is a referent of their oral history, and that constitutes an identification with their ancestors."

THE OPINIONS OF THE MANY
AND THE POWER OF THE FEW

The overwhelming support for returning Saint Biritute to the *comuna* of Sacachún is one of the most interesting elements of the dialogue about and struggle over the monolith's final resting place. The director of the

Municipal Museum of Guayaquil during my stay in Ecuador, Paco Cuesta Caputti, the Archaeology Department of the ESPOL, writers, and reporters overwhelmingly agreed that the *comuna* of Sacachún was the rightful owner of the idol. They also agreed that it was stolen and therefore should be returned. The curator of the museum's archaeological exhibition, Rita Álvarez Litben, concurred that Saint Biritute did not belong in the museum, but in Sacachún. For Álvarez Litben, the monolith was out of its historical context in Guayaquil, and only with its return to its original community could it regain its enormous value (*El Telégrafo* 1993a): "We are undertaking a series of investigations of Saint Biritute not only at the individual level, but also what is behind him at both the social and the ideological levels. This is a very distinctive case, since, through an oral memory, a pre-Hispanic belief has been kept alive. It is very important that the collective memory be kept alive, and with the presence of Saint Biritute that could be done."

Then-director of the museum, Paco Cuesta, also argued that if there was religious freedom in the country, then there was nothing wrong with returning this pre-Hispanic idol to its cultural-historical descendants. He also pointed out that their religious beliefs should be respected, at the least, studied, but definitely not repressed (*El Universo* 1993c). After all,

> they never actually donated it; it was taken from them. So therefore it is logical that it should return to its rightful owners.
>
> —*El Telégrafo* (1993a)

> The *comuna* of Sacachún was deprived of this deity in a clear act of intolerance, disrespect, and ignorant evangelical inquisition. They made use of deceit and of false archaeological arguments that ended with the complete abandonment of the monolith for over twenty years on a sidewalk! from which some charitable hands rescued it to deliver it to the Municipal Museum, in whose files it has not yet been registered and cannot be registered because it is a "living testimony."
>
> —*El Universo* (1993b)

The Saint Biritute controversy was also considered important enough for a professor and students associated with the Center of Archaeological and Anthropological Studies of the ESPOL to write an editorial supporting the return of the idol to Sacachún. For them this incident was another case of an ethnocentric and imperialist ideology implying that there was only one truth or way of understanding reality. It reflected the imposition of a single correct and civilized form of cultural tradition and the belief that all others were savage and uncivilized. The controversy, they stated, indicated that the ravages of the conquest were present in contemporary Ecuador and that there was an incredible bias concerning the essential role of archaeology as the "prime source of knowledge of the pre-Hispanic communities and as such, offering a historical identity for the current nation-states" (*El Universo* N.d.b).

The former director of the Centro de Estudios Arqueológicos y Antropológicos (Center for Archaeological and Anthropological Studies, CEAA), Jorge Marcos, believes it is easy to understand why Saint Biritute was taken from Sacachún. As a traditional archaeologist, Marcos worked with self-trained archaeologists like Francisco Huerta Rendón and Carlos Zevallos Menéndez to provide Guayaquil with some level of historical legitimization. It is clear to him that this initial group of archaeologists, "from their differing perspectives, wanted to give the city [Guayaquil] the symbols of the archaeological discoveries they found, and to conserve and spread among the new generations of Guayaquileños the 'Huancavilca heritage' of the urban center" (*Expreso* 1993d).

But for Marcos, the historical conditions which provided the context in which these monoliths were brought to the economic capital of the country had changed. The historical reasoning that justified the removal of archaeological artifacts from their communities was no longer valid or acceptable. He ended his piece on indigenous and *criollo* ethnicity by inverting the traditional "Huancavilca" values that the city of Guayaquil tried to uphold in its political ideology (*Expreso* 1993d): "Let's demonstrate once again that Guayaquileños are free, are generous, that is, 'huancavilcas,' if you will, and let's return Saint Biritute to those who have had it for generations as a symbol of their relationship with nature. Let's return Saint Biritute to the *comuna* of Sacachún."

Even the newspaper reporters at the time sided with the *comuneros* in different ways. One of the most subtle was to print sympathetic pictures and narratives about the *comuneros'* relationship with the idol. In one of these reports, several *comuneros* related how they felt about the idol and how it was stolen from their community:

A pathetic scene that exemplified the beliefs of our ancestors and their naïveté was carried out yesterday in the halls of the Municipal Museum. The descendants of the *comuna* of Sacachún, just to the east of Cerecita, when they saw "Saint Biritute," a giant monolith, God of Fertility and Rain of their ancestors, after forty years of separation, threw themselves before it and, crying and caressing it, with veneration said: "How can you

be here lying in this position, abandoned, when we have an altar for you,
to adore and treat you as you deserve?"

—*Expreso* (1993e)

For the reporter the enormous emotion expressed by the *comuneros* of
Sacachún when they were allowed to see Saint Biritute "was the object
of an enormous respect, since it faithfully expressed part of our culture,
our past, our history, from where we have come" (*Expreso* 1993e).
This type of article is very different from the more explicit approach
taken by Alex Riva Toledo for the October 16, 1993, edition of *Hoy*. In
this page-long article, Riva presents the Saint Biritute controversy in a
very factual manner, but then argues for the *comuneros* in a strikingly
unapologetic way. Riva states that the religious practice of this rural
community is not to be respected or defended, but simply to be accepted
for what it is: another type of religious practice. There is no question
that Riva believed the urban authorities were in the wrong, that the taking of Saint Biritute from Sacachún was a literal "castration of the community," and that the idol should be returned to its rightful owners: "To
recognize that this stone idol belongs to its people would be an act that
would go beyond mere justice, it would be to recognize that there are
differences among human beings and that the peace which we all desire
has to be constructed every single day."

Even though most favored returning Saint Biritute to the *comuna* of
Sacachún, the Catholic Church was strongly opposed. Surprisingly, the
church's highest authority in Ecuador at the time, Pablo Cardinal Muñoz Vega, was the most willing to negotiate the return of the idol, but
only if the community promised to view it as a "historical memory," not
as a deity (*El Universo* 1993d). The cardinal's position was much more
lenient than that of the archbishop of Guayaquil.

For Guayaquil's archbishop, Juan Larrea Holguín, the artifact belonged in a museum, not in a community where it might contribute to
cultism. Even the name "Saint Biritute" was preposterous to the archbishop, since it bestowed sainthood on a mere idol. He conceded that
Catholics should respect other religious beliefs, but he said that did not
mean encouraging erroneous practices, especially since "a society that
owes everything to Christianity must collaborate so that the people do
not return to a period of primitivism and paganism through error or
confusion. Respecting the culture and work of the people does not mean
wishing for or favoring a return to an ancient time" (*Expreso* 1993c).

Significantly, Guayaquil's conservative mayor and former president,
León Febres Cordero, sided with the archbishop. After weeks of articles

arguing to the contrary, he decided that Saint Biritute should stay in the city's museum, where it could be visited, but not worshiped (*Expreso* 1993c). The monument remains in the museum to this day.

THE ANALYTICAL CONSTRAINTS OF SAINT BIRITUTE

The story of Saint Biritute concerns the struggle between a rural community and the city of Guayaquil over a monolith known as Saint Biritute. The central characters in this saga were the members of the *comuna*, many of whom were singled out by reporters because they were elected leaders, or because of their gender, age, or knowledge of ritual. Other characters were the museum curator and staff, who had physical possession of the monolith; intellectuals of all persuasions, who considered it their duty to state their opinion on the matter; the newspapers and reporters who deemed the story worthy of coverage; the Catholic Church; and the mayor of Guayaquil and former president León Febres Cordero. All of the characters can be placed into two camps. On one side was the church and the mayor, who sided against the *comuna*; on the other was everybody else.

The story could be interpreted as a simple one of a small "indigenous" community fighting for something that history says belonged to it. Even the newspapers, through their "objective" reporting, supported this claim. But once again, official agencies, in this instance, represented by the religious and political authorities, discarded reasons based on history and disregarded the community's claim to ownership of a tangible piece of the past. Using both religious and political authority, the mayor was able to decide ownership of the past. He considered it more appropriate to have the monolith exhibited at the city's Municipal Museum than to return it to the community. The decision ran counter to popular opinion (an important contradiction), including that of the experts: the anthropologists and archaeologists.

The narrative also reveals an insight into a better understanding of the ownership of the past. The newspapers were faithful to their mission in their objective approach to the historical truth, and once the decision was made, they made very few objections, even though their pages had been filled with articles arguing the contrary. What comes across in most newspaper articles and editorials is the community's right to its past, in this case, a past Saint Biritute tangibly represented and was even a part of. Also expressed is the belief that ownership of the past has very little to do with historical reasoning per se and much more to do with history's relationship with political authority and power. It also appears that the newspapers were unwilling to get involved in the struggle, to side completely with the cause because, ultimately, that would have resulted in questions about their objectivity—the indisputable basis of their ability to present a valid and acceptably neutral history of the nation. At the same time, this "neutral" discussion of issues from a distance becomes a much more effective way to produce an official historical truth.

The structure the newspapers utilized to report historical accounts is quite different from that of other historical narratives. The newspapers' structure, especially in terms of their coverage of the Saint Biritute story, is much more dialogic than official versions in textbooks or the CONAIE's national version (discussed in chapter 5). From the media one gets a sense that the historical truth is something that is not readily apparent, but very much contested. For newspapers, only a dialogic structure which allows for a multiplicity of voices leads to an understanding and investigation of historical reality.

The print media's dialogic structure understands history as a hidden truth that needs to be discovered (or uncovered) by reporters. This structure also reveals that there is an inherent historical truth, a truth that, no matter how hidden or erased, can be put back together objectively and recognized (note the similarity to Cochasquí's production of historical truth). The reporters' job is not to overemphasize or interpret particular voices; it is to allow different viewpoints to emerge and contribute their own understanding of the historical puzzle under discussion. In this structure, objectivity becomes the supreme, and perhaps only, medium through which the historical truth can be retrieved. This objectivity as a regulating device is far more explicit and pervasive than that in history textbooks and propounded by the Indian movement. Objectivity becomes the ultimate system within which the historical facts will be measured.

This objectivity was evidenced in the multiple single-page articles about Saint Biritute that tried to present all voices in the historical debate by interviewing different protagonists, by using sections to separate opinions, and by providing context. This is evident even in editorials, which re-created the context within which they could make their opinion stand out. Other articles, such as those about pre-Columbian cultures, archaeological excavations, or historical heritage (*El Universo* 1992–1997; *El Comercio* 1995, 1997a, 1997b), signal a recognition that history is not static, that there will always be a number of sources to be incorporated and that provide for a more objective and authentic rendering of the historical reality.

The newspaper's structure is related to journalism's objective stance. More important, it highlights the print media's reliance on academic politics for support and legitimization. The print media's interest in objectivity is more closely related to academic concerns with truth than to the official or alternative versions. This is not to say that other historical discourses do not espouse some notion of objectivity; rather, the written media, like academics, consider objectivity to be integral to their methodology. Objectivity, then, defines and legitimizes the media's endeavor by making it scientific. This structure therefore allows the print media to borrow historians' objectivity, thereby legitimizing this particular form of historical truth (Ayala Mora 1983, 1985a, 1985b).

The print media also borrow from other social sciences, including anthropology. An ethnographic approach allows the media to get close to the historical truth, or at least to hear the other side, the local side, of the story. This approach also illustrates the print media's understanding that there is always another side to any story, especially when history is being actively contested. It is precisely in this struggle that the news is created, or, as in the story of Saint Biritute, where history becomes news. The acknowledgment of the inimical nature of historical issues is not a self-evident reality so much as the characteristic that allows history to be sold as news, a daily commodity in the form of the written word.

Different notions of power also become apparent in the discussion of the structures of the varied historical versions, with each discourse having a different relationship within the power relations that sustain it. In the textbooks' version, the powerful entity represented by the nation is reified. Every element in this history serves to elevate patriotic feelings and contribute to a national heritage that takes on mythic proportions. In this version, power relations are not questioned or even made apparent. Instead, they are actively, although somewhat simplistically, constructed to seem natural. Although the print media have the most dialogic structure, they are still far from placing demands on the power structure itself. As is clearly visible in the case of Saint Biritute, the print media can go a long way toward presenting a particular case and exploring the uneven power relations that permeate the struggle, but there is no challenge to the authorities before or after a decision. Newspapers have no qualms about exposing the decision-making power of the municipal authority, especially when the city's highest authority defies the consensus. Yet the print media have no interest in battling the uneven power structure. For this reason, once the decision over Saint Biritute was made, there was no more news, no longer a need for articles. The newspapers moved on to other histories to be commodified and converted into news.

This "multivocal" newspaper history is, interestingly, also expressed in its own medium, or, rather, the medium is what helps establish the newspaper's history as objective and neutral. Thus, being a newspaper with a national audience assures a level of neutrality that offers an aura in which the contents of the historical discourse may be discussed and understood. However, even though each of the newspapers claims a national audience, all of them have very clear regional and political inclinations which color the events and actions they strive to describe objectively. For example, the coastal newspapers (e.g., *El Universo*) never sided as openly with the *comuna* as *Hoy,* a more progressive paper, did. The more conservative political outlook also reflects the traditionally less supportive understanding of ethnic history and property in the coastal region, where there are only four surviving coastal Indian groups (there are four times as many indigenous communities in the highlands). This political element, and many other regional factors, greatly influences who reads each newspaper and who is exposed to the different uncontested and unofficial historical narrative.

We also must take into account the literacy rate of the population, especially in Guayaquil and Quito. Although literacy has increased in the last couple of decades, not everyone has access to newspapers. The economic constraints on newspaper consumption are evident in the low number of copies sold during the week. Around sixty thousand more copies are sold on weekends than on a daily basis, since the weekend editions tend to synthesize the week's news and provide more leisure articles or in-depth coverage of contemporary issues.

All of these factors inhibit exposure to all the information in the different newspapers. A lack of knowledge of the full story also explains why the articles about Saint Biritute recapitulate the entire debate to make their own story intelligible. But even the general articles elaborate the full story and incorporate all the sides, making each article stand alone and making references to other articles largely unnecessary.

In essence, the written word has the potential to reach a significant national audience. However, due to constraints that largely reflect a class dynamic, such as literacy, financial limitations, regionalism, and political inclinations, the most likely audience for newspapers is the educated and economic elite. At the same time, and not surprisingly, it is these two groups that are most typically represented and actively engaged in the production of newspapers.

Academics are most likely to be interviewed by or to offer their opinions to newspapers. This intellectual spotlight is present in the articles on Saint Biritute, where academics express enormous interest in the outcome of this rural-urban struggle over a historical artifact. Traditional families also have a say in the establishment and management of newspapers. All the major newspapers were founded by one of the leading elite families, that is, the Febres-Cordero family in Guayaquil, the Corderos in Cuenca, the Ortiz family in Quito. Class is an even greater issue in that most academics are part of this close network of elite families, giving credence to Ayala Mora's notion that to understand Ecuadorian history one must, above all, be knowledgeable about Ecuador's elite genealogy (Enrique Ayala Mora, personal communication).

Although the elite is most invested in producing and consuming the independent historical narratives elaborated in the national newspapers, it is not the only target population. For example, grade school and high school students are encouraged to buy and read newspapers, television and radio news is based on reports from the print media, and the emerging middle class also uses the print media to express its concern about public safety and survival in the two major cities.

All of these instances point to ways in which independent historical narratives get disseminated and the influence they have on a wider range of nonelite national communities. The country's stark class division, evident in differences in economic resources and literary interests, closely circumscribes the national newspapers' historical influence. The country's class structure does not alone determine the print media's coverage, but it plays a large part in sustaining a structure that narrows plausible interpretations and ultimate impacts on national historical production and popular dissemination.

⌒

SEVEN

CONCLUSION
Power, Hegemony, and National Identity

⌒

But it is sensible to begin by asking the beginning questions,
why imagine power in the first place, and what is the
relationship between one's motive for imagining power
and the image one ends up with.

— EDWARD W. SAID (2000)

In general, I view the present work as a contribution to the understanding of the political production of hegemony in Ecuador. I am particularly interested in highlighting the role of historical representation and hermeneutics in the maintenance and functioning of national political domination. This book is not exclusively, or even primarily, an assessment of archaeological research on Ecuador so much as a case study of hegemonic articulation. I use archaeological and historical material as a vehicle through which to research the production of national domination in the same way that other areas of hegemonic production—sentiment, education, art, political structure—are and should be researched.

I do not wish to imply that historical production does not have a unique and essential role in hegemonic domination; rather, I am arguing for a reassessment of earlier scholarship, particularly in Ecuador and Latin America, that narrowly focuses on disciplinary interests. I believe that, instead of merely increasing anthropological and historical knowledge, we need a broader and more incisive research agenda to study the implications of different types of intellectual production. There is no doubt that anthropological (and other forms of) knowledge is useful, yet discipline-specific agendas will continue to expand without extraordinary justification. It is this semiautomatic production of knowledge that

I wish to mark as an important and interesting avenue for intellectual exploration (Said 1989).

This book therefore explores the political implications of archaeological knowledge (strategically situated as both anthropological and historical) instead of just looking to increase disciplinary knowledge per se. In this context, this book clearly falls within Foucault's poststructuralist endeavor of assessing the power of discourses and forms of knowledge and their impact on the postmodern/postcolonial subject. I have also striven to assess how history contributes to the political forms of domination inherited from the colonial period. At the same time, I am taking into account how the European form of domination transformed local forms of control and contributed to more modern forms of power dynamics. However, I have tried to make these contrasting forms of power articulation culturally meaningful by restating less-institutionalized forms of deployment in terms of ethnic, racial, gendered, and sexualized forms of identity. The contemporary picture of Ecuador's national hegemony presents a postmodern process that incorporates varied identity deployments into a continual reworking and transformation of hegemonic maintenance (McClintock, Mufti, and Shohat 1997; D. Miller 1992; Monsiváis 1995, 1997).

Thus, this study can also be seen as an analysis of the political effects and implications of anthropological and historical knowledge. I analyze history as a richly productive intellectual and political endeavor rather than as a neutral enterprise. I see it as closely associated with a national enterprise implicit in its research agenda. In a sense, history's fundamental emphasis on empirical objectivity has placed it in a privileged position vis-à-vis the reproduction of the national ideal and the state's political production. History as an academic discipline in Ecuador, as in other Latin American nation-states, has carved itself a space of "neutral" activity with wider-reaching social implications than those initially accepted by the majority of historians.

History's inherent relationship with national hegemony is constructed on the discipline's supposed objectivity and neutrality (Alonso 1988). Because of this power effect (see J. Miller 1993), understanding the impact of a presumed intellectual objectivity is important for assessing the colonial legacy of established academic forms (Asad 1982; Said 1978). Anthropology is particularly involved in this process; thus, it could benefit the most from applying its own methodological approach to its own established forms of knowledge production. Ultimately, the deconstruction of Western academic disciplines helps us assess the identity of the European subject as it is normalized via these intellectual discourses and strongly involved with the effects of power throughout disciplinary practices and reproduction (Mignolo 1994, 2000; Mitchell 1988). This book also contributes to understanding how anthropological and historical knowledge supports domination by creating a normalized national subject (including a recognized homogeneous state entity). Ecuador, and many other Latin American nation-states, provides these academic disciplines with social advantages as they define, legitimize, and even "invent" (in the Andersonian sense) the national subject. History is particularly burdened as it must sustain the existence of a national subject not open to question or critical analysis as the sine qua non of its intellectual conduct. Thus, history seems a more useful vehicle than other disciplines for understanding hegemonic articulation and its fragile constitution from necessarily diverse, and even contradictory, elements.

As I have argued throughout this book, nothing is unworthy of historical reproduction and representation. Even archaeological pyramids and mounds constructed a thousand years ago are essential markers for the reproduction of the nation and the maintenance of the state (i.e., for a constant national political project). Far from being unimportant, pre-Hispanic knowledge holds a privileged place in the discourse that initializes and furthers the nation's embodiment. Part of this essential and inherent practice of subtly incorporating national pre-Hispanic narratives is highlighted by the invisibility of the historical process. Invisibility becomes an innate feature of successful hegemonic practice. The promised invisibility may be compared to the emperor's new clothes and the startling effect of his (i.e., hegemony's) nudity. But the dramatic impact of physical repression (Abrams 1988) and paralyzing fear (Taussig 1992b) in destabilizing communities while maintaining a homogeneous national subject cannot be overestimated.

Hegemony therefore is far from the monolithic and static reality that it traditionally has been presented as or, more accurately, as it (re)presents itself in historical studies and other political practices. Hegemony is successful above all in its ability to adapt to changing national conditions and the ever-present institutional and individual deployments (Joseph and Nugent 1994; Silverblatt 1988). Yet hegemony's ability to adapt lies not so much in its external capacity or even in its predictive ability as in its connection to human beings as national subjects and, above all, as socially identifiable beings (Foucault 1980, 1991). Hegemony is part of our daily life and of those actions that make up the agenda of social institutions and national norms.

Because of its ability to adapt, hegemony can sustain dialectical tension among the many elements that seem to question its homogenizing efforts (Lorde 1997; Wylie 1995). That it can balance on this trapeze is not surprising if we remember that hegemony is a fundamental part of our social identity, cultural practice, and personal beliefs; that is, it is internal and not imposed from above.

What also becomes clearer as we size up the hegemonic process is the fundamental role counter-hegemonic discourses play in the effort to dominate. Far from being disruptive, as they are presented in traditional narratives, counter-hegemonic elements are actually central to the hegemonic enterprise. National hegemony could not be sustained without alternative ways of understanding and assessing social reality. In reaction to challenges, hegemony changes its strategy of domination (i.e., of cohesion) as national conditions shift. This is possible because hegemony is inherent in all social action, especially the most meaningful nationally. Thus, counter-hegemonic discourses, which we might have thought devastating to the nation-state's survival, are relatively easily incorporated into a new metanarrative of national appropriation and redefinition of the national subject.

As I have shown, Ecuador's indigenous origin is handily reconstructed in the nation's historical imagination without any real rupture in the country's structure of domination. In this manner, the Indian movement's success will be measured to a large degree by its ability to impose its ideas on others in similar fashion.

One must also look for an explanation of how counter-hegemonic discourses evolve, however. Their original context is important for understanding the constant transformations of hegemonic production, the field of force if you will (Roseberry 1994), that establishes the social setting without fully defining or limiting all plausible social action. To some degree, it is as if the rules of the game are determined, but exceptions (and a rule is not made unless it has exceptions that delineate it) are still possible. The invisibility of these exceptions, or non-normative maneuvers, is the main testament to the success of counter-hegemonic discourses and assures their impact. It is their very success of the rules (that is, their application to a broader national audience), however, that immediately causes them to change.

This fact implies two things: first, a direct impact on the game, that is, the field of force itself; and, second (and less understood in contemporary analyses of hegemony), that what once was an exception, an illegal maneuver, has now been hegemonized. By succeeding, counter-hegemonic devices, and not hegemony, are ultimately defeated.

I have emphasized the fragile nature of hegemonic transformation and its ambivalent form of consolidation in my analysis of history's agenda for the study of Ecuador. I have highlighted how necessary it is to question counter-hegemonic production, to consider it as not exclusively concerned with the deconstruction of alternative modes of interpretation, but also with understanding where and how is it that these alternative modes are generated. We must assess and analyze how the national imagination constructs and gives meaning to ideas, emotions, sentiments, and trends. Perhaps this historical research of emotion and sentiment has been considered more a concern of the humanities than of the social sciences; however, I hope this book demonstrates the need for an interdisciplinary and organic approach (in the Gramscian sense) to the study of the roots and methods (what Foucault [2000] refers to as the "how") of different modes of interpretation.

Interdisciplinary and organic research could be useful in defining how social (and therefore hegemonic) identities reflect transitions and transformations within a field of force with rules that are constantly questioned and changed. Even though the rules might be different, the game is not necessarily changed, or, perhaps more precisely, is still understood in homogeneous and unique ways. The challenge may be to study counter-hegemonic devices from their emergence so as to better understand the process of hegemonic articulation. This research method is key because it encompasses the struggle between established forms of social identity and their dynamic transformation that most of us spend our lives identifying, interacting, and legitimizing. There are several ways to understand this shifting, humanizing struggle; the use of a hermeneutical tool such as "structures of feeling" (R. Williams 1977) might prove productive in this regard.

AGENCY, COUNTER-HEGEMONY, AND SOCIAL CHANGE

> *But nowhere is this engagement more gripping than in the conflict between Foucault's archaeologies and social change itself, which it must remain for his students, like ourselves on such occasions, to expose and if possible to resolve.*
>
> —EDWARD SAID (2000)

Perhaps one of the most important issues raised by my research is the problematic articulation of counter-hegemonic devices within the production of dominant forms of control. The degree to which the past is an active element of contention, and of multiple and varied meanings, is also the degree to which hegemony is contested. It is never secure even when it is constantly presenting itself as such. I have presented and analyzed scenarios of historical production and hegemonic articulation in which the past is active in political manufacture, not in the sense of the past's not existing, but of "the past's" being many things to many people at the same time.

Although at Cochasquí the pre-Hispanic past is constantly represented and displayed, it never means the same thing to everyone, even when the enormous state apparatus (à la Althusser 1977) is constantly reformulating historical narratives that sanctify the nation and protect the state's political machinery. After all, the state is independent of the nation, but it needs the nation's façade or mask to make it officially legitimate. Even when the state invests explicitly in the Programa Cochasquí, historical variation cannot be completely denied. "Sliding signifiers" are always at work and constantly demand newer forms of domination and escape (Hall 1981, 1986).

This sliding signification is even more apparent in the Saint Biritute debate, in which a pre-Hispanic monolith becomes the focus of varied positions signaling the enormous investment of contemporary politics in the emblems, and therefore the representation, of the past. The Saint Biritute debate allowed an alienated and formerly indigenous coastal community to recover its heritage by reclaiming an ancient monolith which in many ways represented the community's expropriation and domination by whites and mestizos for more than five centuries. This conflict permitted a professional group of archaeologists, journalists, and social scientists to side with the coastal community, thereby relieving themselves of the race and class guilt they embodied as normative members of the national community. However, the sliding signification afforded by the monolith was laid to rest, in a manner of speaking, by the city's religious and political authorities' (the archbishop and the mayor) agreeing that Saint Biritute belonged to Guayaquil, not to Sacachún. The real question is whether the conflict over Saint Biritute was for naught, if the authorities could so easily decide the monolith's future to their advantage, even when the experts, that is, the archaeologists, advocated the contrary.

It would seem that the Indian movement's efforts are paradigmatic in this regard. Like Sacachún, the Indian movement, particularly but not exclusively in the person of the CONAIE, is questioning the nation's control of its territory and resources in terms of historical rights and cultural authenticity. In this initial stage, there is no radical difference between the CONAIE's and Sacachún's claims: both use history to legitimize their demands and, in the process, question the nation's (or their sociopolitical representatives') claim to their past. The articulation of authenticity in cultural terms and in terms of legitimizing power is of enormous importance, central to the nation's future, and embedded in the contemporary debate over globalization and development strategies (Arce and Long 2000). However, this is where the similarities end.

The most obvious difference is one of range. It is clear that the Saint Biritute debate was considered a regional issue of some national consequence; the Indian movement's concerns are always considered national in scope, even when it is claiming very specifically regional rights to land and access to resources. This national dimension is not afforded merely by the Indian movement's use of a national ethos of pan-Indianness; rather, the visibility of the Indian protest, at many ideological, political, and economic levels, hits at the heart of the nation's self-representation. As I have argued throughout this work, the "Indian" wields enormous power in the creation of the Ecuadorian nation. Although the Indian is repeatedly silenced as being inconsequential and trivial to the concerns of the ruling majority, the lie is exposed at key moments when the Indian movement contests the past.

It would seem that the Indian movement, however, takes this social knowledge—acquired during years of oppression and political organizing—to a higher logistical level. The movement's political and social "success" since the 1990s is not based exclusively on its historical validation or even its moral right. If it were, Saint Biritute would have been returned to Sacachún. What makes both its historical claim and its moral superiority successful is the political muscle that the different Indian organizations, like the CONAIE, are able to muster to support their ideology and, more important, their claims. There is no doubt that no political leader would have negotiated with the Indian leadership unless forced to do so by nationwide strikes, interruption of agricultural production, civil unrest in the capital, and, perhaps most telling, pressure from international NGOs and financial institutions like the World Bank and the IMF. There is no doubt that the Indians in Ecuador have learned to play the game quite well, as they have repeatedly beat the state by transforming themselves into an intriguing and complicated postmodern creation.

It is clear, however, that the movement's political savvy is a testament to its authenticity and not a renunciation of it (Spivak 1999). It is also clear that the Indians' political organizing has paid off; otherwise, they would not be in the position of contributing to the toppling of "democratically" elected presidents and to the election of their own candidates in the November 17, 2002, election. This political success was made possible by years of massive grassroots organizing, marches, hunger strikes, international support, lawsuits against transnational oil companies, and the like. The Indian movement's agenda not only has moved into the national spotlight, but also, most important, has made its way onto the stage of the state's machinery.

It is also at this moment of transformation from a counter-hegemonic stance to a more hegemonic one that a myriad of other issues arise. Will the Indian movement, like other powerful movements, *fail through its success?* In other words, what happens to social movements once they make the dangerous transition from outsiders to insiders and are then blamed by their constituency for being like those they used to criticize? To put it in theoretical terms, does the success of counter-hegemonic complaints signal their hegemonic demise?

Muratorio's (1998) and Guerrero's (1991) analyses might prove insightful in the Ecuadorian case. Muratorio, more than any other researcher, honestly outlines the hegemonic constraints visible in the Indian movement even before its first successful presidential election. According to her (also see chapter 5), the Indian movement was forced to construct itself within Western parameters of social organization: men fill most of the important organizational roles; Quechua speakers are more important in the movement because they are bilingual and can engage with the national population; those Indians with academic degrees have more responsibility than those with only political organizing background. Thus, questions of sex, race, and class or status are intimately embedded in the Indian movement's organization, making one wonder how successful the movement can be in destabilizing a state organization when it orders itself along similar lines. What will change when the Indian movement's claims to land and resources are satisfied if its ideological and social structure are so intimately shared that one racial group will supplant another, but, structurally, things may not change very much?

Guerrero's (1991) ethnographic foray into the colonial legacy of Indian social structure tellingly explores the "semantics of domination" encapsulated within a colonial institution that has organized Indian communities throughout the Ecuadorian Andes since the early republic. To Guerrero's credit, he is concerned not only with both the forms of power within the state-sanctioned structures and how the native indigenous communities repeat or even further their domination as part of their position within a larger web of hegemonic constraints. He does not equate domination with official forms of control, but with a larger social dynamic of interaction and position invested with enormous power and identity.

Perhaps Guerrero's approach is instructive in terms of the current indigenous requestioning of national hegemonic composition. Rather than thinking of the Indian movement in absolute terms of domination or resistance, it reflects a more realistic assessment: working within looser constraints than those visible to any single character (or in any analysis) of the problem. Thus, the CONAIE's contribution is not measured by its distance from the oppressive structures it resists or even by changes in exploitative conditions, but, instead, by the realistic shift in the hegemonic field of force (Roseberry 1994) within which it originally worked.

But it is also this quota of reality, the movement's willingness to get its hands dirty and engage with the very oppressive forces it is fighting that is most problematic. At the same time, it is the movement's involvement in the articulation of hegemony that both secures its political success and kills its "authentic" representation of the voices for which it purports to fight. It is this ambiguous reality, fraught with uncertainty and complex developments, that is most tellingly present in the Indian movement's engagement with hegemony, particularly as Ecuador now has a president the movement vigorously supported and helped elect. The movement's contribution can therefore be defined, by Foucault's analysis of power, not as an all-or-nothing matter, or even as one of contingencies; instead, the movement is a medium through which to make mechanisms of domination more conspicuous in the hopes of shifting relations of power and generating a convincing escape from subjugation (Foucault 1991: 173–174).

There is no doubt, therefore, that the Indian movement's political agency makes it much more successful in contesting the officializing scripts, especially compared with efforts at Cochasquí or to get Saint Biritute returned to its indigenous home. However, the movement's greater counter-hegemonic success does not translate into an immediate disruption of domination, since, as discussed throughout this work, hegemony is more than official rhetoric; it is a larger social machinery that incorporates antagonistic narratives as well as official ones. Therefore, the Indian movement has been successful in revealing the state's territorial control and transnational vulnerability, but, in succeeding, it has come closer to embracing the officializing game it has disrupted so well since the 1990s.

The movement's failure is perhaps more productive than it might seem at first glance. If one takes Lessing's (1987) insights seriously, it is good to know beforehand that all progressive movements will fail once they succeed—not because this might be their original objective, or even because they do not deliver total liberation, but because this failure is an inherent political reality. And if this is the case, there is no movement "more real" in the Ecuadorian landscape at present than the Indian movement. As such, it has rightfully beat the nation and the state at their own game of bestowing historical rights and naturalizing culturally authentic ones. The CONAIE, however, like all national movements that preceded it, will undoubtedly need a "justifying" state and a "caring" nation to survive.

NATIONAL IDENTITIES IN LATIN AMERICA: THE VIEW FROM ECUADOR

*If for the time being, I grant a certain privileged position
to the question of "how," it is not because I would wish to
eliminate the questions of "what" and "why." Rather, it is that
I wish to present these questions in a different way—better
still, to know if it is legitimate to imagine a power that unites in
itself a what, a why, and a how. To put it bluntly, I would say
that to begin the analysis with a "how" is to introduce the
suspicion that power as such does not exist.*

—MICHEL FOUCAULT (2000)

Since this work addresses the maintenance of hegemonic domination in Ecuador and the role of national histories and identities in this political process, its findings are particular to Ecuador's social reality. However, I maintain that a more theoretical elaboration of my findings may have a wider geographical application, in terms of how contemporary national hegemonic production works and, more specifically, how postcolonial race, class, and gender are invested in the nationalizing process of identity; and in terms of the analysis of national historical production and history's investment in the hegemonic production of contemporary Latin American national identities.

I portray hegemony as a political project in the making, with no unidirectional or single form of control. This does not mean that the hegemonic project is not limited by parameters of class and social institution. Such criteria by themselves do not produce the national outcome; rather, socially constituted human subjects and socially institutionalized deployments are implicated in hegemonic production—production that is inherent in each subject's and institution's own form of national identification. This dynamic understanding of hegemony is most readily applicable to a Latin American context that is intersected by new "old" global concerns (Hall 1997) that provide new meaning to old cultural forms (or "reconversion," as García-Canclini [1992] calls it).

Reconversion is probably the most common way in which the continent has been historically constituted from a colonial reality of European, African, and indigenous traditions. Latin America and the Caribbean have never been free of global influences; throughout the last five centuries, they have readily responded to European and African influences and cultural forms pierced by differing notions of power and identity (D. Miller 1992). In this manner, Latin America has been supported by constant reformulations of meaningful cultural embodiments and symbols that adapt to the changing social conditions of the reconquered territories. This process of cultural reconversion is also inherent in a national identity which has been transformed in the last two hundred years by the needs of the new postcolonial reality (Appiah 1997).

Paramount in postcolonial life has been the emergence of new forms of political control, suitably expressed in neocolonial forms of domination, with no further need for direct political occupation (Fanon 1967). This neocolonial experience has also produced new cultural forms, forms of nationalism, and social identities that themselves have been adapted to the fluctuating political and cultural scene (D. Miller 1992). It is in this setting that the present book's understanding of hegemony could prove insightful and politically useful. In a poststructural approach, hegemony is never too far, or disengaged, from cultural production or social reconversion. This means both a more political interpretation of culture and its hegemonizing role and the deconstruction of hegemony as a much more open-ended and transformative identity process, one that includes, but is not limited to, the nation.

This particular approach, although far from complete, is better able to incorporate the contradictions inherent in the continent's historical and cultural production. Far from seeing ruling elites and hidden agendas on the one side and romanticized natives and pristine popular culture on the other, it provides for a broader and more realistic assessment of cultural forms (Rowe and Schelling 1991). It is in this regard that global discourses about transnational capital exploitation, international financial institutions, demands on Third World debtor economies, development loans, and international NGOs are more easily related to diverse local populations creating and responding to different national socioeconomic realities. It is within this configuration that the continent's national communities may be viewed as actively involved in and responding to their own projected future. It provides an alternative to understanding local populations as blindly responding to coercive economic and political forces with nothing other than outright resistance and revolution. Instead, a middle ground in which local populations neither exclusively resist nor are co-opted seems to be essential for analyzing the modern production of cultural identities.

At the same time, the configuration of hegemony discussed here provides more realistic parameters for the many postmodern discourses that do not take into account the oppressive and exploitative conditions in which most postcolonial subjects must re-create their lives in personally and socially significant ways. To this end, the understanding of national identity I have presented here is intended to better represent the Latin American and Caribbean subject as compounded of both global and local repressive mechanisms and personal agency that allows that subject to respond, adapt, resist, and contribute to the transformation of these political mechanisms. This new form of representation, it is hoped, will contribute to a better understanding of how people, simply by living their lives, are inherently involved in political situations that strongly implicate their own historical subjugation.

The idea of historical subordination leads us to the continent's original form of historical production and its contribution to nationally hegemonizing political identities. The study of nation-states like Peru and Mexico, which occupy areas traditionally represented as cultural cores, are the least likely to benefit from the present analysis, not necessarily because I do not believe that the hegemonic production of national identities might work in similar fashion there, but because in these two state projects, history has always been an issue of debate. Unlike in the rest of the continent, history has never been overlooked in Peru's and Mexico's production of a national identity. The national investment of these two countries in their history is so clear that history to them is a political question. It is not so much that my analysis might not contribute to understanding the Peruvian and Mexican forms of historiography, but that Peru's and Mexico's state sanctioning of and involvement with historical production produce cultural reconversion and social identification.

This explicit type of historical investment has begun to be addressed in areas of the world (Kohl and Fawcett 1995; Abu El-Haj 2001) other than Mexico (Castañeda 1996; Gándara 1992) and Peru (De la Cadena 2000; Patterson 1995a). But it is perhaps more interesting that researchers are slowly reevaluating the dynamic forms of historical representation invested in each nation's cultural identity as expressed in public forums such as the media, film, education, and social mobilization (Franco 1992; Monsiváis 1995).

My analysis could lead to interesting research on the other countries of the continent, I believe. Most Latin American and Caribbean nation-states, like Ecuador, do not figure prominently in the historical representation of the continent's pre-Hispanic past. Rather, as in Ecuador, many of these nation-states have unconsciously incorporated a pre-Hispanic narrative of the past into their national identity. In this regard, it would be instructive to assess the initial mechanism of hermeneutical representation and hegemonic devices used to build these nation-states' identities and to reconvert their present-day cultural reality.

Without exception, all the Caribbean islands saw the decimation of their indigenous population within a couple of decades of the European conquest (Greenblatt 1993). The Caribbean islands not only were the main entry points of European maritime explorers, but also saw themselves continually conquered by warring European monarchs and their emerging national projects (quite possibly in an earlier version of a colonial playing-out of a larger global war. One must ask what role colonial expansion and the Caribbean islands themselves played in Europe's configuration as nation-states [Mignolo 1994, 2000]). At the same time, the Caribbean's indigenous population found itself involved in the rise of military conflicts, sometimes resisting, sometimes helping different European powers until the indigenous groups were completely destroyed (Adorno 1993).

The Caribbean presents a unique historical hypothesis of its pre-Hispanic past (Trouillot 1995). One of the ways in which this complex colonial legacy is imagined is as a cultural heritage, particularly a specific genealogical kind. Throughout the Caribbean, a social discourse that claims direct lineage to many of the decimated Indian groups is quite common. The claim of Puerto Ricans in Manhattan to Taíno culture is one of the most visible transformations of this historical production. Throughout the islands, whole national communities imagine themselves to be the descendants of brave Indian populations, a belief that contributes enormously to their understanding of their historical heritage, social identification, and cultural production.

The Caribbean discourse of a pre-Hispanic lineage is quite different from the *mestizaje* ideology developed on the Latin American mainland, since it does not have a contemporary Indian population for contrast. This historically imagined genetic discourse is crucial in providing racial identification (in the Dominican Republic), national legitimization (in Jamaica), and popular cultural symbols (e.g., carnival celebrations in Trinidad and other islands).

Indigenous Carib and Arawak populations (as well as their regional variations) are also continually elaborated because they no longer exist and implicitly contribute to the Caribbean nation-states' historical heritage and identity. As in Ecuador, the Caribbean does not explicitly sanction the pre-Hispanic past as an essential and, even worse, volatile political subject. Yet, as I argue, pre-Hispanic discourses cannot help but be an important element in a nation's historical legitimization, importantly expressed in its implicit construction and explicit political denial. The Caribbean's historiography is constructed along the lines of a significant postcolonial aftermath much more recent because of the longer domination of the islands by the different European nation-states, the islands' recent struggles for national liberation, and their more direct encounter with U.S. neocolonial domination and territorial occupation.

It would be useful to explore the role history has played in the islands' national identifications and their transformation into an exploited and impoverished region in the postmodern global market. It would be also useful to explore historical production in the Caribbean, as each island has lived the last four centuries without an Indian presence, and yet all have maintained a vivid ideal of Indian heritage from the pre-Hispanic past. The presence of a large slave population, mostly but not exclusively from the African continent, provides broader identity markers and historically exploitative relationships that further complicate each Caribbean nation-state's identity.

The large African presence also could be insightfully explored in the largest nation-state of the South American continent, Brazil. This former Portuguese colony could benefit from an assessment along the lines presented in this book—an analysis that would contribute to rounding out our findings about the constitution of Latin Americans as historical subjects. Three distinct areas would refine our analysis of Brazil from a poststructural historical viewpoint: the presence of large diasporic African populations, similar to those found in other areas of the continent; Brazil's unique process for winning independence, which made the country rival Portugal in power and status; and the large contemporary presence of Indian groups in the Amazon. These three areas would provide for an interesting case study into other possible ways in which historical imagination has contributed to the continent's articulation of national identity. Brazil more than any other country in South America possesses a large Indian and black population that has contributed significantly to the country's national portrayal. Analysis of Brazil's historiography within the structure I present in this book would demand understanding the manner in which these two populations simultaneously have been historically constructed as "native" and excluded from mainstream social structures and the official political stage. It is important to assess history's role in this regard, and the way in which both the Indian and the black communities have consistently contested and contributed to the country's representation of them and other national communities. Understanding the role of history in the national production of Brazil would help us understand the political subjugation of similar communities throughout the continent and their relationship to this exploitative process.

Assessing the actual comparative historical appearance of Latin American subjects as a whole could be most paradigmatic, however. Up to now, scholars have taken for granted the continent's historical process and the development of a particular kind of Latin American and Caribbean national identity/population. What this study, and similar ones highlighted for other nation-states, points to is the essentially political nature of the historical enterprise. Far from being a neutral intellectual endeavor, historical production is necessarily implicated in hegemonic articulation, even more pervasively so in nation-states that do not explicitly recognize their "primeval dance" with historical representation. There is nothing "natural" or taken for granted in historical research or, for that matter, in the appearance of Latin American historical subjects as such. Rather, the nature of a Latin American historical subject should be critically assessed and deconstructed, particularly since pre-Hispanic elements are one of the most essential components of this historical subjugation/creation of national identity. The production of national, continental, and regional identities is implicit in hegemonic devices that must be explained, not simply described, narrated, contested, or, worse, legitimized. Furthermore, these national identities are fundamentally inscribed within cultural forms that have evolved from an initial representation as colonial territories to cultural markers for a new postcolonial citizen.

Historical research for too long has effaced its political counterpart. Generations of elites have found in an "objective" history the legitimization of their class; other communities have either been robbed of their history or have had to reclaim it through the hegemonic process of reconstituting their national identity. But both sides of the equation are equally involved in the hegemonic articulation of the Latin American subject and, through that articulation, in the cultural representation of groups, regions, nations, and even the continent itself. As I have argued throughout this book, history is also an imagined cultural form, and both history and culture are implicated in political production by the effects of power and agency.

Just as studies of national identity and historical deconstruction would be useful in assessing the continent's reality, the assessment of popular culture and agency is another area that needs study. Cultural production, particularly contemporary everyday popular culture, is another area needing investigation for a broader understanding of hegemony. As outlined throughout this book, without culture or agency, no history would have occurred to be reconstructed; therefore, no national hegemonic articulation could have been secured for the domination of the people of Latin America or any other continent.

REFERENCES

Abelove, Henry; Michele Aina Barale; and David Halperin. 1993. *The Lesbian and Gay Studies Reader*. New York: Routledge.

Abrams, Phillip. 1988. "Notes on the Difficulty of Studying the State (1977)." *Journal of Historical Sociology* 1(1): 58–89.

Abu El-Haj, Nadia. 2001. *Facts on the Ground: Archaeological Practice and Territorial Self-Fashioning* in Israeli Society. Chicago: University of Chicago Press.

Academia de las Lenguas Quichua-Castellano. 1993. "Historia sobre la cultura india en Cayambe-Pesillo." In Federación Indígena Pichincha Runacunapac Riccharimui, *Historia de la Organización Indígena en Pichincha*, pp. 11–24. Quito: Abya-Yala.

Acción Ecológica. 2001. "Protesters Occupy IMF Offices in Quito, Ecuador." Press release.

Acosta, Alberto, et al. 1997. *Identidad nacional y globalización*. Quito: Instituto Latinoamericano de Investigaciones Sociales, Facultad Latinoamericana de Ciencias Sociales (FLACSO), and Instituto de Altos Estudios Nacionales.

Adorno, Rolena. 1993. "The Negotiation of Fear in Cabeza de Vaca's *Naufragios*." In *New World Encounters*, edited by S. Greenblatt, pp. 48–84. Berkeley & Los Angeles: University of California Press.

Adoum, Jorge Enrique. 2000. *Ecuador: Señas particulares*. Quito: Eskeltra.

———. 1976. *entre Marx y una mujer desnuda*. Quito: Editorial El Conejo.

Agoglia, Rodolfo, ed. 1985. *Historiografía ecuatoriana*. Quito: Banco Central del Ecuador and Corporación Editora Nacional.

Alameddine, Rabih. 1998. *Koolaids: The Art of War*. New York: Picador.

Alarcón, Norma. 1990. "The Theoretical Subject(s) of *This Bridge Called My Back* and Anglo-American Feminism." In *Making Face, Making Soul/Haciendo Caras: Creative and Critical Perspectives by Feminists of Color*, edited by G. Anzaldúa, pp. 356–364. San Francisco: Aunt Lute Foundation Books.

Alarcón, Norma; Cherríe Moraga; and Ana Castillo, eds. 1993. *The Sexuality of Latinas*. Berkeley, Calif.: Third Woman Press.

Allauca, José María. 1993. "La historia de mi organización." In *Primer con-curso de testimonio: La historia de mi organización*, pp. 17–64. Quito: Escuela de Formación Popular "Fernando Velasco" and Centro de Educación Popular.

Allen, Catherine J. 1988. *The Hold Life Has: Coca and Cultural Identity in an Andean Community*. Washington, D.C.: Smithsonian Institution Press.

Almeida, Ileana, et al. 1992. *Indios: Una reflexión sobre el levantamiento indígena de 1990*. Quito: Instituto Latinoamericano de Investigaciones Sociales (ILDIS) and Abya-Yala.

Alonso, Ana María. 1995. *Thread of Blood: Colonialism, Revolution, and Gender on Mexico's Northern Frontier*. Tucson: University of Arizona Press.

———. 1988. "The Effects of Truth: Re-Presentation of the Past and the Imagining of a Community." *Journal of Historical Sociology* 1(1): 33–57.

Althusser, Louis. 1977. *Lenin and Philosophy, and Other Essays*. London: New Left Books.

Álvarez, Julia. 1991. *How the García Girls Lost Their Accents*. New York: Plume Books.

Amin, Samir. 1997. *Capitalism in the Age of Globalization: The Management of Contemporary Society*. London: Atlantic Highlands.

Anderson, Benedict. 1991. *Imagined Communities: Reflections on the Origin and Spread of Nationalism*. Rev. and expanded ed. London: Verso.

———. 1983. *Imagined Communities: Reflections on the Origin and Spread of Nationalism*. London: Verso.

Andrade, Xavier. 1997. "Carnaval de masculinidades." *ICONOS* 2: 71–84.

———. 1995. "Pancho Jaime: Masculinidad, violencia, imágenes y textos de una narrativa popular." *Ecuador Debate* 36 (December): 95–108.

Andrade Reimers, Luis. 1995. *Biografía de Atahualpa*. Quito: Fundación Ecuatoriana de Desarrollo.

Antiquity. 1971. Editorial. 45(177): 1.

Anzaldúa, Gloria. 1987. *Borderlands/La Frontera: The New Mestiza*. San Francisco: Aunt Lute Foundation Books.

———, ed. 1990. *Making Face, Making Soul/Haciendo Caras: Creative and Critical Perspectives by Feminists of Color*. San Francisco: Aunt Lute Foundation Books.

Anzaldúa, Gloria, and Ann Louise Keating. 2000. *Gloria E. Anzaldúa: Interviews and Entrevistas*. New York: Routledge.

Appiah, Kwame Anthony. 1997. "Is the 'Post' in 'Postcolonial' the 'Post' in Postmodern?" In *Dangerous Liaisons: Gender, Nation, and Postcolonial Perspectives*, edited by A. McClintock et al., pp. 420–444. Minneapolis: University of Minnesota Press.

Arce, Alberto, and Norman Long, eds. 2000. "Reconfiguring Modernity and Development from an Anthropological Perspective." In *Anthropology, Development and Modernities: Exploring Discourses, Counter-Tendencies, and Violence*, pp. 1–31. London: Routledge.

Arenas, Reinaldo. 1993. *Before Night Falls*. New York: Viking Press.

———. 1991. *El asalto*. Miami: Ediciones Universal.

Arnold, Bettina. 1992. "Germany's Nazi Past: How Hitler's Archaeologists Distorted European Prehistory to Justify Racist and Territorial Goals." *Archaeology* (July/August): 30–37.

———. 1990. "The Past as Propaganda: Totalitarian Archaeology in Nazi Germany." *Antiquity* 64(244): 464–478.

Asad, Talal. 1982. "A Comment on the Idea of Non-Western Anthropology." In *Indigenous Anthropology in Non-Western Countries*, edited by H. Fahim, pp. 284–287. Durham, N.C.: Carolina Academic Press.

———. 1985. "Primitive States and the Reproduction of Production Relations." *Critique of Anthropology* 5(2): 21–33.

Aspiazu Carbo, Miguel. 1970. "Acta de fundación de la Ciudad de Santiago de Guayaquil (Santiago de la Provincia de Quito) 15 de Agosto de 1534." *Cuadernos de Historia y Arqueología* 20(37): 225–253.

Ayala Mora, Enrique. 1993. *Estudios sobre historia ecuatoriana*. Quito: Tehisladap.

———. 1991. *Las nacionalidades indígenas en el Ecuador: Contribución para su estudio*. Ibarra, Ecuador: Corporación Imbabura.

———. 1986. *Los partidos políticos en el Ecuador: Síntesis histórica*. Quito: Ediciones La Tierra.

———. 1985a. *La historia del Ecuador: Ensayos de interpretación*. Quito: Corporación Editora Nacional.

———. 1985b. *Lucha política y origen de los partidos en Ecuador*. Quito: Corporación Editora Nacional.

Ayala Mora, Enrique, ed. 1983. *Nueva historia del Ecuador*. 13 vols. Quito: Corporación Editora Nacional and Editorial Grijalbo. Ayala Mora, Enrique, et al. 1992. *Pueblos indios, estado y derecho*. Quito: Corporación Editora Nacional.

Babb, Valerie. 1998. *Whiteness Visible: The Meaning of Whiteness in American Literature and Content*. New York: New York University Press.

Baldwin, James. 1990. *Just above My Head*. New York: Laurel Books.

———. 1988a. *Another Country*. New York: Laurel.

———. 1988b. *The Fire Next Time*. New York: Laurel.

———. 1984. *Notes of a Native Son*. Boston: Beacon Press.

Balibar, Etienne, and Immanuel Wallerstein. 1991. *Race, Nation, Class: Ambiguous Identities*. New York: Routledge.

Barbero, Jesús Martín. 1993. "Latin American: Cultures in the Communication Media." *Journal of Communication* 43(2): 18–30.

———. 1987. *De los medios a las mediaciones*. Barcelona: Gustavo Gil.

Barsky, Osvaldo. 1984. *La reforma agraria ecuatoriana*. Biblioteca de Ciencias Sociales, vol. 3. Quito: Corporación Editora Nacional.

Barthes, Roland. 1992. *Incidents*. Berkeley & Los Angeles: University of California Press.

———. 1982. *A Barthes Reader*. New York: Hill and Wang.

———. 1972. *Mythologies*. New York: Noonday Press.

Baudin, Louis. 1961. *A Socialist Empire: The Incas of Peru*. Princeton, N.J.: Van Nostrand.

Beach, David. 1998. "Cognitive Archaeology and Imaginary History at Great Zimbabwe." *Current Anthropology* 39(1): 47–72.

Becker, Marc. 1992. "Nationalism and Pluri-Nationalism in a Multi-Ethnic State: Indigenous Organization in Ecuador." Paper presented at the Mid-America Conference on History, Chicago, September.

Benavides, O. Hugo. 2001. "My Deep Dark Pain Is Love: Reflections on an Acquired Identity." In "Gay Rights at the End of the Twentieth Century." *Occasional Paper Number 5*, edited by B. Abed. School of Continuing and Professional Studies, Paul McGhee Division, New York University.

———. 1998. "The Homosexual and the Homonational: Discourse on Sex and Race in Post–Neo Colonial Ecuador." Paper presented at the Queer Globalization and Local Homosexualities Conference, New York, June.

———. 1994. "Archaeology and Politics: The Struggle for Historical Legitimacy." Paper presented at the Meetings of Applied Anthropology, Cancún, Mexico, April.

Benavides Solís, Jorge. 1986. *La arquitectura y el urbanismo de Cochasquí.* Quito: Fundación Saber.

Bender, Barbara. 1998. *Stonehenge: Making Space.* New York: Berg.

Benítez, Silvia, and Gaby Costa. 1983. "La Familia, la ciudad y la vida cotidiana en el período colonial." In *Nueva historia del Ecuador,* vol. 5, edited by E. Ayala Mora, pp. 187–230. Quito: Corporación Editora Nacional and Editorial Grijalbo.

Benítez Vinueza, Leopoldo. 1986. *Ecuador: Drama y paradoja.* Quito: Banco Central del Ecuador and Corporación Editora Nacional.

Benzoni, Girolamo. 1995. *La historia del mundo nuovo (relatos de su viaje por Ecuador, 1547–1550).* Guayaquil: Banco Central del Ecuador.

Bergmann, Emilie, and Paul Julian Smith, eds. 1995. *¿Entiendes?: Queer Readings, Hispanic Writings.* Durham, N.C.: Duke University Press.

Bernard, H. Russell. 1994. *Research Methods in Cultural Anthropology.* Newbury Park, Calif.: Sage Publications.

Berris, David. 1996. "Introduction: If You're Gay and Irish, Your Parents Must Be English." *Identities: Global Studies in Culture and Power* 2(3): 189–196.

Bhabha, Homi, ed. 1990. *Nation and Narration.* London: Routledge.

Birken, Lawrence. 1988. *Consuming Desire: Sexual Science and the Emergence of a Culture of Abundance.* Ithaca, N.Y.: Cornell University Press.

Blakey, Michael. 1995. "Race, Nationalism, and the Afrocentric Past." In *Making Alternative Histories: The Practice of Archaeology and History in Non-Western Settings,* edited by T. Patterson and P. Schmidt, pp. 213–228. Santa Fe, N.M.: School of American Research Press.

———. 1991. "Man and Nature, White and Other." In *Decolonizing Anthropology: Moving Further toward an Anthropology for Liberation,* edited by F. Harrison, pp. 15–23. Washington, D.C.: Association of Black Anthropologists, American Anthropological Association.

Bommes, M., and Patrick Wright. 1982. "Charms of Residence: The Public and the Past." In *Making Histories: Studies in History-Writing and Politics,* edited by R. Johnson et al., pp. 253–302. Minneapolis: University of Minnesota Press.

Bond, George, and Angela Gilliam, eds. 1994. *Social Construction of the Past: Representation as Power.* London: Routledge.

Bourdieu, Pierre. 1993. *The Field of Cultural Production: Essays on Art and Literature.* New York: Columbia University Press.

Bray, Tamara. 1991. *The Effects of Inca Imperialism in the Northern Frontier,* Ph.D. diss., State University of New York at Binghamton, microfilm #AAC9110795.

Brettell, Caroline, and Carolyn Sargent, eds. 1997. *Gender in Cross-Cultural Perspective.* Upper Saddle River, N.J.: Prentice Hall.

Bronfen, Elizabeth. 1996. "Killing Gazes, Killing in the Gaze: On Michael Powell's Peeping Tom." In *Gaze and Voice as Love Objects,* edited by R. Saleci and S. Zizek, pp. 59–89. Durham, N.C.: Duke University Press.

Browning, Frank. 1991. *The Culture of Desire: Paradox and Perversity in the Lives of Gay Men.* New York: Vintage Books.

Bruhns, Karen. 1994. *Ancient South America.* Cambridge: Cambridge University Press.

Burns, Kathryn. 1999. *Colonial Habits: Convents and the Spiritual Economy of Cuzco, Peru.* Durham, N.C.: Duke University Press.

Bustos-Aguilar, Pedro. 1995. "Mister, Don't Touch the Banana: Notes on the Popularity of the Ethnosexed Body South of the Border." *Critique of Anthropology* 15(2): 149–170.

Butler, Judith. 1997a. "Gender Is Burning." In *Dangerous Liaisons: Gender, Nation and Postcolonial Perspectives,* edited by Anne McClintock, Aamir Mufti, and Ella Shohat, pp. 381–395. Minneapolis: University of Minnesota Press.

———. 1997b. *The Psychic Life of Power.* Stanford, Calif.: Stanford University Press.

———. 1993. *Bodies That Matter: On the Discursive Limits of "Sex."* New York: Routledge.

Cabral, Amilcar. 1974a. *Return to the Source.* New York: Monthly Review Press.

———. 1974b. *Unity and Struggle: Speeches and Writing.* New York: Monthly Review Press.

Campaña Continental (500 Años de Resistencia Indígena y Popular). 1990. *Queremos que nos escuchen.* Quito.

Carrera Andrade, Jorge. 2002. *El camino del sol I y II.* Colección Luna Tierna, Campanha Nacional Eugenio Espejo por el Libro y la Lectura, vols. 3, 6. Quito: Cargraphics.

———. 1957. "Los franceses incendian Guayaquil." *Cuadernos de Historia y Arqueología* 7(19–21): 55–61.

Carrier, Joseph. 1995. *De los Otros: Intimacy and Homosexuality among Mexican Men.* New York: Columbia University Press.

Carrión, Benjamín. 2002. *El cuento de la patria.* Colección Luna Tierna,

Campanha Nacional Eugenio Espejo por el Libro y la Lectura, vol. 1. Quito: Cargraphics.

Castañeda, Quetzil. 1996. *In the Museum of Maya Culture: Touring Chichén Itzá.* Minneapolis: University of Minnesota Press.

———. 1995. "'The Progress That Chose a Village': Measuring Zero-Degree Culture and the 'Impact' of Anthropology." *Critique of Anthropology* 15(2): 115–147.

Castillo, Ana. 1996. *Loverboys.* New York: Plume.

———. 1992. *The Mixquiahuala Letters.* New York: Anchor Books.

Centro de Documentación e Información de los Movimientos Sociales del Ecuador (CEDIME). 1987. *Derechos de la mujer indígena.* Quito: CEDIME.

Centro de Educación Popular (CEDEP). 1986. *Primer concurso de testimonio: La historia de mi organización.* Quito: Escuela de Formación Popular "Fernando Velasco" and CEDEP.

Centro de Estudios y Difusión Social (CEDIS). 1992. *Indios, tierra y utopía.* Quito: CEDIS.

Cervone, Emma, and Fredy Rivera, eds. 1999. *Ecuador racista: Imágenes e identidades.* Quito: FLACSO-Ecuador.

Corporación Ecuatoriana de Turismo (CETURIS). 1972. "Marco de referencia para la creación del parque arqueológico y la preservación de sus monumentos." Manuscript. Quito: Dirección Nacional de Turismo.

Cevallos, Pedro Fermín. 1870. *Historia del Ecuador.* Quito: Clásicos Ariel.

Cevallos García, Gabriel. 1960. *Visión teórica del Ecuador.* Biblioteca Ecuatoriana Mínima. Puebla, Mexico: J. M. Cajica.

Chatterjee, Partha. 1993. *The Nation and Its Fragments: Colonial and Postcolonial Histories.* Princeton, N.J.: Princeton University Press.

———. 1986. *Nationalist Thought and the Colonial World: A Derivative Discourse?* Tokyo: Zed Books for United Nations University.

Chela, Tránsito. 1992. "Somos hijos de Pachacamac: Entrevista a los mayores de su comunidad." In *Indios, tierra y utopía,* pp. 39–57. Quito: CEDIS.

Churuchumbi, Guillermo. 1993. "Encuentros culturales con las comunidades indígenas en la provincia de Pichincha." In *Historia de la organización indígena en Pichincha,* pp. 39–55. Quito: Abya-Yala.

Cieza de León, Pedro de. 1986. *La crónica del Perú, primera parte.* Lima: Pontificia Universidad Católica del Perú, Fondo Editorial, Academia Nacional de la Historia.

———. [1553] 1971. *La crónica del Perú.* Buenos Aires: Colección Austral.

———. [1553] 1945. *La crónica del Peru.* Buenos Aires: Colección Austral.

Cifuentes, María Ángela. 1999. *El placer de la representación: La imagen femenina ante la moda y el retrato (Quito, 1880–1920).* Quito: Abya-Yala.

Classen, Constance. 1993. *Inca Cosmology and the Human Body.* Salt Lake City: University of Utah Press.

Clifford, James. 1992. "Traveling Culture." In *Cultural Studies,* edited by L. Grossberg, C. Nelson, and P. Treichel, pp. 92–116. London: Routledge.

———. 1988. "On Collecting Art and Culture." In *The Predicament of Culture: Twentieth-Century Ethnography, Literature, and Art*, edited by J. Clifford, pp. 215-252. Cambridge: Harvard University Press.

Cobham, Rhonda. 1992. "Misgendering the Nation: African Nationalist Fictions and Nuruddin Farah's *Maps*." In *Nationalisms and Sexualities*, edited by A. Parker et al., pp. 42-49. New York: Routledge.

Cobo, Father Bernabé. [1653] 1983. *History of the Inca Empire: An Account of the Indians' Customs and Their Origin, Together with a Treatise on Inca Legends, History, and Social Institutions*. Translated and edited by Roland Hamilton. Austin: University of Texas Press.

Cole, John, and Eric Wolf. 1974. *The Hidden Frontier: Ecology and Ethnicity in an Alpine Valley*. New York: Academic Press.

Collier, Donald. 1982. "One Hundred Years of Ecuadorian Archaeology." In *Primer Simposio de Correlaciones Antropológicas Andino-Mesomericano*, edited by P. Norton and J. Marcos, pp. 5-33. Guayaquil: ESPOL.

Comaroff, John, and Jean Comaroff. 1992. *Ethnography and the Historical Imagination*. San Francisco: Westview Press.

El Comercio (Quito). 1997a. "La antropología es una ficción: Hugo Burgos." (June 4).

———. 1997b. "De viaje hasta el pasado" (March 16).

———. 1995. "Pistas para armar una nación" (November 29).

———. 1994. "La cultura huancavilca rescata su emblema" (October 10).

———. 1993. "San Biritute, ídolo o santo?" (August 22).

Comisión por la Defensa de los Derechos Humanos (CDDH). 1996. *El levantamiento indígena y la cuestión nacional*. Quito: Abya-Yala and CDDH.

Confederación Nacional de Indígenas del Ecuador (CONAIE). 1998. *Las nacionalidades indígenas y el estado plurinacional*. Quito: CONAIE.

———. 1997. *Proyecto político de la CONAIE*. Quito: CONAIE.

———. 1989. *Las nacionalidades indígenas en el Ecuador: Nuestro proceso organizativo*. Quito: Editorial TINCUI/CONAI, Ediciones Abya-Yala.

———. 1988a. *Derechos humanos y solidaridad de los pueblos indígenas*. Quito: CONAIE.

———. 1988b. *Primer encuentro de derechos humanos CONAIE-ECUARUNARI*. Quito: CONAIE.

Coronil, Fernando. 1997. *The Magical State: Nature, Money, and Modernity in Venezuela*. Chicago: University of Chicago Press.

Corrigan, Phillip, and Derek Sayer. 1985. *The Great Arch: English State Formation as Cultural Revolution*. Oxford: Basil Blackwell.

Cortez, Jaime. 1999. *Virgins, Guerrillas, and Locas: Gay Latinos Write about Love*. New York: Cleis Press.

Costales, Piedad, and Alfredo Costales. 1990-1991. *Historia india de Cochasquí: Ensayo de interpretación etnográfica con documentos*. Quito: H. Consejo Provincial de Pichincha.

Crain, Mary. 1990. "The Social Construction of National Identity in Highland Ecuador." *Anthropological Quarterly* 63(1): 43-59.

———. 1989. *Ritual, memoria popular y proceso político en la sierra ecuatoriana.* Quito: Corporación Editora Nacional, Ediciones Abya-Yala.

Cueva, Agustín. 1988. *Las democracias restringidas de América Latina: Elementos para una reflexión crítica.* Quito: Planeta.

———. 1987. *La teoría marxista: Categorías de base y problemas actuales.* Quito: Planeta.

———. 1986. *Lecturas y rupturas: Diez ensayos sociológicos sobre la literatura del Ecuador.* Quito: Planeta.

———. 1981. *Entre la ira y la esperanza: Ensayos sobre la cultura nacional.* Cuenca, Ecuador: Núcleo del Azuay de la Casa de la Cultura Ecuatoriana.

Cypess, Sandra Messinger. 1991. *La Malinche in Mexican Literature: From History to Myth.* Austin: University of Texas Press.

Davidow, Joie. 2000. Foreword to *Las Mamis: Favorite Latino Authors Remember Their Mothers,* edited by E. Santiago and J. Davidow. New York: Alfred A. Knopf.

Dávila, Arlene. 1997. *Sponsored Identities: Cultural Politics in Puerto Rico.* Philadelphia: Temple University Press.

De Certeau, Michel. 1984. *The Practice of Everyday Life.* Berkeley & Los Angeles: University of California Press.

de la Cadena, Marisol. 2000. *Indigenous Mestizos: The Politics of Race and Culture in Cuzco, Peru, 1919–1991.* Durham, N.C.: Duke University Press.

de la Cuadra, José. 1973. *Los sangurimas, hornos y otros relatos.* Guayaquil: Ariel.

de las Casas, Fray Bartolomé. 1982. *Los indios de México y Nueva España: Antología.* Mexico City: Porrúa.

de la Torre Espinosa, Carlos. 1996. *El racismo en Ecuador: Experiencias de los indios de clase media.* Quito: Centro Andino de Acción Popular.

Deler, Jean-Paul. 1994. "Transformaciones regionales y organización del espacio nacional ecuatoriano entre 1830–1930." In *Historia y región en el Ecuador, 1830–1930,* edited by J. Maiguashca, pp. 295–354. Quito: FLACSO and Ediciones Abya-Yala.

del Valle, Teresa. 1993. *Gendered Anthropology.* London: Routledge.

El Día (Quito). 1930. "Búsqueda de madre de Atahualpa" (September).

Díaz, Junot. 1997. *Drown.* New York: Riverhead Books.

Dirks, Nicholas; Geoff Eley; and Sherry Ortner. 1994. *Culture/Power/History: A Reader in Contemporary Social Theory.* Princeton, N.J.: Princeton University Press.

Domínguez, Virginia. 1996. "Engendering the Sexualized State of the Nation?" *Identities: Global Studies in Culture and Power* 2(3): 301–305.

———. 1986. "The Marketing of Heritage." *American Ethnologist* 13(3): 546–555.

Donoso Pareja, Miguel. 2000. *Ecuador: Identidad o esquizofrenia.* Quito: Eskeltra Editorial.

Dyer, Richard. 1997. "The White Man's Muscles." In *Race and the Subject of Masculinities,* edited by H. Stecopoulos and M. Uebel, pp. 286–314. Durham, N.C.: Duke University Press.

Echeverría Almeida, José. 1995. "La construcción de lo prehispánico: Aproximación antropológica a la arqueología ecuatoriana." M.A. thesis, FLACSO, Quito.

Efrén Reyes, Oscar. 1967. *Breve historia general del Ecuador.* 3 vols. Quito: Chávez.

Elon, Amos. 1997. "Politics and Archaeology." In *The Archaeology of Israel: Constructing the Past, Interpreting the Present,* edited by N. Silberman and D. Small, pp. 18–28 Sheffield, Eng.: Sheffield Academic Press.

Enloe, Cynthia. 1990. *Bananas, Beaches, and Bases.* Berkeley & Los Angeles: University of California Press.

Escobar, Arturo. 1995. *Encountering Development: The Making and Unmaking of the Third World.* Princeton, N.J.: Princeton University Press.

Escobar, Arturo, and Sonia Álvarez, eds. 1992. *The Making of Social Movements in Latin America: Identity, Strategy, and Democracy.* Boulder, Colo.: Westview Press.

Espejo, Eugenio de Santa Cruz y. 1791. "Primicias de la cultura de Quito." In *Obras escogidas,* pp. 201–221. Quito: Clásicos Ariel.

———. 1786. "Defensa de los curas de Riobamba." In *Obras escogidas,* pp. 9–86. Quito: Clásicos Ariel.

Espinosa, Simón. 1995. "Hacia un nuevo Ecuador." In *Tiwintsa,* pp. 58–73. Quito: Editorial El Conejo.

Espinosa Apolo, Manuel. 1995. *Los mestizos ecuatorianos y las señas de identidad cultural.* Quito: Centro de Estudios Felipe Guamán de Ayala.

Espinosa Soriano, Waldemar. 1988. *Los cayambes y carangues: Siglos xv–xvi, el testimonio de la etnohistoria,* vols. 1 and 2. Otavalo, Ecuador: Instituto Otavaleño de Antropología.

Estrada, Emilio. 1962a. *Arqueología de Manabí Central.* Publicación del Museo Víctor Emilio Estrada, no. 7. Guayaquil: Museo Víctor Emilio Estrada.

———. 1962b. "Correlaciones entre la arqueología de la costa del Ecuador y Perú." *Humanitas* (Quito) 2(2): 31–61.

———. 1961. *Nuevos elementos de la cultura valdivia: Sus posibles contactos transpacíficos.* Guayaquil: Sub-comité Ecuatoriano de Antropología Dependiente del Instituto Panamericano de Geografía e Historia.

———. 1958. *Las culturas pre-clásicas, formativas o arcaicas del Ecuador.* Publicación del Museo Víctor Emilio Estrada, no. 5. Guayaquil: Museo Víctor Emilio Estrada.

———. 1957a. "Cronología de la Cuenca del Guayas." *Cuadernos de Historia y Arqueología* (Guayaquil) 7: 232–236.

———. 1957b. *Los Huancavilcas: Últimas civilizaciones pre-históricas de la Costa del Guayas.* Publicación del Museo Víctor Emilio Estrada, no. 3. Guayaquil: Museo Víctor Emilio Estrada.

———. 1957c. *Prehistoria de Manabí.* Publicación del Museo Víctor Emilio Estrada, no. 4. Guayaquil: Museo Víctor Emilio Estrada.

———. 1957d. "Sumario de las características Milagro-Quevedo." *Cuadernos de Historia y Arqueología* (Guayaquil) 7: 237–239.

———. 1957e. *Últimas civilizaciones pre-históricas de la Cuenca del Río Gua-*

yas. Publicación del Museo Víctor Emilio Estrada, no.2. Guayaquil: Museo Víctor Emilio Estrada.

———. 1956. *Valdivia: Un sitio arqueológico formativo en la costa de la provincia del Guayas, Ecuador.* Publicación del Museo Víctor Emilio Estrada, no.1. Guayaquil: Museo Víctor Emilio Estrada.

———. 1954. *Ensayo preliminar sobre la arqueología de milagro.* Guayaquil: Editorial Cervantes.

Estrada Ycaza, Julio. 1987. *Andanzas de cieza por tierras americanas.* Guayaquil: Banco Central del Ecuador and Archivo Histórico del Guayas.

———. 1975. "Alrededor de la fundación de Guayaquil." *Revista del Archivo Histórico del Guayas* 4(7): 9–63.

Expreso (Guayaquil). 1993a. "Una muestra del pasado" (October 9).

———. 1993b. "San Biritute y la independencia 2000" (September 6).

———. 1993c. "La etnicidad indígena y criolla" (August 24).

———. 1993d. "La controversia de San Biritute" (August 23).

———. 1993e. "Lágrimas por San Biritute en el museo" (August 4).

Fabian, Johannes. 1983. *Time and the Other: How Anthropology Makes Its Object.* New York: Columbia University Press.

Fanon, Frantz. 1967. *A Dying Colonialism.* New York: Grove Press.

———. 1966. *Black Skin, White Masks.* New York: Grove Press.

———. 1965. *The Wretched of the Earth.* New York: Grove Press.

Fausto-Sterling, Anne. 1992. *Myths of Gender: Biological Theories about Women and Men.* New York: Basic Books.

Federación Indígena Pichincha Runacunapac Riccharimui. 1993. *Historia de la organización indígena en Pichincha.* Quito: Ediciones Abya-Yala.

Ferguson, James. 1994. *The Anti-Politics Machine: "Development," Depoliticization, and Bureaucratic Power in Lesotho.* Minneapolis: University of Minnesota Press.

Fernández de Oviedo, Gonzalo. [1535] 1959. *Historia general y natural de las Indias.* 5 vols. Madrid: Ediciones Atlas.

Foster, Robert. 1990. "Making Cultures in the Global Ecumene." *Annual Review of Anthropology* 20: 235–260.

Foucault, Michel. 2000. "The Subject and Power." In *Power/Essential Works of Foucault,* no.3, edited by J. Faubion, pp. 326–348. New York: New Press.

———. 1998. "A Preface to Transgression." In *Aesthetics, Method and Epistemology: Essential Works of Foucault,* no. 2, edited by J. Faubion, pp. 69–88. New York: New Press.

———. 1995. *Discipline and Punish: The Birth of the Prison.* New York: Vintage Books.

———. 1994. *The Birth of the Clinic: An Archaeology of Medical Perception.* New York: Vintage Books.

———. 1993. "Nietzsche, Genealogy and History." In *Language, Counter-Memory, Practices: Selected Essays and Interviews,* edited by D. Bouchard, pp. 139–164. Ithaca, N.Y.: Cornell University Press.

———. 1991. *Remarks on Marx.* New York: Semiotext(e).

———. 1990. *The History of Sexuality: An Introduction,* vol. 1. New York: Vintage Books.

———. 1988. *Madness and Civilization: A History of Insanity in the Age of Reason.* New York: Viking Books.

———. 1980. *Power/Knowledge: Selected Interviews and Other Writings, 1972–1977.* New York: Pantheon Books.

———. 1972. *The Archaeology of Knowledge and the Discourse on Language.* New York: Pantheon Books.

Fox, Richard, ed. 1990. *Nationalist Ideologies and the Production of National Cultures.* American Ethnological Society Monograph Series, no. 2. Washington, DC: American Anthropological Association.

Franco, Jean. 1992. "Going Public: Reinhabiting the Private." In *On Edge: The Crisis of Contemporary Latin American Culture,* edited by G. Yudice, J. Franco, and J. Flores, pp. 65–83. Minneapolis: University of Minnesota Press.

———. 1991. "'Manhattan Will Be More Exotic This Fall': The Iconisation of Frida Kahlo." *Women: A Cultural Review* 2(3): 220–226.

Freire, Paulo. 1992. *Pedagogy of the Oppressed.* New York: Continuum.

Friedlander, Judith. 1975. *Being Indian in Hueyapan: A Study of Forced Identity in Contemporary Mexico.* New York: St. Martin's Press.

Friedman, Jonathan. 1992. "The Past in the Future: History and the Politics of Identity." *American Anthropologist* 94(4): 837–859.

Fuentes, Carlos. 1988. "En América Latina se escribe porque falta decirlo todo." *Hoy* (February).

Fusco, Coco. 1995. *English Is Broken Here: Notes on Cultural Fusion in the Americas.* New York: New Press.

———. 1994. "The Other History of Intercultural Performance." *The Drama Review: The Journal of Performance Studies* 38(1): 143–167.

Gable, Eric; Richard Handler; and Anna Lawson. 1992. "On the Uses of Relativism: Fact, Conjecture, and Black and White Histories at Colonial Williamsburg." *American Ethnologist* 19(4): 791–805.

Gailey, Christine. 1987. *Kinship to Kingship: Gender Hierarchy and State Formation in the Tongan Islands.* Austin: University of Texas Press.

Gallardo, José, et al., eds. 1995. *Tiwintsa.* Quito: Editorial El Conejo.

Gallardo, Gen. José. 1995. "La defensa militar del Alto Cenepa." In *Tiwintsa,* edited by J. Gallardo et al., pp. 7–31. Quito: Editorial El Conejo.

Gallegos Lara, Joaquín; Demetrio Aguilera Mata; and Enrique Gil Gilbert. 1970. *Los que se van: Cuentos del cholo y del montuvio.* Guayaquil: Publicaciones Educativas Ariel.

Gándara, Manuel. 1992. *La arqueología oficial mexicana: Causas y efectos.* Mexico City: Instituto Nacional de Antropología e Historia.

Garcés, Víctor Gabriel. 1933. "Ensayo de interpretación histórico-sociológica de las nacionalidades en América." *Anales de la Universidad Central* (Quito) 51(285): 171–200.

García, Cristina. 1992. *Dreaming in Cuban.* New York: Ballantine Books.

García-Canclini, Néstor. 1993. *Transforming Modernity: Popular Culture in Mexico.* Austin: University of Texas Press.

———. 1992a. "Cultural Reconversion." In *On Edge: The Crisis of Contemporary Latin American Culture,* edited by G. Yudice, J. Franco, and J. Flores, 29–43. Minneapolis: University of Minnesota Press.

———. 1992b. *Culturas híbridas: Estrategias para entrar y salir de la modernidad.* Buenos Aires: Editorial Suramericana.

García González, Luis. 1997. *Resumen de geografía, historia y cívica, primer curso, ciclo básico.* Quito: Editora Andina.

García Márquez, Gabriel. 1971. *One Hundred Years of Solitude.* New York: Avon Books.

Garcilaso de la Vega, "El Inca." [1609] 1998. *Comentarios reales.* Mexico City: Porrúa.

Garcilaso de la Vega, "El Inca." [1609] 1974. *Comentarios reales de los Incas.* Madrid: Círculo de Amigos de la Historia.

Gellner, Ernest. 1983. *Nations and Nationalism.* Ithaca, N.Y.: Cornell University Press.

Gero, Joan. 1990. "Facts and Values in the Archaeological Eye: Discussion of 'Powers and Observation.'" In *Powers of Observation: Alternative Views in Archaeology,* edited by S. Nelson and A. Kehoe, pp. 113–119. Archeological Papers of the American Anthropological Association, no. 2. Washington, D.C.: American Anthropological Association.

Gero, Joan, and Margaret Conkey, eds. 1990. *Engendering Archaeology: Women and Prehistory.* London: Basil Blackwell.

Gilroy, Paul. 1987. *"There Ain't No Black in the Union Jack": The Cultural Politics of Race and Nation.* Chicago: University of Chicago Press.

Girardi, Giulio. 1994. *Los excluidos: Construirán la nueva historia? Movimiento indígena, negro y popular.* Quito: Centro Cultural Afroecuatoriano.

Gómez-Peña, Guillermo. 1996. "The Artist as Criminal." *The Drama Review: The Journal of Performance Studies* 40(1): 112–118.

———. 1994. "The Multicultural Paradigm: An Open Letter to the National Arts Community." In *Negotiating Performance: Gender, Sexuality, and Theatricality in Latin/o America,* edited by D. Taylor and J. Villegas, pp. 17–29. Durham, N.C.: Duke University Press.

———. 1991. "Border Brujo." In *Being America: Essays on Art, Literature, and Identity from Latin America,* edited by R. Weiss and A. West, pp. 194–236. New York: White Pine Press.

González, Ray, ed. 1996. *Muy Macho: Latino Men Confront Their Manhood.* New York: Anchor Books.

González, Víctor. 1986. *Historia del Ecuador: Razas y clases en la colonia.* Guayaquil: Graba.

González Suárez, Federico. [1892]. *Atlas arqueológico ecuatoriano.* Quito: Clásicos Ariel.

———. 1890. *Historia general de la República del Ecuador.* 3 vols. Quito: Ariel.

———. 1878. *Estudio histórico sobre los Cañaris, antiguos habitantes de la provincia del Azuay en la República del Ecuador.* Quito: Imprenta del Clero.

Gould, Jeffrey. 1996. "Gender, Politics, and the Triumph of *Mestizaje* in Early 20th Century Nicaragua." *Journal of Latin American Anthropology* 2(1): 4–33.

Gramsci, Antonio. 1971. *Selections from the Prison Notebooks*, edited by Q. Hoare and G. Nowell-Smith. New York: International Publishers.

Greenblatt, Stephen, ed. 1993. *New World Encounters*. Berkeley & Los Angeles: University of California Press.

Gregory, Steven, and Roger Sanjek, eds. 1994. *Race*. New Brunswick, N.J.: Rutgers University Press.

Guamán Poma de Ayala, Felipe. [1613] 1980. *El primer nueva crónica y buen gobierno*, edited by J. Murra and R. Adorno. 3 vols. Mexico City: Siglo XXI.

Guerra, Erasmo. 1999. *Latin Lovers: True Stories of Latin Men in Love*. New York: Painted Leaf Press.

Guerrero, Andrés. 1994. "Una imagen ventrílocua: El discurso liberal de la 'desgraciada raza indígena' a fines del siglo XIX." In *Imágenes e imagineros: Representaciones de los indígenas ecuatorianos, siglos XIX y XX*, edited by B. Muratorio, pp. 197–252. Quito: FLACSO.

———. 1991. *La semántica de la dominación: El concertaje de indios*. Quito: Ediciones Libri Mundi and Enrique Grosse-Luemern.

Guha, Ranajit, and Gayatri Chakravorty Spivak, eds. 1985. *Selected Subaltern Studies*. New York: Oxford University Press.

Gutiérrez, Ramón A. 1991. *When Jesus Came, the Corn Mothers Went Away: Marriage, Sexuality, and Power in New Mexico, 1500–1846*. Stanford, Calif.: Stanford University Press.

Gutmann, Matthew. 1996. *The Meanings of Macho: Being a Man in Mexico City*. Berkeley & Los Angeles: University of California Press.

———. 1994. "The Meaning of Macho: Changing Mexican Male Identities." *Masculinities* 2(1): 21–33.

Hale, Charles. 1996. "Introduction." *Journal of Latin American Anthropology* 2(1): 2–3.

Hall, Stuart. 1997. "The Local and the Global: Globalization and Ethnicity." In *Culture, Globalization and the World-System: Contemporary Conditions for the Representation of Identity*, edited by A. King, pp. 19–39. Minneapolis: University of Minnesota Press.

———. 1986. "Popular Culture and the State." In *Popular Culture and Social Relations*, edited by Tony Bennett, C. Mercer, and J. Woollcott, pp. 22–49. Philadelphia: Open University Press.

———. 1981. "Notes on Deconstructing the Popular." In *People's History and Socialist Theory*, edited by R. Samuel, pp. 227–240. London: Routledge.

Handler, Richard. 1988. *Nationalism and the Politics of Culture in Quebec*. Madison: University of Wisconsin Press.

———. 1986. "Authenticity." *Anthropology Today* 2(1): 2–4.

Handler, Richard, and Eric Gable. 1997. *The New History in an Old Museum: Creating the Past at Colonial Williamsburg*. Durham, N.C.: Duke University Press.

Haraway, Donna. 1989. "Teddy Bear Patriarchy: Taxidermy in the Garden of

Eden, New York City, 1908–36." In *Primate Visions: Gender, Race, and Nature in the World of Modern Science*, pp. 26–58. New York: Routledge.

Harke, Heinrich. 1998. "Archaeologists and Migrations: A Problem of Attitude?" *Current Anthropology* 39(1): 19–45.

Harrison, Faye, ed. 1991. *Decolonizing Anthropology: Moving Further toward an Anthropology for Liberation*. Washington, D.C.: Association of Black Anthropologists, American Anthropological Association.

Hellman, Lillian. 1980. *Maybe*. Boston: Little, Brown and Company.

Heredia, Víctor. 1986. *Taki Ongoy*. Polygram Records.

Herzfeld, Michael. 1987. *Anthropology through the Looking Glass: Critical Ethnography in the Margins of Europe*. New York: Cambridge University Press.

———. 1982. *Ours Once More: Folklore, Ideology and the Making of Modern Greece*. Austin: University of Texas Press.

Hesse, Hermann. 1994. *The Journey to the East*. New York: Noonday Press.

Heyer, Judith; Pepe Roberts; and Gavin Williams, eds. 1981. *Rural Development in Tropical Africa*. New York: St. Martin's Press.

Hill, Jonathan. 1992. "Contested Pasts and the Practice of Anthropology." *American Anthropologist* 94(4): 809–815.

———, ed. 1988. *Rethinking History and Myth: Indigenous South American Perspectives on the Past*. Urbana: University of Illinois Press.

Hill, Mike. 1997. *Whiteness: A Critical Reader*. New York: New York University Press.

Hobsbawm, Eric. 1990. *Nations and Nationalisms since 1780: Programme, Myth, Reality*. Cambridge: Cambridge University Press.

Hobsbawm, Eric, and Terence Ranger, eds. 1983. *The Invention of Tradition*. Cambridge: Cambridge University Press.

Hodder, Ian. 1986. *Reading the Past*. Cambridge: Cambridge University Press.

———. 1982. *Symbols in Action*. Cambridge: Cambridge University Press.

Holm, Olaf. 1986. *Cultura manteño-huancavilca*. Guayaquil: Museo Antropológico y Pinacoteca and Banco Central del Ecuador.

Holm, Olaf, and Hernán Crespo. 1980. *Historia del Ecuador; Período de integración*. Vol. 70. Quito: Salvat Editores.

hooks, bell. 1994. *Teaching to Transgress: Education as the Practice of Freedom*. New York: Routledge.

———. 1990. *Yearning: Race, Gender and Cultural Politics*. Boston: South End Press.

La Hora (Guayaquil). 1993a. *San Viritute* (September 18).

———. 1993b. *Cayambe* (April 3).

Hoy (Quito). 1997. "Historia con fondo de mar: La ruta de la costa" (February 15).

———. 1993. "San Biritute quiere volver" (October 16).

Humboldt, Alexander von. 1993. *Breviario del nuevo mundo*. Colección "La Expresión Americana." Caracas: Biblioteca de Ayacucho.

Hurtado, Osvaldo. 1981. *El poder político en el Ecuador*. Barcelona: Editorial Planeta Ariel.

Ibarra, Hernán. 1992. *Indios y cholos, orígenes de la clase trabajadora ecuatoriana.* Quito: Editorial El Conejo.

Icaza, Jorge. 1993. *Huasipungo.* Quito: Ediciones Guayacán.

———. 1983. *El chulla Romero y Flores.* Quito: Libresa.

———. 1981. *Cholos.* Bogotá: Plaza y Janes.

———. 1936. *En las calles.* Buenos Aires: Publicaciones Atlas.

Isbell, Billie Jean. 1985. *To Defend Ourselves: Ecology and Ritual in an Andean Village.* Prospect Heights, Ill.: Waveland Press.

Jackson, Jean. 1989. "Is There a Way to Talk about Making Culture without Making Enemies?" *Dialectical Anthropology* 14: 127–143.

James, C. L. R. 1938. *The Black Jacobins: Toussaint Louverture and the San Domingo Revolution.* New York: Secker and Warburg.

———. 1933. *The Case for West-Indian Self-Government.* London: Hugarth Press.

Jaramillo Alvarado, Pío. 1993. "Situación política, económica y jurídica del indio en el Ecuador." In *Indianistas, indianófilos, indigenistas,* edited by J. Trujillo, pp. 453–494. Quito: ILDIS and Abya-Yala.

———. 1988. "El indio ecuatoriano (texto seleccionado)." In *Pensamiento indigenista del Ecuador,* edited by C. Malo González, pp. 99–186. Quito: Banco Central del Ecuador and Corporación Editora Nacional.

Jijón y Caamaño, Jacinto. 1997. *Antropología prehispánica del Ecuador.* Quito: Embajada de España and Museo Jacinto Jijón y Caamaño.

———. [1943] 1992. "La ecuatorianidad." *Museo Histórico* 59: 233–268.

———. 1952. *Antropología prehispánica del Ecuador: Resumen 1945.* Quito: La Prensa Católica.

———. 1941/1946. *El Ecuador interandino y occidental antes de la conquista española.* 4 vols. Quito: Editorial Ecuatoriana.

———. 1933. *Curso de prehistoria ecuatoriana dictado en la Universidad Central de Quito.* Publicaciones de la Universidad Central. Quito.

———. 1930. "Una gran marea cultural en el noroeste de Sudamérica." *Journal de la Société des Americanistes de Paris* 22: 107–197.

———. 1929. "Notas de arqueología cuzqueña." *Dios y Patria* 1 (Riobamba) 2–3.

———. 1927. *Puruhá: Contribución al conocimiento de los aborígenes de la provincia del Chimborazo.* 2 vols. Quito: N.p.

———. 1922. "La edad del bronce en América del Sur." *Boletín de la Academia Nacional de Historia* 4(9): 119–126.

———. 1920a. "Nueva contribución al conocimiento de los aborígenes de la provincia de Imbabura." *Boletín de la Sociedad Ecuatoriana de Estudios Históricos* 4(10): 1–120; 4(11): 183–245.

———. 1920b. "Los Tincullpas y notas acerca de la metalurgia de los aborígenes del Ecuador." *Boletín de la Sociedad Ecuatoriana de Estudios Históricos* 5(13–14): 4–45.

———. 1919a. "Artefactos prehistóricos del Guayas." *Boletín de la Sociedad Ecuatoriana de Estudios Históricos* 2(5): 169–172.

———. 1919b. "Contribución al conocimiento de las lenguas indígenas, que se hablaron en el Ecuador interandino y occidental, con anterioridad a la conquista española." *Boletín de la Sociedad Ecuatoriana de Estudios Históricos* 2(6): 340–413.

———. 1918a. "Artefactos prehistóricos del Guayas." *Boletín de la Sociedad Ecuatoriana de Estudios Históricos* 1(3): 253–275.

———. 1918b. "Examen crítico de la veracidad de la historia del Reino de Quito del P. Juan de Velasco de la Compañía de Jesús." *Boletín de la Sociedad Ecuatoriana de Estudios Históricos Americanos* 1(3): 33–63.

———. 1918c. "Una punta de Labalina de Puegasí (Pichincha)." *Boletín de la Sociedad Ecuatoriana de Estudios Históricos* 1(3): 109–111.

———. 1914. *Contribución al conocimiento de los aborígenes de la provincia de Imbabura en la República del Ecuador.* Estudios de Prehistoria Americana II. Madrid: Blass y Cía.

———. 1912. *El tesoro de Itschimbía.* Estudios de Prehistoria Americana I. London: J. Bale, Sons & Danielsson.

Joseph, Gilbert, and Daniel Nugent, eds. 1994. *Everyday Forms of State Formation: Revolution and the Negotiation of Rule in Modern Mexico.* Durham, N.C.: Duke University Press.

Karakasidou, Anastasia. 1997. *Fields of Wheat, Hills of Blood: Passages to Nationhood in Greek Macedonia, 1870–1990.* Chicago: University of Chicago Press.

Karakras, Ampam. 1990. *Las nacionalidades indias y el estado ecuatoriano.* Quito: Editorial TINCUI-CONAIE.

Kincaid, Jamaica. 1997. *My Brother.* New York: Farrar, Straus and Giroux.

Kinsman, Gary. 1987. *The Regulation of Desire: Sexuality in Canada.* Montreal: Black Rose Books.

KIPU (Quito). 1995. "Kipu 25: El mundo indígena en la prensa ecuatoriana" (July–December).

———. 1991. "Kipu 16: El mundo indígena en la prensa ecuatoriana" (January–June).

Knight, Alan. 1990. "Racism, Revolution and *Indigenismo*: Mexico, 1910–1940." In *The Idea of Race in Latin America, 1870–1940,* edited by Richard Graham, 71–114. Austin: University of Texas Press.

Kohl, Phillip, and Clare Fawcett, eds. 1995. *Nationalism, Politics, and the Practice of Archaeology.* Cambridge: Cambridge University Press.

Kowii, Ariruma. 1992. "El derecho internacional y el derecho de los pueblos indios." In *Pueblos indios, estado y derecho,* edited by E. Ayala Mora et al., p. 213–227. Quito: Corporación Editora Nacional.

Kuklick, Henrika. 1991. "Contested Monuments: The Politics of Archaeology in Southern Africa." In *Colonial Situations: Essays on the Contextualization of Ethnographic Knowledge,* edited by G. Stocking, pp. 135–169. History of Anthropology, vol. 7. Madison: University of Wisconsin Press.

Kulik, Don. 1998. *Travesti: Sex, Gender, and Culture among Brazilian Transgendered Prostitutes.* Chicago: University of Chicago Press.

Kulik, Don, and Margaret Wilson. 1995. *Taboo, Sex, Identity and Erotic Subjectivity in Anthropological Fieldwork*. London: Routledge.

Lamas, Marta, et al. 1998. *Para entender el concepto de género*. Quito: Abya-Yala.

Lancaster, Roger. 1996. *Life Is Hard: Machismo, Danger, and the Intimacy of Power in Nicaragua*. Berkeley & Los Angeles: University of California Press.

———. 1986. "Comment on Argüelles and Rich's 'Homosexuality, Homophobia, and Revolution': Notes toward an Understanding of the Cuban Lesbian and Gay Male Experience, Part II." *Signs* 12(1): 111–125.

Lancaster, Roger, and Micaela di Leonardo, eds. 1997. *The Gender/Sexuality Reader: Culture, History, Poltical Economy*. New York: Routledge.

Lang, Sabine. 1998. *Men as Women, Women as Men: Changing Gender in Native American Cultures*. Austin: University of Texas Press.

Larraín Barros, Horacio. 1977. *Demografía y asentamientos indígenas en la sierra norte del Ecuador en el siglo XVI: Estudio etnohistórico de las fuentes tempranas, 1525–1600*. Colección Pendoneros, vols. 11–12. Otavalo, Ecuador: Instituto Otavaleño de Antropología.

Layton, Robert, ed. 1989a. *Conflict in the Archaeology of Living Traditions*. London: Unwin Hyman.

———. 1989b. *Who Needs the Past?: Indigenous Values and Archaeology*. London: Unwin Hyman.

León Mera, Juan. 1989. *Cumandá o un drama entre salvajes*. Seville: Alfar.

Lessing, Doris. 1987. *Prisons We Choose to Live Inside*. New York: Harper and Row.

Lewin, Ellen, and William Leap, eds. 1996. *Out in the Field: Reflections of Lesbian and Gay Anthropologists*. Urbana: University of Illinois Press.

Leyland, Winston, and E. A. Lacey, eds. 1983. *My Deep Dark Pain Is Love: A Collection of Latin American Gay Fiction*. San Francisco: Gay Sunshine Press.

Lipsitz, George. 1995. "The Possessive Investment in Whiteness: Racialized Social Democracy and the 'White' Problem in American Studies." *American Quarterly* 47(3): 369–394.

Lizárraga, Fray Reginaldo de. [1605] 1968. *Descripción breve de toda la tierra del Perú, Tucumán, Río de la Plata y Chile*. Biblioteca de Autores Españoles, vol. 216. Madrid: Editorial Atlas.

L.N.S. N.d. *Historia del Ecuador: Primera Parte*. Cuenca, Ecuador: Editorial Don Bosco.

Lomnitz-Adler, Claudio. 1992. *Exits from the Labyrinth: Culture and Ideology in the Mexican National Space*. Stanford, Calif.: Stanford University Press.

Lorde, Audre. [1977] 1997. "Age, Race, Class, and Sex: Women Redefining Difference." In *Dangerous Liaisons: Gender, Nation, and Postcolonial Perspectives*, edited by A. McClintock, A. Mufti, and E. Shohat, pp. 374–380. Minneapolis: University of Minnesota Press.

Lowenthal, David. 1985. *The Past Is a Foreign Country*. New York: Cambridge University Press.

Lucena Salmoral, Manuel. 1994. *Sangre sobre piel negra*. Colección Mundo Afro 1. Quito: Centro Cultural Afroecuatoriano and Ediciones Abya-Yala.

Lumbreras, Luis. 1990. *Cronología arqueológica de Cochasquí.* Quito: H. Consejo Provincial de Pichincha.

Macas, Luis. 1992. "El levantamiento indígena visto por sus protagonistas." In *Indios: Una reflexión sobre el levantamiento indígena de 1990,* pp. 17–36. Quito: ILDIS and Ediciones Abya-Yala.

———. 1991. *El levantamiento indígena visto por sus protagonistas.* Quito: ILDI and Ediciones Abya-Yala..

Macas Ambuludí, Luis, and Edisón Ramiro Miño. 1997. *Por que cayó Bucaram: Entretelones y actores.* Quito: Imprefepp.

Maiguashca, Bice. 1992. "The Role of Ideas in a Changing World Order: The Case of the International Indigenous Movement, 1975–91." Paper delivered at the Conference on Changing World Order and the United Nations System, Yokohama, Japan, March.

———, ed. 1994. *Historia y región en el Ecuador 1830–1930.* Quito: Corporación Editora Nacional.

Maldonado, Luis E. 1992. "El movimiento indígena y la propuesta multinacional." In *Pueblos indios, estado y derecho,* edited by E. Ayala Mora et al., pp. 151–162. Quito: Corporación Editora Nacional.

Malkki, Liisa. 1995. *Purity and Exile: Violence, Memory, and National Cosmology among Hutu Refugees in Tanzania.* Chicago: University of Chicago Press.

Mallon, Florencia. 1996. "Constructing *Mestizaje* in Latin America: Authenticity, Marginality, and Gender in the Claiming of Ethnic Identities." *Journal of Latin American Anthropology* 2(1): 170–181.

———. 1995. *Peasant and Nation: The Making of Postcolonial Mexico and Peru.* Berkeley & Los Angeles: University of California Press.

Malo González, Claudio. 1988. "Estudio introductorio." In *Pensamiento indigenista del Ecuador,* edited by C. Malo González, pp. 9–98. Biblioteca Básica del Pensamiento Ecuatoriano, no. 34. Quito: Banco Central del Ecuador and Corporación Editora Nacional.

Mamani Condori, Carlos. 1989. "History and Prehistory in Bolivia: What about the Indians?" In *Conflict in the Archaeology of Living Traditions,* edited by R. Layton, pp. 46–59. London: Unwin Hyman.

Manalansan, Martin, IV, and Arnaldo Cruz-Malavé, eds. 2002. *Queer Globalizations: Citizenship and the Afterlife of Colonialism.* New York: New York University Press.

Manrique, Jaime. 1997. *Twilight at the Equator.* Boston: Farber and Farber.

———. 1992. *Latin Moon in Manhattan.* New York: St. Martin's Press.

Manrique, Jaime, and Jesse Dorris, eds. 1999. *Bésame Mucho: New Gay Latino Fiction.* New York: Painted Leaf Press.

Mantilla, Ramiro. N.d. *Manejo sustentable de Cochasquí.* N.p.: Programa Cochasquí.

Marcos, Jorge. 1986a. "Breve prehistoria del Ecuador." In *Arqueología de la costa ecuatoriana: Nuevos enfoques,* edited by J. Marcos. Quito: Escuela Superior Politécnica del Litoral and Corporación Editora Nacional.

———. 1986b. "La situación actual y las perspectivas de las investigaciones arqueológicas en el Ecuador." In *Arqueología de la costa ecuatoriana: Nuevos enfoques*, edited by J. Marcos, pp. 25–40. Quito: Escuela Superior Politécnica del Litoral and Corporación Editora Nacional.

———, ed. 1986c. *Arqueología de la costa ecuatoriana: Nuevos enfoques.* Quito: Escuela Superior Politécnica del Litoral and Corporación Editora Nacional.

Mariátegui, José Carlos. 1955. *Siete ensayos interpretativos de la realidad peruana.* Santiago de Chile: Editorial Universitaria.

Martínez, Rubén. 1998. "Technicolor." In *Half and Half: Writers on Growing up Biracial and Bicultural*, edited by C. O'Hearn, pp. 245–264. New York: Pantheon Books.

———. 1992. *The Other Side: Notes from the New L.A., Mexico City and Beyond.* New York: Vintage Books.

Martínez-Alier, Verena. 1974. *Marriage, Class and Colour in Nineteenth-Century Cuba: A Study of Racial Attitudes and Sexual Values in a Slave Society.* Cambridge: Cambridge University Press.

Martínez Estrada, Alejandro. N.d. *Historia del Ecuador.* Quito: DIMAXI.

McClintock, Anne. 1995. *Imperial Leather: Race, Gender, and Sexuality in the Colonial Contest.* New York: Routledge.

McClintock, Anne; Aamir Mufti; and Ella Shohat, eds. 1997. *Dangerous Liaisons: Gender, Nation, and Postcolonial Perspectives.* Minneapolis: University of Minnesota Press.

McEwan, Colin. 1990. "El sitio arqueológico de Agua Blanca, Manabí, Ecuador." Report, Instituto Nacional de Patrimonio Cultural, Guayaquil.

McEwan, Colin, and Chris Hudson. N.d. "Como despertar el orgullo por el propio pasado: El ejemplo de Agua Blanca, Ecuador." Manuscript.

McGuire, Randall. 1992. *A Marxist Archaeology.* San Diego: Academic Press.

McGuire, Randall, and Robert Paynter. 1991. *The Archaeology of Inequality.* Oxford: Basil Blackwell.

Mead, Margaret. 1949. *Male and Female: A Study of the Sexes in a Changing World.* New York: William Morrow.

Meggers, Betty. 1966. *Ecuador.* London: Praeger.

Memmi, Albert. 1991. *The Colonizer and the Colonized.* Boston: Beacon Press.

Menchú, Rigoberta. 1998. *Crossing Borders.* New York: Verso.

———. 1985. *Me llamo Rigoberta Menchú y así me nació la conciencia*, edited by E. Burgos. Mexico City: Siglo Veintiuno Editores.

Meridiano (Guayaquil). 1993. "Comuna Sacachún solicita devolución de "San Biritute" (August 5).

Merleau-Ponty, Maurice. 1964. *The Primacy of Perception, and Other Essays on Phenomenological Psychology, the Philosophy of Art, History, and Politics.* Evanston, Ill.: Northwestern University Press.

———. 1963. *The Structure of Behavior.* Boston: Beacon Press.

Mignolo, Walter. 2000. *Local Histories/Global Designs: Coloniality, Subaltern Knowledges, and Border Thinking.* Princeton, N.J.: Princeton University Press.

———. 1994. *The Darker Side of the Renaissance: Literacy, Territoriality, and Colonization.* Ann Arbor: University of Michigan Press.

Miller, Daniel. 1992. "The Young and the Restless in Trinidad: A Case of the Local and the Global in Mass Consumption." In *Consuming Technologies: Media and Information in Domestic Spaces*, edited by R. Silverstone and E. Hirsch, pp.163–182. New York: Routledge.

Miller, James. 1993. *The Passion of Michel Foucault*. New York: Anchor Books.

Mills, Nick. 1983. "Economía y sociedad en el período de la independencia." In *Nueva Historia del Ecuador*, vol. 6, edited by E. Ayala Mora, pp. 127–164. Quito: Corporación Editora Nacional and Grijalbo.

Minh-ha, Trinh. 1997. "Not You/Like You: Postcolonial Women and the Interlocking Questions of Identity and Difference." In *Dangerous Liaisons: Gender, Nation, and Postcolonial Perspectives*, edited by A. McClintock, A. Mufti, and E. Shohat, pp. 415–419. Minneapolis: University of Minnesota Press.

Mirande, Alfredo. 1997. *Hombres y Machos: Masculinity and Latino Culture*. Boulder, Colo.: Westview Press.

Mistral, Gabriela. 1998. *Desolación, ternura, tala y lagar*. Mexico City: Porrúa.

Mitchell, Timothy. 1988. *Colonising Egypt*. Cambridge: Cambridge University Press.

Mohanty, Chandra T., and M. Jacqui Alexander, eds. 1997. *Feminist Genealogies, Colonial Legacies, Democratic Futures*. New York: Routledge.

Mohanty, Chandra T.; Ann Russo; and Lourdes Torres, eds. 1991. *Third World Women and the Politics of Feminism*. Bloomington: Indiana University Press.

Molloy, Sylvia, and Robert M. Irwin, eds. 1998. *Hispanisms and Homosexualities*. Durham, N.C.: Duke University Press.

Monsiváis, Carlos. 1997. *Mexican Postcards*. Translated and introduced by J. Jraniauskas. London: Verso.

———. 1995. "Literatura latinoamericana e industria cultural." In *Cultura y pospolítica: El debate sobre la modernidad en América Latina*, compiled by N. García-Canclini, pp. 187–208. Mexico City: Consejo Nacional para la Cultura y las Artes.

Montesinos, Fernando de. [1644] 1957. *Memorias antiguas historiales y políticas del Perú*. Revista del Museo and Instituto Arqueológico de la Universidad Nacional del Cuzco, no. 16–17. London: The Hakluyt Society.

———. [1644] 1920. *Memorias antiguas historiales del Perú*. Translated and edited by Philip Ainsworth Means. London: The Hakluyt Society.

Moore, Henrietta. 1988. *Feminism and Anthropology*. Cambridge: Polity Press.

Moore, James, and Arthur Keene, eds. 1983. *Archaeological Hammers and Theories*. New York: Academic Press.

Moraga, Cherríe. 1997. *Waiting in the Wings: Portrait of a Queer Motherhood*. Ithaca, N.Y.: Firebrand Books.

———. 1994. "Art in América con Acento." In *Negotiating Performance: Gender, Sexuality, and Theatricality in Latin/o America*, edited by D. Taylor and J. Villegas, pp. 30–36. Durham, N.C.: Duke University Press.

———. 1986. "From a Long Line of Vendidas: Chicanas and Feminism." In *Feminist Studies, Critical Studies*, edited by T. de Lauretis. Bloomington: Indiana University Press.

Moraga, Cherríe, and Gloria Anzaldúa, eds. 1983. *This Bridge Called My Back: Writings by Radical Women of Color.* New York: Kitchen Table Press.

Moreno Yánez, Segundo. 1992. *Antropología ecuatoriana: Pasado y presente.* Colección Primicias de la Cultura de Quito 1. Quito: Ediguías.

———. 1981. "Una evaluación de los aportes de las investigaciones arqueológicas en Cochasquí." In *Cochasquí: Estudios arqueológicos,* vol. 3, edited by U. Oberem, pp. 11–38. Colección Pendoneros. Otavalo, Ecuador: Instituto Otavaleño de Antropología.

Moreno Yánez, Segundo, and José Figueroa. 1992. *El levantamiento indígena del Inti Raymi de 1990.* Quito: Fundación Ecuatoriana de Estudios Sociales and Editorial Abya-Yala.

Morrison, Toni. 1993. *Playing in the Dark: Whiteness in the Literary Imagination.* New York: Vintage Books.

Morse, Michael. 1994. "Seeking an Ethical Balance in Archaeological Practice in Ecuador." *Journal of Anthropological Research* 50: 169–185.

Mort, Frank. 1987. *Dangerous Sexualities: Medical-Moral Politics in England since 1830.* London: Routledge and Kegan Paul.

Moscoso, Lucia, and Gaby Costa. 1989. *Historia oral de Cochasquí.* Quito: Programa Cochasquí and H. Consejo Provincial de Pichincha.

Mosse, George. 1985. *Nationalism and Sexuality: Respectability and Abnormal Sexuality in Modern Europe.* New York: H. Fertig.

Mullo, Mario. 1993. "Las luchas de las comunidades indígenas en la zona de Olmedo." In *Historia de la organización indígena en Pichincha,* by Federación Indígena Pichincha Runacunapac Riccharimui, pp. 31–38. Quito: Abya-Yala.

Muñoz Vernaza, Alberto. [1937] 1984. *Orígenes de la nacionalidad ecuatoriana, y otros ensayos.* Biblioteca de Historia Ecuatoriana, vol. 8. Quito: Corporación Editoria Nacional.

Muratorio, Blanca. 1998. "Indigenous Women's Identities and the Politics of Cultural Reproduction in the Ecuadorian Amazon." *American Anthropologist* 100(2): 409–420.

Murra, John. 1989. *La organización económica del estado inca.* Mexico City: Siglo XXI.

Murray, David, and Richard Handler, eds. 1996. *Identities: Global Studies in Culture and Power* 2(3), Special Issue: *The Nation/State and Its Sexual Dissidents.*

Murray, Stephen. 1987. *Male Homosexuality in Central and South America.* New York: Gay Academic Union.

———. 1980. "Lexical and Institutional Elaboration: The 'Species Homosexual' in Guatemala." *Anthropological Linguistics* 22: 177–185.

Muse, Michael. 1991. "Products and Politics of a Milagro Entrepot: Peñón del Río, Guayas Basin, Ecuador." *Research in Economic Anthropology* 13: 269–322.

Muteba Rahier, Jean. 1998. "Blackness, the Racial/Spatial Order, Migrations, and Miss Ecuador 1995–6." *American Anthropologist* 100(2): 421–430.

Nacionalidades Indias (Quito). 1996. "Hacemos historia" (December).

———. 1994. "El por qué? de la ingobernabilidad" (April).

———. 1993. "Del año a la década de los pueblos indígenas" (April).

Nadia L., Abu El-Haj. 1995. *Excavating the Land, Creating the Homeland: Archaeology, the State, and the Making of History in Modern Jewish Nationalism.* Ann Arbor, Mich.: University Microfilms.

Nanda, Serena. 1990. *Neither Man nor Woman: The Hijras of India.* Belmont, Calif.: Wadsworth Publishing Co.

Naranjo, Plutarco. 1985. "Las raíces de nuestra historia." In *La historia del Ecuador: Ensayos de interpretación,* edited by E. Ayala Mora, pp. 197–222. Quito: Corporación Editoria Nacional.

Navas Jiménez, Mario. 1994. *Historia, geografía y cívica.* Quito: Gráfica Mediavilla Hnos.

New Yorker. 1997. *The Fiction Issue: India* (June 23 and 30).

Nietzsche, Friedrich. 1966. *Beyond Good and Evil: Prelude to a Philosophy of the Future.* Translated, with commentary, by Walter Kaufmann. New York: Vintage Books.

Norton, Presley, and Jorge Marcos, eds. 1982. *Primer Simposio de Correlaciones Antropológicas Andino-Mesoamericano.* Guayaquil: ESPOL.

Núñez, Frank. 1998. "Who Says That There Is Racism in Ecuador?" Manuscript on file, City College of New York.

Oberem, Udo, comp. 1980. *Cochasquí: Estudios arqueológicos.* Colección Pendoneros 3–5. Otavalo, Ecuador: Instituto Otavaleño de Antropología.

Oberem, Udo, and Roswith Hartmann. 1981. "Informe de trabajo sobre las excavaciones arqueológicas de 1964–1965." In *Cochasquí: Estudios arqueológicos,* pp. 39–58. Colección Pendoneros 3. Otavalo, Ecuador: Instituto Otavaleño de Antropología.

Oberem, Udo, and Wolfgang Wurster. 1989. *Excavaciones arqueológicas en Cochasquí, Ecuador 1964–1965.* Hamburg: Geo.

Oyuela-Caycedo, Augusto, ed. 1994. *History of Latin American Archaeology.* Aldershot, Eng.: Avebury.

Pakari, Nina. 1994. "Nina Pakari." In *Me levanto y digo: Testimonios de tres mujeres quichuas,* edited by M. Bulnes, pp. 41–62. Quito: Editorial El Conejo.

Palomeque, Silvia. 1994. "La sierra sur (1825–1900)." In *Historia y región en el Ecuador, 1830–1930,* edited by J. Maiguashca, pp. 69–142. Quito: FLACSO and Abya-Yala.

———. 1990. *Cuenca en el siglo XIX: La articulación de una región.* Quito: FLACSO and Abya-Yala.

Paredes, Domingo, and Eduardo Estrella. 1989. *Cochasquí: Aspectos socioeconómicos y nutritivos.* Quito: Programa Cochasquí and H. Consejo Provincial de Pichincha.

Pareja Diezcanseco, Alfredo. 1990. *Breve historia del Ecuador.* Quito: Libreas.

Parker, Andrew, et al. 1992. *Nationalisms and Sexualities.* New York: Routledge.

Parker, Richard. 1991. *Bodies, Pleasures, and Passions: Sexual Culture in Contemporary Brazil.* Boston: Beacon Press.

———. 1986. "Masculinity, Femininity, and Homosexuality: On the Anthropological Interpretation of Sexual Meanings in Brazil." *Journal of Homosexuality* 14: 156–163.

Patterson, Thomas. 1995a. "Archaeology, History, *Indigenismo,* and the State in Peru and Mexico." In *Making Alternative Histories: The Practice of Archaeology and History in Non-Western Settings,* edited by T. Patterson and P. Schmidt, pp. 69–86. Santa Fe, N.M.: School of American Research Press.

———. 1995b. *Toward a Social History of Archaeology in the United States.* New York: Harcourt Brace College Publishers.

———. 1991. *The Inca Empire: The Formation and Disintegration of a Pre-Capitalist State.* New York: Berg.

———. 1989. "Political Economy and a Discourse Called 'Peruvian Archaeology.'" *Culture and History* 4: 35–64.

Patterson, Thomas, and Peter Schmidt, eds. 1995. "Introduction: From Constructing to Making Alternative Histories." In *Making Alternative Histories: The Practice of Archaeology and History in Non-Western Settings,* edited by T. Patterson and P. Schmidt, pp. 1-24. Santa Fe, N.M.: School of American Research Press.

Patton, Cindy, and Benigno Sánchez-Eppler, eds. 2000. *Queer Diasporas.* Durham, N.C.: Duke University Press.

Perugachi, Rafael. 1994. *Rafael Perugachi: Un dirigente muerto a puntapies.* Quito: Unión de Organizaciones Campesinas de Cotacachi and CEDIS.

Petersen, Glenn. 1995. "Nan Madol's Contested Landscape: Topography and Tradition in the Eastern Caroline Islands." *ISLA: A Journal of Micronesian Studies* 3(1): 105–128.

Pinto, Amanda. 2001. Ecuador Demonstrators Seek Detention of IMF Delegates. *www.pulsar.org.ec/index.html*

Poole, Deborah. 1997. *Vision, Race, and Modernity: A Visual Economy of the Andean Image World.* Princeton, N.J.: Princeton Universtiy Press.

Popular Memory Group. 1982. "Popular Memory: Theory, Politics and Method." In *Making Histories: Studies in History-Writing and Politics,* edited by R. Johnson et al., pp. 205–252. Minneapolis: University of Minnesota Press.

Pratt, Mary Louise. 1992. *Imperial Eyes: Travel Writing and Trans-culturation.* New York: Routledge.

Price, Richard, and Sally Price. 1995. "Executing Culture: Musée, Museo, Museum." *American Anthropologist* 97(1): 97–109.

Prieur, Annick. 1998. *Mema's House, Mexico City: On Transvestites, Queens, and Machos.* Chicago: University of Chicago Press.

Programa Anual. 1996/1997. "*Informática—Cuarto curso.*" Colegio Nacional Tumbaco, Tumbaco, Ecuador.

———. 1996. "*Historia general del Ecuador—Cuarto curso.*" Colegio Nacional Tumbaco, Tumbaco, Ecuador.

Programa Cochasquí. 1997. *Informe annual.* Quito: H. Consejo Provincial de Pichincha.

———. 1991. *Replanteamiento programático.* Quito: Consejo Provincial de Pichincha.

———. 1990. *Museo arqueológico de sitio "Quilago."* Quito: Consejo Provincial de Pichincha.

———. 1981. *Programa Cochasquí.* Quito: Consejo Provincial de Pichinicha.

———. N.d. *Proyecto y manejo sustentable de Cochasquí.* Quito: Consejo Provincial de Pichincha.

Puga, Miguel, and Fernando Jurado. 1992. *El proceso de blanqueamiento en el Ecuador: De los Puentos a los Egas.* Colección Medio Milenio, vol. 3. Quito: N.p.

Puig, Manuel. 1986. *Pubis Angelical.* New York: Vintage Books.

Pullas de la Cruz, Virgilio. 1997. *Historia hecha en Cangahua: Guía del Centro Monumental Arqueológico y vida socio-cultural de Cochasquí.* Quito: Ediciones Abya-Yala.

Punto de Vista. 1990. *Victorioso levantamiento indígena.* Quito: Semanario del CEDIS.

Quijano, Aníbal. 1993. "América Latina en la economía mundial." *Problemas del Desarrollo* 24: 5–18.

Quimbo, José. 1992. "Derecho indígena." In *Pueblos indios, estado y derecho,* edited by E. Ayala Mora et al., pp. 205–212. Quito: Corporación Editora Nacional.

Quintero, Rafael, and Erika Silva. 1991. *Ecuador: Una nación en ciernes.* 3 vols. Quito: FLACSO and Abya-Yala.

Quintero López, Rafael. 1997. "Identidad nacional y estado nacional." In *Identidad nacional y globalización,* edited by A. Acosta et al., pp. 139–164. Quito: Instituto Latinoamericano de Investigaciones Sociales, FLACSO and Instituto de Altos Estudios Nacionales.

———. 1983. "El estado colonial." In *Nueva historia del Ecuador,* vol. 5, edited by E. Ayala Mora, pp. 9–50. Quito: Corporación Editora Nacional and Grijalbo.

Radcliffe, Sarah, and Sallie Westwood. 1996. *Remaking the Nation: Place, Identity and Politics in Latin America.* New York: Routledge.

Radcliffe-Brown, Alfred Reginald, ed. 1950. *African Systems of Kinship and Marriage.* London: Oxford University Press.

Ramón Valarezo, Galo. 1992. "Estado plurinacional: Una propuesta innovadora atrapada en viejos conceptos." In *Pueblos indios, estado y derecho,* edited by E. Ayala Mora et al., pp. 9–24. Quito: Corporación Editora Nacional.

———. 1990. "Ese secreto poder de la escritura." In *Indios: Una reflexión sobre el levantamiento indígena de 1990,* pp. 351–372. Quito: ILDIS and Ediciones Abya-Yala.

Rappaport, Joanne. 1994. *Cumbe Reborn: An Andean Ethnography of History.* Chicago: University of Chicago Press.

Renan, E. [1882] 1990. "What Is a Nation?" In *Nation and Narration,* edited by H. Bhabha, pp. 19–36. London: Routledge.

Ribeiro, Darcy. 1988. *El dilema de América Latina: Estructuras de poder y fuerzas insurgentes.* Mexico City: Siglo XXI Editores.

———. 1972. *The Americas and Civilization.* New York: E. P. Dutton.

Rodríguez, Evangelista. 1980. "Historia de Cochasquí." Manuscript.

Roediger, David. 1991. *The Wages of Whiteness: Race and the Making of the American Working Class.* Boston: Routledge.

———, ed. 1994. *Towards the Abolition of Whiteness: Essays on Race, Politics, and Working Class History.* London: Verso.

Ron, Alex. 1995. *Quito: Una ciudad de grafitis.* Quito: Editora Luz de América.

Rosaldo, Renato. 1989. *Culture and Truth: The Remaking of Social Analysis.* Boston: Beacon Press.

———. 1986. "From the Door of His Tent: The Fieldworker and the Inquisitor." In *Writing Culture: The Poetics and Politics of Writing Ethnography,* edited by J. Clifford and G. Marcus, pp. 77–97. Berkeley & Los Angeles: University of California Press.

Roscoe, Will. 1998. *Changing Ones: Third and Fourth Genders in Native North America.* London: Macmillan.

Roseberry, William. 1994. "Hegemony and the Language of Contention." In *Everyday Forms of State Formation: Revolution and the Negotiation of Rule in Modern Mexico,* edited by G. Joseph and D. Nugent, pp. 355–366. Durham, N.C.: Duke University Press.

Roura, Valeria, and Frank Núñez. 1991. "El pueblo negro en Guayaquil." Videorecording.

Rowe, William, and Vivian Schelling. 1991. *Memory and Modernity: Popular Culture in Latin America.* London: Verso.

Rowland, Michel. 1989. "Geografía y geología." In *Excavaciones arqueológicas en Cochasquí, Ecuador 1964–1965,* edited by U. Oberem and W. Wurster, pp. 1–14. Hamburg: Geo.

Rowlands, Michael. 1994. "The Politics of Identity in Archaeology." In *Social Construction of the Past,* edited by G. Bond and A. Gilliam, pp. 129–143. London: Routledge.

Rubin, Gayle. 1984. "Thinking Sex: Notes for a Radical Theory of the Politics of Sexuality." In *Pleasure and Danger: Exploring Female Sexuality,* edited by C. Vance, pp. 3–44. Boston: Routledge and Kegan Paul.

Rushdie, Salman. 1994. *East, West.* New York: Pantheon Books.

———. 1989. *The Satanic Verses.* New York: Viking.

———. 1981. *Midnight's Children.* New York: Knopf.

Sacks, Oliver. 1995. *An Anthropologist on Mars: Seven Paradoxical Tales.* New York: Alfred A. Knopf.

Said, Edward. 2000. *Reflections on Exile and Other Essays.* Cambridge: Harvard University Press.

———. 1989. "Representing the Colonized: Anthropology's Interlocuters." *Critical Inquiry* 15: 205–225.

———. 1978. *Orientalism.* New York: Pantheon Books.

Saitta, Dean. 1988. "Marxism, Prehistory, and Primitive Communism." *Rethinking Marxism* 1(4): 145–168.

Salazar, Ernesto. 1997. "Presentación." In *Una gran marea cultural en el noroeste de Sudamérica,* by J. Jijón y Caamaño, pp. 5–8. Quito: Museo Jacinto Jijón y Caamaño.

————. 1995a. "Between Crisis and Hope: Archaeology in Ecuador." In *Society for American Archaeology Bulletin* 13: 4.

————. 1995b. *Entre mitos y fábulas: El Ecuador aborigen.* Quito: Corporación Editora Nacional.

————. 1993/1994. "La arqueología contemporánea del Ecuador (1970–1993)." *Procesos: Revista Ecuatoriana de Historia* 5(Semesters I and II).

————. 1988. *Mitos de nuestro pasado.* Quito: Museo del Banco Central.

Salcedo, José. 1985. "Al rescate de la identidad cultural en Cochasquí." Manuscript.

Saleci, Renata, and Slavoj Zizek, eds. 1996. *Gaze and Voice as Love Objects.* Durham, N.C.: Duke University Press.

Salomon, Frank. 1990. "Ancestors, Grave Robbers, and the Possible Antecedents of Cañari 'Inca-Ism.'" In *Natives and Neighbors in South America: Antropological Essays,* edited by H. Skar and F. Salomon, pp. 207–232. Ethnological Studies 38. Goteborg, Sweden: Goteborgs Etnografiska Museum.

————. 1986. *Native Lords of Quito in the Age of the Incas: The Political Economy of North Andean Chiefdoms.* Cambridge: Cambridge University Press.

Sánchez, Isabel. 2001. "Ecuadorian Government, Indians Sign Accord." Press release (February 7).

Santiago, Esmeralda, and Joie Davidow, eds. 2000. *Las Mamis: Favorite Latino Authors Remember Their Mothers.* New York: Alfred A. Knopf.

Santiana, Antonio. 1966. *Nuevo panorama ecuatoriano del indio,* vol. 1. Quito: Editorial Universitaria.

Sarduy, Severo. 1997. *De donde son los cantantes.* Madrid: Catedra-Letras Hispánicas.

Sarmiento de Gamboa. [1572] 1960. *Historia general llamada indica.* Madrid: Biblioteca de Autores Espanoles.

————. [1572] 1947. *Historia de los incas.* Buenos Aires: Biblioteca Emecé.

Savoia, Rafael, ed. 1988. *El negro en la historia del Ecuador y del sur de Colombia.* Quito: Centro Cultural Afroecuatoriano.

Saxton, Alexander. 1990. *The Rise and Fall of the White Republic: Class Politics and Mass Culture in Nineteenth-Century America.* London: Verso.

Sayer, Derek. 1994. "Everyday Forms of State Formation: Some Dissident Remarks on 'Hegemony.'" In *Everyday Forms of State Formation: Revolution and the Negotiation of Rule in Modern Mexico,* edited by G. Joseph and D. Nugent, pp. 367–378. Durham, N.C.: Duke University Press.

Scham, Sandra. 1998. Mediating Nationalism and Archaeology: A Matter of Trust?" *American Anthropologist* 100(2): 301–308.

Schein, Louisa. 1996. "The Other Goes to Market: The State, the Nation and Unruliness in Contemporary China." *Identities: Global Studies in Culture and Power* 2(3): 197–222.

Scott, James. 1985. *Weapons of the Weak: Everyday Forms of Peasant Resistance.* New Haven, Conn.: Yale University Press.

Selverston, Melina. 1994. "The Politics of Culture: Indigenous Peoples and the State in Ecuador." In *Indigenous People and Democracy in Latin America,* edited by D. Lee Van Cott, pp. 131–152. New York: St. Martin's Press.

Shanks, Michael, and Christopher Tilly. 1987a. *Re-Constructing Archaeology: Theory and Practice.* Cambridge: Cambridge University Press.

———. 1987b. *Social Theory and Archaeology.* Albuquerque: University of New Mexico Press.

Sider, Gerald, and Gavin Smith. 1998. *Between History and Histories: The Making of Silences and Commemorations.* Toronto: University of Toronto Press.

Silberman, Neil Asher. 1997. "Structuring the Past: Israelis, Palestinians, and the Symbolic Authority of Archaeological Monuments." In *The Archaeology of Israel: Constructing the Past, Interpreting the Present,* edited by N. Silberman and D. Small, pp. 73–96. Sheffield, Eng.: Sheffield Academic Press.

———. 1995. "Promised Lands and Chosen People: The Politics and Poetics of Archaeological Narrative." In *Nationalism, Politics, and the Practice of Archaeology,* edited by P. Kohl and C. Fawcett, pp. 249–262. Cambridge: Cambridge University Press.

———. 1989. *Between Past and Present: Archaeology, Ideology, and Nationalism in the Modern Middle East.* New York: Henry Holt and Company.

———. 1982. *Digging for God and Country: Exploration, Archeology, and the Secret Struggle for the Holy Land, 1799–1917.* New York: Alfred A. Knopf.

Silberman, Neil Asher, and David Small, eds. 1997. *The Archaeology of Israel: Constructing the Past, Interpreting the Present.* Sheffield, Eng.: Sheffield Academic Press.

Silva, Erika. 1995. *Los mitos de la ecuatorianidad: Ensayo sobre la identidad nacional.* Quito: Abya-Yala.

Silverblatt, Irene. 1988. "Political Memories and Colonizing Symbols: Santiago and the Mountain Gods of Colonial Peru." In *Rethinking History and Myth: Indigenous South America,* edited by J. Hill, pp. 174–194. Urbana: University of Illinois Press.

———. 1987. *Moon, Sun, and Witches: Gender Ideologies and Class in Inca and Colonial Peru.* Princeton, N.J.: Princeton University Press.

Smith, Anthony. 1995. *Nations and Nationalism in a Global Era.* Cambridge: Cambridge University Press.

———. 1987. *The Ethnic Origins of Nations.* New York: Basil Blackwell.

———. 1983. *State and Nation in the Third World: The Western State and African Nationalism.* New York: St. Martin's Press.

Smith, Carol. 1996. "Myths, Intellectuals, and Race/Class/Gender Distinctions in the Formation of Latin American Nations." *Journal of Latin American Anthropology* 2(1): 148–169.

———. 1990. "Failed National Movements in 19th-Century Guatemala: A Parable for the Third World." In *Nationalist Ideologies and the Production of National Cultures,* edited by R. Fox, pp. 149–177. American Ethnology Monograph Series, no. 2. Washington, D.C.: American Anthropological Association.

Solano, Gonzalo. 2001. "Ecuador, Indians Cease to Protest." Associated Press (January 23).

Spalding, Karen. 1984. *Huarochirí: An Andean Society under Inca and Spanish Rule.* Stanford, Calif.: Stanford University Press.

————. 1970. "Social Climbers: Changing Patterns of Mobility among the Indians of Colonial Peru." *Hispanic American Historical Review* 50(4): 645–664.

————, ed. 1982. *Essays in the Political, Economic and Social History of Colonial Latin America.* Newark: Latin American Studies Program, University of Delaware.

Spivak, Gayatri. 1999. *A Critique of Postcolonial Reason: A History of the Vanishing Present.* Cambridge: Harvard University Press.

————. 1992. "Asked to Talk about Myself." *Third Text* 19 (Summer): 9–18.

————. 1988. "Can the Subaltern Speak?" In *Marxism and the Interpretation of Culture,* edited by C. Nelson and L. Grossberg, pp. 271–313. Urbana: University of Illinois Press.

Spriggs, Matthew, ed. 1984. *Marxist Perspectives in Archaeology.* Cambridge: Cambridge University Press.

Stephen, Lynn. 1989. "Anthropology and the Politics of Facts, Knowledge and History." *Dialectical Anthropology* 14: 259–269.

Stocking, George, ed. 1985. *Objects and Others: Essays on Museums and Material Culture.* Madison: University of Wisconsin Press.

Stoler, Anne. 1996. *Race and the Education of Desire: Foucault's History of Sexuality and the Colonial Order of Things.* Durham, N.C.: Duke University Press.

Stutzman, Ronald. 1981. "El Mestizaje: An All-Inclusive Ideology of Exclusion." In *Cultural Transformations and Ethnicity in Modern Ecuador,* edited by N. Whitten, pp. 45–93. Urbana: University of Illinois Press.

Tamba, Floresmilo. 1993. "El movimiento indígena en la provincia de Pichincha." In *Historia de la organización indígena en Pichincha,* by Federación Indígena Pichincha Runacunapac Riccharimui, pp. 25–30. Quito: Abya-Yala.

Taussig, Michael. 1992a. "Maleficium: State Fetishism." In *The Nervous System,* pp. 111–140. New York: Routledge.

————. 1992b. *The Nervous System.* New York: Routledge.

————. 1989. "History as Commodity in Some Recent American (Anthropological) Literature." *Critique of Anthropology* 9(1): 7–23.

Taxin, Amy. 2001. "Analysis: Ecuador-Indian Accord Quick-Fix in Split Nation." Press release (February 9).

Taylor, Anne Christine. 1994. "El oriente ecuatoriano en el siglo XIX: 'El otro litoral.'" In *Historia y región en el Ecuador, 1830–1930,* edited by J. Maiguashca, pp. 17–68. Quito: FLACSO and Abya-Yala.

Taylor, Diana. 1998. "A Savage Performance: Guillermo Gómez-Peña and Coco Fusco's 'Couple in the Cage.'" *Drama Review: The Journal of Performance Studies* 42(2): 160–175.

El Telégrafo (Guayaquil). 1994. "Totem manteño en museo municipal" (July 24).

————. 1993a. "San Biritute despierta interés internacional" (August 11).

————. 1993b. "San Viritute" (September 21).

Thompson, E. P. 1978. "Eighteenth-Century English Society: Class Struggle without Class?" *Social History* 3(2): 133–165.

Thorpe, Benjamin, ed. [1853] 1968. *Yule-tide Stories: A Collection of Scandi-*

navian and North German Popular Tales and Traditions, from the Swedish, Danish, and German. New York: AMS Press.

Tinajero, Fernando. 1986. "Estudio introductorio." In *Teoría de la cultura nacional,* edited by F. Tinajero, pp. 9–78. Quito: Corporación Editora Nacional and Banco Central del Ecuador.

———. 1982. *El Desencuentro.* Quito: Editorial El Conejo.

Trigger, Bruce. 1995. "Romanticism, Nationalism, and Archaeology." In *Nationalism, Politics, and the Practice of Archaeology,* edited by P. Kohl and C. Fawcett, pp. 263–279. Cambridge: Cambridge University Press.

———. 1984. "Alternative Archaeologies: Nationalist, Colonialist, Imperialist." *Man* 19: 355–370.

Trouillot, Michel-Rolph. 1995. *Silencing the Past: Power and the Production of History.* Boston: Beacon Press.

Ucko, Peter. 1987. *Academic Freedom and Apartheid: The Story of the World Archaeological Congress.* London: Duckworth.

Uhle, Max. 1939. "Las ruinas de Cochasquí." *Boletín de la Academia Nacional de Historia* 18(54): 5–14.

———. 1937. "Las ruinas de Cochasquí." *Revista del Museo Nacional de Lima* 6: 86–91.

———. 1936. "Las antiguas civilizaciones del Ecuador y Perú." *Boletín de la Academia Nacional de Historia* 13: 36–39.

———. 1933. *Estudio sobre las civilizaciones del Carchi e Imbabura.* Informe al Ministerio de Educación. Quito.

———. 1931. "Las antiguas civilizaciones de Manta." *Boletín de la Academia Nacional de Historia* 12(33–35): 5–72.

———. 1930a. "Apuntes arqueológicos acerca de la Isla de Puná." *Revista de la Universidad de Guayaquil* 1(1): 78–88.

———. 1930b. "El Reino de Quito." *Boletín de la Academia Nacional de Historia* 10(27–29).

———. 1929. *Estado actual de la prehistoria ecuatoriana.* Quito: Talleres Tipográficos Nacionales.

———. 1928. "Las ruinas de Cuasmal." *Anales de la Universidad Central* 40.

———. 1927. "Estudios esmeraldeños." *Anales de la Universidad Central* 39.

———. 1926. "Excavaciones arqueológicas en la región de Cumbayá." *Anales de la Universidad Central* 37.

———. 1923. *Las ruinas de Tomebamba.* Quito: Imprenta Julio Saenz Rebolledo.

———. 1922a. "Orígenes centro-americanos." *Boletín de la Academia Nacional de Historia* 4(9): 1–7.

———. 1922b. "Sepulturas ricas de oro en la Provincia del Azuay." *Boletín de la Academia Nacional de Historia* 4(9): 108–114.

———. 1922c. "Influencias mayas en el Alto Ecuador." *Boletín de la Academia Nacional de Historia* 4(10–11): 205–240; 5(12–14): 1–3.

El Universo (Guayaquil). 2001. "Página editorial" (February 12).

———. 1997. "Consulta 97" (May 26).

———. 1993a. "Sacachún pasa a la historia" (August 29).

————. 1993b. "El totem del museo municipal" (August 23).

————. 1993c. "San Biritute, la iglesia y sus detractores" (August 11).

————. 1993d. "La etnicidad indígena y criolla" (June 24).

————. 1992a. "Incas" (November 25).

————. 1992b. "Panzaleo" (November 18).

————. 1992c. "Cañari" (November 11).

————. 1992d. "Carchi y Cuasmal" (November 4).

————. 1992e. "Manteña-Huancavilca" (October 28).

————. 1992f. "Chorrera" (October 21).

————. 1992g. "Bahía de Caraquez" (October 14).

————. 1992h. "El Inga" (October 7).

————. 1992i. "Valdivia" (September 30).

————. 1992j. "La Tolita" (September 23).

————. N.d.a. "Museo con nueva imagen."

————. N.d.b. "Arqueología, tradición oral y San Biritute, Guayaquil."

Unterhalter, Elaine, and G. Gaitskell, eds. 1989. *Apartheid Education and Popular Struggles*. London: Zed.

Urton, Gary. 1990. *The History of a Myth: Pacariqtambo and the Origin of the Inkas*. Austin: University of Texas Press.

Vaquero Dávila, Jesús. 1941. *Génesis de la nacionalidad ecuatoriana*. Quito: Imprenta de la Universidad.

Varese, Stefano, and Michael Kearny. 1995. "Latin America's Indigenous Peoples: Changing Identities and Forms of Resistance." In *Capital, Power, and Inequality in Latin America*, edited by S. Halebsky and R. Harris, pp. 207–232. Boulder, Colo.: Westview Press.

Vargas, Iraida. 1995. "The Perception of History and Archaeology in Latin America: A Theoretical Approach." In *Making Alternative Histories: The Practice of Archaeology and History in Non-Western Settings*, edited by T. Patterson and P. Schmidt, pp. 47–68. Santa Fe, N.M.: School of American Research Press.

————. 1990. *Arqueología, ciencia y sociedad*. Caracas: Editorial Abre Brecha.

Vargas, Father José María. 1991. "Biografía de Jacinto Jijón y Caamaño." In *Obras selectas I*, pp. 187–241. Cuenca: Ediciones del Banco Central del Ecuador.

————. 1982. *La economía política del Ecuador durante la colonia*. Quito: Banco Central del Ecuador and Corporación Editora Nacional.

————. 1964. *Historia del arte ecuatoriano*. Quito: Santo Domingo.

————. 1953. *Ecuador: Monumentos históricos y arqueológicos*. Mexico.

Vasconcelos, José. 1997. *The Cosmic Race*. Baltimore, Md.: Johns Hopkins University Press.

Velasco, Juan de. [1790] 1841. *Historia del reino de Quito en la América meridional. Tres Partes*. Quito: Clásicos Ariel.

Vidal, Hernán Julio. 1993. "A través de sus cenizas: Imágenes etnográficas e identidad regional en Tierra del Fuego (Argentina)." M.A. thesis, FLACSO.

Villacrés Moscoso, Jorge. 1967. *Historia diplomática de la República del Ecuador*. Guayaquil: Imprenta de la Universidad de Guayaquil.

Vistazo. 1997a. "Padre Velasco." No. 723 (October 2).

———. 1997b. "Bank Ad." No. 723 (October 2): 53.

Wade, Peter. 1994. "Representation and Power: Blacks in Colombia." In *Social Construction of the Past: Representation as Power,* edited by G. Bond and A. Gilliam, pp. 59–73. London: Routledge.

———. 1993. *Blackness and Race Mixture: Dynamics of Racial Identity in Colombia.* Baltimore, Md.: Johns Hopkins University Press.

Weismantel, Mary J. 1992. *Food, Gender, and Poverty in the Ecuadorian Andes.* Philadelphia: University of Pennsylvania Press.

West, Cornel. 1994. *Race Matters.* New York: Vintage Books.

Whitten, Norman. 1984. "Etnocidio ecuatoriano y etnogénesis indígena: Resurgencia amazónica ante la colonización andina." In *Temas sobre la continuidad y adaptación cultural ecuatoriana,* edited by M. Naranjo, J. L. Pereira V., and N. E. Whitten, Jr. Quito: EDUC.

———. 1974. *Black Frontiersmen: Afro-Hispanic Culture of Ecuador and Colombia.* Prospect Heights, Ill.: Waveland Press.

———. 1965. *Class, Kinship and Power in an Ecuadorian Town: The Negroes of San Lorenzo.* Stanford, Calif.: Stanford University Press.

———, ed. 1981. *Cultural Transformations and Ethnicity in Modern Ecuador.* Urbana: University of Illinois Press.

Wilk, Richard. 1985. "The Ancient Maya and the Poltical Present." *Journal of Anthropological Research* 41(3): 307–326.

Williams, Brackette. 1991. *Stains on My Name, War in My Veins: Guyana and the Politics of Cultural Struggle.* Durham, N.C.: Duke University Press.

———. 1990. "Nationalism, Traditionalism, and the Problem of Cultural Inauthenticity." In *Nationalist Ideologies and the Production of National Cultures,* edited by R. Fox, pp. 112–129. American Ethnological Society Monograph Series, no. 2. Washington, D.C.: American Anthropological Association.

Williams, Raymond. 1977. *Marxism and Literature.* Oxford: Oxford University Press.

Wolf, Eric. 1982. *Europe and the People without History.* Berkeley & Los Angeles: University of California Press.

Wright, Patrick. 1985. *On Living in an Old Country: The National Past in Contemporary Britain.* New York: Verso.

Wurster, Wolfgang. 1989. "Ruinas existentes." In *Excavaciones arqueológicas en Cochasquí, Ecuador 1964–1965,* edited by U. Oberem and W. Wurster, pp. 11–69. Hamburg: Geo.

Wylie, Alison. 1995. "Alternative Histories: Epistemic Disunity and Poltical Integrity." In *Making Alternative Histories: The Practice of Archaeology and History in Non-Western Settings,* edited by T. Patterson and P. Schmidt, pp. 255–272. Santa Fe, N.M.: School of American Research Press.

———. 1992. "The Interplay of Evidential Constraints and Political Interests: Recent Archaeological Research on Gender." *American Antiquity* 57(1): 15–35.

Xavier, Emanuel. 1999. *Christ-Like.* New York: Painted Leaf Press.

Young, Robert. 1995. *Colonial Desire: Hybridity in Theory, Culture and Race.* New York: Routledge.

Yourcenar, Marguerite. 1963. *Memoirs of Hadrian, and Reflections on the Composition of Memoirs of Hadrian.* Translated by Grace Frick. New York: Farrar, Straus.

Yupanki, Atik Kurikamak. 1992. "Comentario." In *Pueblos indios, estado y derecho,* edited by E. Ayala Mora et al., pp. 163–166. Quito: Corporación Editora Nacional.

Yurevich, Valentin. 1986. "Posibles significaciones astronómicas de las pirámides de Cochasquí." Manuscript on file in site archives.

Zárate, Agustín de. [1555] 1995. *Historia del descubrimiento y conquista del Perú.* Lima: Pontificia Universidad Católica del Perú, Fondo Editorial.

Zea, Leopoldo. 1991. *Precursores del pensamiento latinoamericano contemporáneo.* Mexico City: Secretaría de Educación Pública.

Zimmerman, Larry. 1989. "Human Bones as Symbols of Power: Aboriginal American Belief System toward Bones and 'Grave-Robbing' Archaeologists." In *Conflict in the Archaeology of Living Traditions,* edited by R. Layton, pp. 211–216. London: Unwin Hyman.

Zizek, Slavoj. 1996. "'I Hear You with My Eyes'; or, The Invisible Master." In *Gaze and Voice as Love Objects,* edited by R. Saleci and S. Zizek, pp. 99–126. Durham, N.C.: Duke University Press.

INDEX